HESPERIA: SUPPLEMENT XVII

KALLIAS OF SPHETTOS AND THE REVOLT OF ATHENS IN 286 B.C.

BY

T. LESLIE SHEAR, JR.

AMERICAN SCHOOL OF CLASSICAL STUDIES AT ATHENS
PRINCETON, NEW JERSEY
1978

PUBLISHED WITH THE AID OF A GRANT FROM
THE DEPARTMENT OF ART AND ARCHAEOLOGY,
PRINCETON UNIVERSITY

Library of Congress Cataloging in Publication Data

Shear, Theodore Leslie, 1938–
Kallias of Sphettos and the revolt of Athens in 286 B.C.

(Hesperia: Supplement; 17)
Bibliography: p.
Includes index.
1. Athens—History—Revolution, 286 B.C.
2. Kallias, of Sphettos, fl. 307–269 B.C.
I. Title. II. Series: Hesperia, journal of the American School of Classical Studies at Athens: Supplement; 17.
DF235.7.S53 938′.5 78–8721
ISBN 0–87661–517–5

Printed in Great Britain by Spottiswoode Ballantyne Ltd.
Colchester and London

To My Father

PREFACE

This study presents the first publication of the long honorary decree for Kallias of Sphettos which came to light some years ago in the excavations of the Athenian Agora and is now housed in the epigraphical collection of the Stoa of Attalos. The text of the new inscription has here been edited and translated, and an effort has been made to interpret its contents in a detailed commentary. Because this remarkable document furnishes so much information about so many different aspects of the history of Athens in the early 3rd century B.C., it seemed essential to examine again many of the events of this period in light of the new evidence. When the decree for Kallias takes its place beside other contemporary documents and references to the period in literature, it may be fairly said to provide the key to our better understanding of the stirring events which engulfed the city of Athens during the two decades between the battle of Ipsos in 301 and the battle of Kouroupedion in 281.

Although publication of this decree was planned as an article in *Hesperia*, like that of all other inscriptions found in the Athenian Agora, the historical complexities of the text caused the manuscript to grow beyond the normal limits of periodical literature; and it thus seemed best to publish it as a separate monograph. In the course of my study of the inscription I have learned much in stimulating discussions with numerous colleagues and I have greatly benefited from their suggestions. It is a pleasure to express my warm thanks to Alan L. Boegehold, John McK. Camp II, Peter M. Fraser, John H. Kroll, Benjamin D. Meritt, Ronald S. Stroud, Homer A. Thompson, and Eugene Vanderpool, Sr., all of whom have helped me at different points in the reading, reconstruction, and interpretation of the text. I am most especially grateful to Christian Habicht who has so generously shared with me his knowledge of the Hellenistic period. He undertook to read and criticize the manuscript and suggested many improvements. The photographs of the stele I owe to Eugene Vanderpool, Jr.

To the Publications Committee of the American School of Classical Studies at Athens, and to its editor Marian H. McAllister, I am indebted both for suggesting that this study appear as a book and for supporting and approving its publication. To my colleagues on the Publications Committee of the Department of Art and Archaeology at Princeton University I am indebted for the generous subvention which made it possible to print this book. Mention must be made too of my long-standing debt of gratitude to the officers of the Greek Service of Antiquities and Restoration, particularly to the successive Inspectors General and to George Dontas, Director of the Athenian Acropolis, under whose general supervision the excavations in the Agora are conducted. Without their enthusiastic support of the excavations and their hospitality to scholars from foreign lands, the inscription preserving the decree for Kallias would not have been found.

It is a special pleasure to acknowledge the unflagging support and encouragement of my wife, Ione M. Shear, who in so many ways has given me help, not the least tangible evidence of which was the neatly typed manuscript handed to the editor.

But these words of my appreciation to others are inadequate to express the sense of rare privilege which I have felt at each step in the writing of this book. One of the gifts which a gracious fortune has reserved for excavators in the field is that feeling of powerful immediacy with remote antiquity which comes at the very moment of new discovery. These are haunted moments when the ghosts of the past seem almost to call out to us across the centuries lest they be forgotten wholly and forever. Never have I felt this more strongly than upon my first reading of the decree for Kallias. At the beginning one's whole concern was to decipher and transcribe correctly the individual letters of the inscription, and one had no ear for the words and their meaning; but the stone spoke of the man, Kallias, until that time forgotten but for a single mention of his name, and now suddenly alive in the full and moving narrative of his career. Although six years have passed since my first meeting with Kallias of Sphettos, the memory of that moment is unforgettable. As the writing of this study progressed, my acquaintance with Kallias has ripened, and I now take joy in introducing him to others who may wish to share his company.

T. Leslie Shear, Jr.

Princeton, New Jersey
December 5, 1977

TABLE OF CONTENTS

ABBREVIATIONS AND BIBLIOGRAPHY

Agora XV = B. D. Meritt and J. S. Traill, *The Athenian Agora*, XV, *Inscriptions, The Athenian Councillors*, Princeton 1974

AJP = *American Journal of Philology*

Ἀρχ. Δελτ. = Ἀρχαιολογικὸν Δελτίον

Ἀρχ. Ἐφ. = Ἀρχαιολογικὴ Ἐφημερίς

AthMitt = *Mitteilungen des deutschen archäologischen Instituts, Athenische Abteilung*

Bagnall, *Ptolemaic Possessions* = R. S. Bagnall, *The Administration of the Ptolemaic Possessions outside Egypt*, Leiden 1976

BCH = *Bulletin de correspondance hellénique*

Beloch, *Gr. Gesch.* = K. J. Beloch, *Griechische Geschichte*, 2nd ed., Berlin 1927

Bengtson, *Strategie* = H. Bengtson, *Die Strategie in der hellenistischen Zeit*, I–III, Munich 1937, 1944, 1952

BSA = *The Annual of the British School at Athens*

CAH = *The Cambridge Ancient History*, edd. J. B. Bury, S. A. Cook, F. E. Adcock, M. P. Charlesworth, and N. H. Baynes, Cambridge 1928–1939

CP = *Classical Philology*

Davies, *APF* = J. K. Davies, *Athenian Propertied Families*, Oxford 1971

Deubner, *Attische Feste* = L. Deubner, *Attische Feste*, Berlin 1932

Dinsmoor, *Archons* = W. B. Dinsmoor, *The Archons of Athens in the Hellenistic Age*, Cambridge, Mass. 1931

Dinsmoor, *List* = W. B. Dinsmoor, *The Athenian Archon List in the Light of Recent Discoveries*, New York 1939

Durrbach, *Choix* = F. Durrbach, *Choix d'inscriptions de Délos*, Paris 1921

Edmonds, *Frag. Att. Com.* = J. M. Edmonds, *The Fragments of Attic Comedy*, I–III, Leiden 1957–1961

FD III = *Fouilles de Delphes*, III, *Épigraphie*, fascs. i-iv (various edd.), Paris 1910–1970

Ferguson, *HA* = W. S. Ferguson, *Hellenistic Athens*, London 1911

Ferguson, *Tribal Cycles* = W. S. Ferguson, *Athenian Tribal Cycles in the Hellenistic Age*, Cambridge, Mass. 1932

F. Gr. Hist. = F. Jacoby, *Die Fragmente der griechischen Historiker*, Berlin 1923–1955

Fraser, *Ptol. Alex.* = P. M. Fraser, *Ptolemaic Alexandria*, Oxford 1972

Heinen, *Untersuchungen* = H. Heinen, *Historia*, Einzelschrift XX, *Untersuchungen zur hellenistischen Geschichte*, Wiesbaden 1972

Hicks, *IBM* = *British Museum: Ancient Greek Inscriptions*, I–IV, edd. C. T. Newton, E. L. Hicks, G. Hirschfeld, London 1874–1893

HSCP = *Harvard Studies in Classical Philology*

HTR = *Harvard Theological Review*

ICret = M. Guarducci, *Inscriptiones Creticae*, I–IV, Rome 1935–1950

IDélos = *Inscriptions de Délos*, I–VII (various edd.), Paris 1926–1972

IG II² = *Inscriptiones Graecae, Inscriptiones Atticae*, Editio Minor, II–III, ed. J. Kirchner, Berlin 1923–1940

IG VII = *Inscriptiones Graecae, Inscriptiones Megaridis et Boeotiae*, ed. W. Dittenberger, Berlin 1892

IG IX² 1 = *Inscriptiones Graecae, Inscriptiones Graeciae Septentrionalis*, Editio Minor, fasc. 1, ed. G. Klaffenbach, Berlin 1932

IG XI = *Inscriptiones Graecae, Inscriptiones Deli*, fasc. 2, ed. F. Durrbach; fasc. 4, ed. P. Roussel, Berlin 1912, 1914

IG XII = *Inscriptiones Graecae, Inscriptiones Insularum Maris Aegaei Praeter Delum*, ed. F. Hiller von Gaertringen, Berlin 1895–1939

Jardé, *Céréales* = A. Jardé, *Les céréales dans l'antiquité grecque*, Paris 1925

JdaI = *Jahrbuch des deutschen archäologischen Instituts*

JHS = *Journal of Hellenic Studies*
Kahrstedt, *Magistratur* = U. Kahrstedt, *Untersuchungen zur Magistratur in Athen*, Stuttgart 1936
Kahrstedt, *Staatsgebiet* = U. Kahrstedt, *Staatsgebiet und Staatsgehörige in Athen*, Berlin 1934
Kirchner, *PA* = J. Kirchner, *Prosopographia Attica*, I–II, Berlin 1901–1903
Κρητ. Χρόν. = *Κρητικὰ Χρόνικα*
LeipzStud = *Leipziger Studien zur classischen Philologie*
Lévêque, *Pyrrhos* = P. Lévêque, *Pyrrhos*, Paris 1957
Manni, *Dem. Pol.* = E. Manni, *Demetrio Poliorcete*, Rome 1951–1952
Meritt, *Ath. Year* = B. D. Meritt, *The Athenian Year*, Berkeley 1961
Moretti, *Iscr. stor. ell.* = L. Moretti, *Iscrizioni storiche ellenistiche*, Florence 1967
OGIS = W. Dittenberger, *Orientis Graecae Inscriptiones Selectae*, I–II, Leipzig 1903–1905
P. Cair. Zen. = C. C. Edgar, *Catalogue général des antiquités égyptiennes du musée du Caire, Zenon Papyri*, I–V, Cairo 1925–1940
Pfuhl, *de pompis* = E. Pfuhl, *de Atheniensium pompis sacris*, Berlin 1900
P. Oxy. = *Oxyrhynchus Papyri*, edd. B. P. Grenfell, A. S. Hunt, *et al.*, I–XLIV, London 1898–1976
Pritchett and Meritt, *Chronology* = W. K. Pritchett and B. D. Meritt, *The Chronology of Hellenistic Athens*, Cambridge, Mass. 1940
Pros. Ptol. = W. Peremans, E. Van't Dack, *et al.*, *Prosopographia Ptolemaica*, I–VI, Louvain 1950–1954
RE = *Paulys Realencyclopädie der classischen Altertumswissenschaft*, ed. G. Wissowa, W. Kroll *et al.*
REA = *Revue des études anciennes*
RhMus = *Rheinisches Museum für Philologie*
Rhodes, *Athenian Boule* = P. J. Rhodes, *The Athenian Boule*, Oxford 1972
RivFil = *Rivista di filologia*
Rostovtzeff, *SEHHW* = M. I. Rostovtzeff, *Social and Economic History of the Hellenistic World*, Oxford 1953
Schmitt, *Staatsverträge* = H. H. Schmitt, *Die Staatsverträge des Altertums*, III, Munich 1969
SEG = *Supplementum Epigraphicum Graecum*
*SIG*³ = W. Dittenberger, *Sylloge Inscriptionum Graecarum*, I–IV, 3rd ed. (F. Hiller von Gaertringen), Leipzig 1915–1924
TAPA = *Transactions of the American Philological Association*
Tarn, *Ant. Gon.* = W. W. Tarn, *Antigonos Gonatas*, London 1913
Will, *Monde hellénistique* = E. Will, *Histoire politique du monde hellénistique*, I, Nancy 1966
ZPE = *Zeitschrift für Papyrologie und Epigraphik*

CHAPTER I

THE DECREE FOR KALLIAS

The epigraphical records of Hellenistic Athens offer eloquent testimony to the good services of her citizens to a city which, if one could judge only from the increasing proliferation of monuments congratulating them, would seem to have been largely populated with zealous benefactors and worthy public officials who performed honorable service. Moreover, they were honored each according to his deserts by the Demos which always remembered to praise worthy deeds and rendered thanks to all good men. With the passage of time, as the economic and political fortunes of Athens fell to ever lower estate, the honorific decrees of the Athenian assembly appear to increase in inverse proportion. The good services are recorded in more fulsome detail, the praises are proclaimed in more ringing tones, and the rewards become more tangible. Indeed, as the documents show an ever increased refinement in the formula for giving thanks, one is left with the feeling that the gratitude of the Demos was largely an expression of its eager anticipation of more good deeds to come.

To the historian, however, the honorary decrees provide the most valuable primary sources for the reconstruction of the history of Athens in one of its darkest periods, the first half of the 3rd century B.C. A welcome addition to the series of honorary decrees is a new inscription from the Athenian Agora, the text of which is presented here for the first time. Like all the documents of its class it dwells myopically upon the career of a single man and upon his contributions both great and small to the events of his time. His was a time, however, of which we know only the broadest outlines and some scattered details; thus any new text which comes to light contributes a few new facts and helps to fit a few more pieces into the puzzle of 3rd-century Athens.

Inv. No. I 7295 (Pls. 1–4). Complete stele of Pentelic marble preserved intact. The shaft terminates in a slight apophyge and is crowned by a molding, consisting of a cavetto above an ovolo, which runs across the front and returns on both sides. Sides and top are worked smooth, but the latter is slightly pitted from exposure to the weather. The bottom is left rough and a rough-picked band (0.065 m. wide) across the lower edge of the shaft indicates the depth to which the stele was inserted in its base. The back is only roughly worked with a point, but bands of irregular width have been slightly smoothed along the sides of the shaft. The stele was evidently erected in such a position that the back was not exposed to view.[1]

[1] There is no way of determining exactly where Kallias' monument originally stood. The text provides (lines 96, 107) that the inscribed stele be placed beside the bronze statue of Kallias which was to be erected in the Agora. The stele appears as it was found on the plan *Hesperia* 42, 1973, p. 123, fig. 1 where it may be

Found on May 20, 1971, lying face upwards and re-used as a cover slab in a late repair of the Great Drain.[2]

Height, 1.655 m.; width, including molding, 0.524 m.; top of shaft, 0.456 m.; bottom of shaft, 0.536 m.; thickness, 0.122 m.

Height of the letters, lines 1–4, 0.008 m.; lines 5ff., 0.005 m., except line 10, 0.007 m.

TEXT

a. 270/69 *a.* NON-*ΣΤΟΙΧ.* 42–49

ὁ δῆμος
Καλλίαν
Θυμοχάρου
Σφήττιον

ἐπὶ Σωσιστράτου ἄρχοντος ἐπὶ τῆς Πανδιονίδος ἕκκτης
πρυτανείας εἶ Ἀθηνόδωρος Γοργίππου Ἀχαρνεὺς ἐγραμμ
άτευεν· Ποσιδεῶνος ὀγδόει ἐπὶ δέκα, μιᾶι κ[α]ὶ εἰκοστε[ῖ τ]
ῆς πρυτανείας· ἐκκλησία κυρία· τῶν προέδρων ἐπεψήφιζε
ν Ἐπιχάρης Φειδοστράτου Ἐρχιεὺς καὶ συμπρόεδροι·
ἔδοξεν τεῖ βουλεῖ καὶ τῶι δήμωι·
Εὐχάρης Εὐάρχου Κονθυλῆθεν εἶπεν· ἐπειδὴ Κ̣αλλία[ς],
γενομένης τῆς ἐπαναστάσεως ὑπὸ τοῦ δήμου ἐπὶ το
ὺς κατέχοντας τὴν πόλιν καὶ τοὺς μὲν ἐκ τοῦ ἄστεως
στρατιώτας ἐγβαλόντος, τοῦ δὲ φρουρίου τοῦ ἐν τῶι
Μουσείωι ἔτι κατεχομένου καὶ τῆς χώρας ἐμ πολέμω
ι οὔσης ὑπὸ τῶν ἐκ τοῦ Πειραέως, καὶ Δημητρίου παρα
γιγνομένου ἐκ Πελοποννήσου μετὰ τοῦ στρατοπέδο
υ ἐπὶ τὸ ἄστυ, πυθόμενος Καλλίας τὸν κίνδυνον τὸν π
ερὶ τὴν πόλιν καὶ ἐπιλεξάμενος τῶν στρατιωτῶν χι
λίους τῶν μεθ' αὐτοῦ τεταγμένων ἐν Ἄνδρωι καὶ ἀναδ
οὺς ὀψώνια αὐτοῖς καὶ σιτομετρήσας παρεγένετο βο
ηθῶν εὐθὺς εἰς τὸ ἄστυ τῶι δήμωι ἀκόλουθα πράττων τεῖ τοῦ
βασιλέως Πτολεμαίου πρὸς τὸν δῆμον εὐνοίαι, καὶ ἐξά
γων εἰς τὴν χώραν τοὺς στρατιώτας τοὺς μεθ' αὐτοῦ προ
εκάθητο τῆς τοῦ σίτου συνκομιδῆς πᾶσαν ποιούμενος

---

identified as the second cover slab from the south on the Great Drain, just east of the south annex of the Stoa Basileios. Since the stele is intact, it was possibly not moved far from its original position at the time of its re-use. It is interesting to observe that the small triangular area, forming the northwest corner of the square and lying only a few meters east of the Great Drain, was found crowded with the foundations of monument bases, *ibid.*, p. 125. Many of these are probably to be dated to the Hellenistic period and are of appropriate size and shape to accommodate single statues. The statue of Kallias may have stood on one of them.

[2] Found in square J 5. The grid coordinates of the general plan of the Agora are conveniently consulted in *Agora* XV, pl. 2.

σπουδὴν ὅπως ἂν εἰς τὴν πόλιν σῖτος ὡς πλεῖστος εἰσκ
ομισθεῖ· καὶ ἐπειδὴ παραγενόμενος Δημήτριος καὶ πε
ριστρατοπεδεύσας ἐπολιόρκει τὸ ἄστυ, ἀγωνιζόμενο
ς ὑπὲρ τοῦ δήμου Καλλίας καὶ ἐπεξιὼν μετὰ τῶν στρατι
ωτῶν τῶν μεθ' αὑτοῦ καὶ τραυματίας γενόμενος κίνδυ
νον οὐθένα ὑποστελλόμενος οὐδὲ ἐν ἑνὶ καιρῶι ἕνεκα
τῆς τοῦ δήμου σωτηρίας· καὶ τοῦ βασιλ{ιλ}έως Πτολεμαί
ου ἀποστείλαντος Σώστρατον τὰ συμφέροντα πράξοντ
α τεῖ πόλει, καὶ Σωστράτου μεταπεμπομένου πρεσβεία
ν πρὸς ἑαυτὸν εἰς Πειραιᾶ μεθ' ἧς συνθήσει τὰ περὶ τὴν
εἰρήνην ὑπὲρ τῆς πόλεως πρὸς Δημήτριον, ὑπακούσας ε
ἰς ταῦτα τοῖστρατηγοῖς καὶ τεῖ βουλεῖ Καλλίας καὶ π
ρεσβεύων ὑπὲρ τοῦ δήμου καὶ [π]άντα πράττων τὰ συμφέρ
οντα τεῖ πόλει, καὶ συμπαραμ[ε]ίνας ἐν τῶι ἄστει μετὰ τ
ῶν στρατιωτῶν ἕως ἡ εἰρήνη σ[υ]νετελέσθη, καὶ ἀναπλεύσ
{σ}ας πρὸς τὸν βασιλέα Πτολεμαῖον ταῖς πρεσβείαις τα
ῖς ἀποστελλομέναις ὑπὸ τοῦ δήμου συναγωνιζόμενος
εἰς πάντα καὶ συνεργῶν εἰς τὰ συμφέροντα τεῖ πόλει· κ
αὶ παραλαβόντος τὴν βασιλε[ί]αν Πτολεμαίου τοῦ νεωτ
έρου βασιλέως ἐπιδημήσας ε[ἰ]ς τὸ ἄστυ Καλλίας, καὶ τῶ
ν στρατηγῶν καλεσάντων αὐτ[ὸ]ν καὶ ἐμφανιζ̣όντων τὰ
κατὰ τὴν πόλιν ἐν οἷς ἦν καὶ παρακαλούντω[ν] αὐτὸν σπου
δάσαι ὑπὲρ τῆς πόλεως πρὸς τὸν βασιλέα Πτ[ο]λεμαῖον ὅ[π]
ως ἂν βοήθειά τις γένηται τὴν ταχ[ί]στην εἰς τὸ ἄστυ σίτ
ωι καὶ χρήμασιν, καὶ ἀναπλεύσα[ς] αὐτὸς ἰδί⟨α⟩ι Καλλίας
εἰς Κύπρον καὶ ἐντυχὼν ἐκεῖ τῶ[ι β]ασιλεῖ φιλοτίμως ὑ
πὲρ τῆς πόλεως ἐκόμισεν τῶι δήμωι ἀργυρίου μὲν τάλαν
τα πεντήκοντα, πυρῶν δὲ δισμυρίους μεδίμνους δωρεὰν
οἳ παρεμετρήθησαν ἐγ Δήλου τοῖς ἀποσταλεῖσιν ὑπὸ τ[ο]
ῦ δήμου· καὶ ὡς ὁ βασιλεὺς πρῶτον ἐπόει τὰ̣ Πτο[λ]εμαῖα τ[ὴ]
ν θυσίαν καὶ τοὺς ἀγῶνας τῶι πατ[ρί], ψηφι[σ]α[μένου τ]ο̣ῦ̣ [δή]
μου θεωρίαν πέμπειν καὶ ἀξιώσαν̣τος ὑπακ[οῦσαι Καλλί]
αν ἀρχεθέωρον καὶ ἀγαγεῖν ὑπὲρ τ[ο]ῦ δήμου [τὴν θεωρίαν, ὑ]
πακούσας εἰς ταῦτα φιλοτίμως Κ[αλ]λίας κα̣[ὶ τὰς ἐψηφισ]
μένας αὐτῶι ὑπὸ τοῦ δήμου εἰς τὴ̣ν ἀρχεθεω[ρίαν πεντήκον]
τα μνᾶς ἀφεὶς καὶ ἐπιδοὺς τῶι δή[μωι], αὐτὸ[ς τὴν μὲν θεωρία]
ν ἀγαγὼν ἐκ τῶν ἰδίων καλῶς καὶ ἀ[ξίως] τοῦ δ̣[ή]μου, [τῆς δὲ] θ̣
υσίας ἐπιμεληθεὶς ὑπὲρ τῆς πόλεω[ς] καὶ τῶν ἄλλω̣[ν] ἀπ̣ά̣[ντ]
ων ὧν προσῆκεν μετὰ τῶν θ̣ε̣ω[ρ]ῶ̣ν· κ̣[αὶ τ]οῦ δήμ[ο]υ τότε [πρῶτο]
ν τὰ Παναθήναια τεῖ Ἀρχηγέτι[δι] μέλλοντος π̣ρ̣ο̣[εῖν] ἀ[φ'] ο̣[ὗ τ]
ὸ ἄστυ ἐκεκόμιστο, διαλεχθεὶς τῶι βασιλεῖ Κ̣[αλλίας ὑπὲ]
ρ τῶν ὅπλων ὧν εἰς τὸν πέπλον ἔδει παρασκευάσ̣α̣ι̣ [καὶ ἐπι]

δόντος τεῖ πόλει τοῦ βασιλ{ι}έως ἐ[σ]πούδ̣ασεν ὅπ[ως ἂν ὡς]
βέλτιστα τεῖ θεῶι γένηται καὶ οἱ θ[ε]ωροὶ̣ οἱ μ̣ε̣θ̣' [αὐτοῦ χε]
ιροτονηθέντες εὐθὺς ἀποκομίζωσ[ιν] ἐ̣[ν]ταῦ[θα τὰ ὅπλα· καὶ]
νῦν ἐν Ἁλικαρνασσῶι καθηστηκὼς ὑ[π]ὸ τ[οῦ βασιλέως Πτολ]
εμαίου Καλλίας διατελεῖ φιλοτιμο[ύ]μενο[ς πρός τε τὰς π]
ρεσβείας καὶ τὰς θεωρίας τὰς ὑπὸ το[ῦ] δήμ[ου πρὸς τὸν βασ]
ιλέα Πτολεμαῖον ἀποστελλομένας, καὶ ἰ̣δ̣ί[αι ἑ]κ̣[άστου τῶν]
πολιτῶν τῶν τε παραγιγνομένων πρὸς αὐτὸν [τὴν πᾶσαν ἐπ]
ιμέλειαν ποιούμενος καὶ τῶν στρατ[ιωτῶν τῶν ἐκεῖ τεταγ]
μένων μεθ' αὐτοῦ, περὶ πλείστου ποιούμ[ενος τὸ σύμφερον]
καὶ κοινεῖ τὸ τῆς πόλεως εὔσχημον· κ̣[.......16–17.......]
ν τεῖ πατρίδι Καλλίας οὐδεπώποθ' ὑ⟨π⟩ομείνας [...]ε[....κ]
αταλελυμένου τοῦ δήμου ἀλλὰ καὶ τὴν οὐσίαν τὴν ἐ̣[αυτοῦ]
προέμενος δόσιν δοθῆναι ἐν τεῖ ὀλιαρχίαι ὥστε μ[ηδὲν ὑ]
πεναντίον πρᾶξαι μήτε τοῖς νόμοις μήτε τεῖ δημοκ̣[ρατί]
α̣ι τεῖ ἐξ ἁπάντων Ἀθηναίων· ὅπως ἂν οὖν εἰδῶσι πάντες [οἱ βο]
υλόμενοι φιλοτιμεῖσθαι πρὸς τὴν πόλιν διότι ὁ δῆμος [ἀε]
ὶ μέμνηται τῶν εὐεργετησάντων ἑαυτὸν καὶ χάριν ἑκάστο
ις ἀποδίδωσιν· ἀγαθεῖ τύχει δεδόχθαι τεῖ βουλεῖ τοὺς π
ροέδρους οἵτινες ἂν λάχωσιν προεδρεύειν εἰς τὴν ἐκ⟨κ⟩λη[σ]
ίαν τὴν ἐκ τοῦ νόμου χρηματίσαι περὶ τούτων, γνώμην δὲ ξυμβ[ά]
λλεσθαι τῆς βουλῆς εἰς τὸν δῆμον, ὅτι δοκεῖ τεῖ βουλεῖ ἐ̣[π]
αινέσαι Καλλίαν Θυμοχάρου Σφήττιον ἀρετῆς ἕνεκα καὶ ε̣
ὐνοίας ἣν ἔχων διατελεῖ περὶ τὸν δῆμον τὸν Ἀθηναίων καὶ σ
τεφανῶσαι αὐτὸν χρυσῶι στεφάνωι κατὰ τὸν νόμον, καὶ ἀ
νειπεῖν τὸν στέφανον Διονυσίων τῶν μεγάλων τραγωιδῶ[ν]
τῶι ἀγῶνι τῶι καινῶι· τῆς δὲ ποιήσεως τοῦ στεφάνου καὶ τῆ[ς]
ἀναγορεύσεως ἐπιμεληθῆναι τοὺς ἐπὶ τεῖ διοικήσει· στῆσα[ι]
δὲ αὐτοῦ τὸν δῆμον καὶ εἰκόνα χαλ⟨κ⟩ῆν ἐν τεῖ ἀγορᾶι, εἶναι δ̣
ὲ καὶ προεδρίαν αὐτῶι ἐν ἅπασιν τοῖς ἀγῶσιν οἷς ἡ πόλις τ[ί]
θησιν καὶ τὸν ἀρχιτέκτονα τὸν ἐπὶ τὰ ἱερὰ χειρο⟨το⟩νούμεν[ο]
ν κατ⟨α⟩νέμειν αὐτῶι τὴν προεδρίαν· χειροτονῆσαι δὲ τὸν δ̣[ῆ]
μον ἤδη τρεῖς ἄνδρας ἐξ Ἀθηναίων ἁπάντων οἵτινες ἐπιμ[ελ]
ήσονται τῆς τε ποιήσεως τῆς εἰκόνος καὶ τῆς ἀναθέσεως· [ε]
ἰσαγαγεῖν δὲ καὶ τοὺς θεσμοθέτας τὴν δοκιμασίαν τῆς δ[ωρ]
εᾶς αὐτῶι εἰς τ⟨ὴ⟩ν ἡλιαίαν ἐπειδὰν αἱ ἡμέραι αἱ ἐκ τοῦ νόμ [ου]
διεξέλθωσιν· ⟨ὅ⟩π⟨ω⟩ς δ' ἂν καὶ εἰς τὸν λοιπὸν χρόνον ὑπόμνημα [δ]
ιαμένει τῶν πεφιλοτιμημένων εἰς τὸν δῆμον Καλλίαι, ἀναγ[ρά]
ψαι τόδε τὸ [ψή]φισμα τὸν γραμματέα τὸν κατὰ πρυτανείαν [ἐν]
στήλει λιθίνει καὶ στῆσαι παρὰ τὴν εἰκόνα, εἰς δὲ τὴν ἀν[αγ]
ραφὴν ⟨κ⟩αὶ τὴν στήλην μερίσαι τοὺς ἐπὶ τεῖ διοικήσηι τὸ [ἀν]
άλωμα τὸ γενόμενον.

Translation

The Demos
Kallias
son of Thymochares
of Sphettos

5 In the archonship of Sosistratos, in the sixth prytany of Pandionis for which Athenodoros, son of Gorgippos of Acharnai was secretary; on Posideon 18th, 21st of the prytany; assembly with full power. The chairman of the proedroi Epichares, son of Pheidostratos of Erchia and his colleagues put the question to a vote. Resolved by the Council and the Demos; Euchares, son of Euarchos of Konthyle made the motion:

11 Whereas Kallias--when the revolution of the Demos took place against those who were occupying the city, and they expelled the mercenary soldiers from the City, but the fort on the Mouseion was still occupied, and the countryside was in a state of war at the hands of the troops from the Peiraieus, and while Demetrios with his army was approaching from the Peloponnese to attack the City—Kallias learned the impending danger to the state, and choosing a thousand of the mercenary troops stationed with him on Andros, paying their wages and providing rations of grain, he came at once to the City to help the Demos, acting in accordance with the good will of King Ptolemy toward the Demos; and he marched his troops into the countryside and made every effort to protect the harvest of the grain so that as much grain as possible could be brought into the city.

27 And whereas, when Demetrios had arrived and encamped to besiege the City, Kallias fought on the side of the Demos, and attacking with his troops, although a wounded man, he did not shrink from any danger, not at any moment, for the sake of the deliverance of the Demos; and when King Ptolemy dispatched Sostratos to negotiate in the city's interests, and Sostratos summoned an embassy to meet him at Peiraieus with which he would conclude terms of peace with Demetrios on behalf of the city, Kallias complied with the request of the generals and the Council, acted as envoy for the Demos, and worked in every way for the city's interests, and he remained in the City with his mercenaries until the peace had been concluded; and after he had sailed back to King Ptolemy, he continued to cooperate in every way with the embassies sent out by the Demos and to work for the city's advantage.

43 And whereas, upon the succession to the monarchy of the younger King Ptolemy, Kallias was staying in the City and when the generals called upon him, explained the situation in which the city found itself, and begged him for the sake of the city to hasten to King Ptolemy in order that aid in the form of grain and money might be forthcoming as quickly as possible for the City, Kallias himself sailing at his own expense to Cyprus and there conversing earnestly with the king in behalf of the city brought back fifty talents of silver for the Demos and a gift of twenty thousand medimnoi of wheat, which were measured out from Delos to the agents sent by the Demos.

55 And whereas, when the king first established the Ptolemaia, the sacrifice and the

games for his father, and the Demos voted to send a sacred delegation and deemed it appropriate for [Kallias] to accept appointment as chief delegate and to lead [the delegation] on behalf of the Demos, Kallias complied zealously and, declining the [fifty?] minas which had been [appropriated] for him by the Demos for the conduct of his office, and giving them freely to the Demos, he himself both led the [delegation] well and in a manner [worthy] of the Demos at his private expense and also, together with the sacred delegates, took charge of the sacrifice in behalf of the city and of all other things that were appropriate; and since the Demos was then about to [celebrate] the Panathenaia for Athena Archegetis [for the first time after] they had recovered the City, [Kallias] conversed with the king about the ropes which it was necessary to prepare for the peplos, and the king having donated them to the city, he endeavored to see that they be as fine as possible for the Goddess and that the delegates elected with him bring [the ropes back here] at once.

70 And whereas, now assigned by King Ptolemy to duty in Halikarnassos, Kallias continues to strive eagerly toward the success of the embassies and the sacred delegations dispatched by the Demos to King Ptolemy, and privately he devotes [every] attention [to each] of the citizens who comes to him and takes all possible care too of the soldiers stationed [there] with him, his main aim being [the advantage] and generally the dignity of the city; [and --] of the fatherland Kallias could never for a moment endure [to --], when the democracy was overthrown, but rather his own property he allowed to be confiscated in the oligarchy so as to act in no way in opposition either to the laws or to the democracy which is the democracy of all Athenians.

83 Now therefore, in order that all men who wish to contribute emulously toward the greatness of the city may know that the Demos remembers forever those who serve it well and renders gratitude to each, with good fortune, be it resolved by the Council that the proedroi, who are chosen by lot to preside in the assembly which meets according to the law, deliberate about these matters and submit the resolution of the Council to the Demos, that the Council resolves to praise Kallias, son of Thymochares of Sphettos for his merit and for the good will which he continues to have toward the
92 Demos of the Athenians, and to crown him with a golden crown according to the law, and to proclaim the crown at the contest for new tragedies at the Great Dionysia; that the board of administration have charge of making the crown and the proclamation; further that the Demos shall erect a bronze statue of him in the Agora; and that he shall have a front seat at all the contests which the city holds, and that the duly elected architect in charge of sanctuaries shall assign him the front seat; that the Demos shall forthwith elect three men from all the Athenians who will supervise the making
101 and the installation of the statue; that the thesmothetai shall introduce the scrutiny of his award in the Heliaia when the days prescribed by law shall have elapsed; in order that there may remain for the future a record of Kallias' honorable deeds to the Demos, that the prytany-secretary shall inscribe this decree on a marble stele and place it beside the statue; and the board of administration shall apportion the expenditure incurred for the inscription and the stele.

Epigraphical Notes

The text is disposed on the stone so that the prescript of the decree begins 0.21 m. below the molding and an uninscribed space, 0.15 m. high, is left at the bottom of the shaft. Centered in the space above the main body of the text is the citation (lines 1–4) indicating the award of a golden crown which would originally have been shown in paint as was the practice at this period on inscriptions honoring the prytaneis of the Council.[3]

In general the lettering is neat and quite carefully executed so that large portions of the text are readily legible. The spacing, however, shows considerable irregularities, and the lines vary in length from a minimum of 42 letters (lines 11, 30) to a maximum of 49 (lines 88, 105), those toward the bottom being regularly two or three letters longer than those at the top because of the taper of the stele. Line 10 with only 26 letters is, of course, a deliberate exception since it records, in slightly larger and more widely spaced letters, only the formula of resolution which thus clearly separates the prescript from the main body of the decree. For the most part the readings are not in doubt since the stone has survived with remarkably little damage. Only on the lower part of the stele toward the right edge has the surface been worn so smooth as to obliterate the letters (Pl. 1), though even here very little has been lost.

Line 5: The first four letters were originally cut one half line lower on the stone and then re-cut without erasure in their present positions.

Line 8: The 25 letters before the final epsilon are all inscribed *in rasura*. The erasure, like four others in lines 9, 22, 50, and 109, simply represents an effort on the part of the stone cutter to correct errors in his transcription of the text which he himself happened to notice. As will be noted below, there are a number of other passages which would have benefited from still further erasure.

Line 9: The name of the chairman of the proedroi has been erased and corrected from the iota of Epichares through the rho of his patronymic.

Line 22: The last 27 letters of the line are cut *in rasura*. In view of the fact that at the beginning of the line the spacing is unusually crowded, whereas the letters are exceptionally widely spaced toward the end, we may surmise that the erasure was employed to delete letters, or a word, which the mason had mistakenly duplicated.

Line 50: From the 14th letter to the end of the line, all letters are inscribed *in rasura*. Again the spacing is unusually wide and the letters are a bit larger toward the right end. The mason inadvertently carved the ninth letter from the right edge as delta instead of alpha, so that the stone reads *IΔIΔI*.

Line 62: The 34th letter preserves only the left diagonal of a triangular letter and possibly the lower angle of a delta. The next letter has been completely obliterated, but after it faint outlines of mu, omicron and upsilon can be seen. In the sixth space further to the right are clear indications of a circular letter. This is separated from the upsilon by no more than five letters, and although there is space for two letters between it and the right edge of the stone, this was seemingly uninscribed. In lines 30 and 92 the last letter also falls two spaces from the right edge.

Line 63: The readings of the last two letters are doubtful. Part of the left vertical stroke and of an upper horizontal as of pi seem to be visible, but gamma is also possible epigraphically. The letter has been damaged

[3] See S. Dow, *Hesperia*, Suppl. I, *Prytaneis*, Athens 1937, p. 20. With few exceptions the wreaths of the citations were regularly painted until *ca.* 125 B.C.

in such a way that a circular letter is not altogether excluded. The last preserved letter in the line was clearly triangular, either alpha or lambda.

Line 64: There is space for no more than four or five letters at the right end of the line.

Line 65: The 36th letter was clearly rectangular, the left vertical stroke and upper left angle being preserved. Gamma and epsilon are also possible epigraphically as well as pi. Traces of a circular letter are preserved in the next space, and there is room for no more than three letters between this and the alpha. Only faint traces of another circular letter can be seen in the second space beyond the alpha.

Line 66: There is only the slightest trace of a stroke in the lower left corner of the last preserved letter space.

Line 67: Of the three dotted letters at the right end of the line only the lowest tips of the strokes are preserved.

Line 74: In the 31st letter space there are traces of two vertical strokes. Epigraphically eta is a possible reading, but the preceding kappa and alpha make it preferable to read both strokes as iotas. The next space preserves the left diagonal of a triangular letter, followed by a centered vertical stroke which can only be read as iota. In the fourth space further to the right, there is visible a left vertical stroke which is more likely to have been joined by other strokes at the middle than at the top or bottom, so that eta or kappa is most probable.

Line 78: The last visible letter in the line had a left vertical stroke, but no other traces survive. There is space for 16 or 17 letters to the right edge of the stone.

Line 79: The 29th letter was mistakenly carved on the stone as mu instead of pi. The last visible letter is epsilon preceded by no more than three missing letters to the left, and followed by five or six letters to the right edge.

Line 80: There is space for no more than five letters to be restored at the right end of the line.

Line 82: The dotted kappa preserves only the lowest tip of the vertical stroke.

Line 83: The initial letter shows only the lower part of a right diagonal stroke.

Line 87: The mason inadvertently omitted one of the kappas from the last word in the line.

Line 95: After cutting the left vertical stroke for the first eta of *ἐπιμεληθῆναι*, the mason then carved the circle for the theta immediately next to it. Seeing his mistake, he proceeded to cut the right vertical of the eta through the middle of the circle, joined the two with a rather long cross bar, and then went on to cut another theta.

Line 96: In the 28th letter space, the stone has chi instead of kappa.

Line 98: The stone reads *ΧΕΙΡΟΝΟΥΜΕΝ*, one syllable of the word having been omitted by mistake.

Line 99: In the fifth letter space the stone has epsilon instead of alpha.

Line 103: The stone reads *ΕΙΣΤΝΗΛ*, the eta of the definite article being omitted.

Line 104: Omicron and omega have been mistakenly reversed so that the stone reads *ΩΠΟΣ*.

Line 108: The sixth letter was mistakenly cut as tau instead of kappa.

Line 109: All the letters beginning with the fourth are inscribed *in rasura*.

CHAPTER II

COMMENTARY ON THE DECREE

Lines 1–4: The new document is a decree of the Athenian assembly which confers a golden crown and other honors (lines 90–99) upon Kallias, son of Thymochares of Sphettos in consideration of his services to Athens at various times in his career. The man's deme and his characteristic prosopography identify him at once as the scion of a wealthy and prominent Athenian family whose members were active in politics and held a number of different public offices throughout much of the 4th and 3rd centuries B.C. Kallias himself, however, has left no other record of his activities among the Athenian documents. Indeed, his name has hitherto been known only from a Delian decree of the early 3rd century (*IG* XI 4, 527), which calls him Kallias, son of Thymochares the Athenian, and his relationship to the family was first recognized by J. K. Davies.[4]

Kallias' brother Phaidros, his father Thymochares, and his grandfather Phaidros are all well known as men of public affairs. The last was elected general on at least three occasions in the third quarter of the 4th century.[5] Thymochares, who as a young man seems to have belonged to the circle of Lykourgos, also served as general under the regime of Demetrios of Phaleron; and he commanded Athenian forces fighting with Antigonos in Cyprus probably in 316 B.C., and later with Kassandros in 313/2.[6] The public career of Kallias' brother Phaidros[7] began during the tyranny of Lachares when

[4] *APF*, p. 526; cf. Kirchner, *PA* 7824. It may be noted that in the Athenian inscriptions the genitive of the patronymic is spelled without exception *Θυμοχάρου* as here lines 3, 90. Cf. *IG* II², 682, lines 57, 72; 700, line 1; 7385; *Hesperia* 15, 1946, p. 192, no. 37, line 15. Only in the Delian text (*IG* XI 4, 527, line 5) does the name appear in the form *Θυμοχάρους*, as it is transcribed by Kirchner (*PA* 13963) and Davies (*APF*, pp. 526, 528).

[5] Kirchner, *PA* 13964; Davies, *APF*, p. 525. He was elected general in 347/6: *IG* II², 213, line 8; before 334/3: *IG* II², 1623, line 240, and cf. lines 174–175, 329, 342; in 323 B.C.: Strabo, X.1.6. Cf. Aischines, I.43,50. From this grandfather Kallias' brother Phaidros took his name. This indicates that Phaidros was the elder brother and Kallias the younger. Kallias was named for his great grandfather, Kallias of Sphettos, Kirchner, *PA* 7891; Davies, *APF*, p. 525.

[6] Kirchner, *PA* 7412; Davies, *APF*, pp. 525–526. In 329/8 he was elected, along with Lykourgos and other prominent Athenians, as one of the hieropoioi of the Amphiareia at Oropos (*IG* VII, 4254=*SIG*³, 298, lines 29–30). For his military commands, *IG* II², 682, lines 3–18; Appendix **1**. If his first generalship in Asia and Cyprus was in command of Athenian ships cooperating with Antigonos and Demetrios, this will explain the excision of some 20 letters in line 6, where the names of Antigonos and Demetrios should presumably be restored, cf. Dittenberger's note, *SIG*³, 409 *ad loc.*, and for the date of the campaign, C. Habicht, *AthMitt* 72, 1957, p. 162, note 26.

[7] Kirchner, *PA* 13963; Davies, *APF*, pp. 526–527. For the details of his career, *IG* II², 682, lines 21–63; Appendix **1**, the only source. As a political figure of the early 3rd century he has been much discussed,

in 296/5 he was elected general ἐπὶ τὴν παρασκευὴν twice, both before and after the dissolution of the Boule in that year. In the years after Athens' capitulation to Demetrios Poliorketes, when the city was subject to Demetrios as king of Macedon and occupied by his garrisons on the Mouseion and in Peiraieus, Phaidros apparently held office almost continuously, several times as general ἐπὶ τὴν χώραν, three times as commander of the foreign mercenaries, once as ambassador to Ptolemy I Soter, and twice as hoplite general. Later, during the years of the nationalist government, Phaidros' public activities were confined to the organization of festivals and athletic events, to various liturgies and public subscriptions, services which drew more heavily upon his personal fortune than upon his political experience or military prowess. Our knowledge of the family, and of the career of Phaidros in particular, is based in large part upon the honorary decree for him (*IG* II^2, 682) to which reference has already been made. This document forms a striking parallel for the new decree in honor of Kallias: a parallel in that both brothers won by their good deeds the highest honors which the Demos could bestow, but striking in that the careers of these two men, exactly contemporary and closely related, should in the event be so different and their politics so divergent. Indeed, a close comparison of the two decrees will show in graphic detail the extent to which the political dislocations of the late 4th and early 3rd centuries had disrupted some of the most substantial families of Athens and polarized their politics.

It was long ago recognized by Tarn[8] that the complexion of Phaidros' politics was pro-Macedonian, even if moderate, as he has often been called. Many details of *IG* II^2, 682 serve to bear out this interpretation. There can be no doubt that the decree was promulgated during the period of Macedonian control following Athens' defeat in the Chremonidean War, for the golden crown and the stele were paid for by the single Officer of Administration (ὁ ἐπὶ τεῖ διοικήσει, lines 79–80, 91), the characteristic administrative official of the Macedonian period.[9] The date can be determined more precisely because the last recorded event of Phaidros' career is dated by the archon Euboulos III of 256/5 (line 58), in whose year Phaidros' son Thymochares was agonothetes. Moreover, both the decree and its amendment were moved by Lyandros, son of Lysiades of Anaphlystos, who served as treasurer of the Council in Philinos' archonship (254/3) and also proposed a decree in honor of a prytany of that year.[10] Since Lyandros specified that Phaidros' honors should be proclaimed at the Great Panathenaia (line 77), his decree was probably passed in a year prior to the celebration of that

---

and the events and chronology of his career have been variously interpreted. See W. S. Ferguson, *Klio* 5, 1905, p. 161; Ferguson, *HA*, pp. 133, 137, 141f.; W. W. Tarn, *Ant. Gon.*, pp. 45f., 422; K. J. Beloch, *RivFil* 51, 1923, pp. 273–286; W. B. Dinsmoor, *Archons*, pp. 70f., 77–80; W. Hoffmann, *RE* XIX, 1938, cols. 1553–1555, *s.v.* Phaidros (4). For the chronology and interpretation followed here, see below, pp. 65–72.

[8] *Ant. Gon.*, pp. 45–46; followed by Dinsmoor, *Archons*, p. 77; Dinsmoor, *List*, p. 51.

[9] Dinsmoor, *Archons*, pp. 65–66.

[10] *Agora* XV, no. 89 = *Hesperia* 38, 1969, p. 418, no. 1, lines 5–6, 32, and for the date, cf. Meritt, *Hesperia* 38, 1969, p. 433.

quadrennial festival. It follows, then, that the most likely date is 255/4, the year which intervened between the archonship of Euboulos III and the Great Panathenaia in the summer of 254 B.C.[11]

In the context of these years of most stringent Macedonian domination at Athens, it is readily understandable that the family's pro-Macedonian leanings should receive public acclaim. Phaidros' son Thymochares was not only elected agonothetes of 256/5, but he had previously served as archon of 258/7, at a time when election by lot had been abrogated and the city's highest civic office was in the appointment of the Macedonian king.[12] Furthermore, the decree for Phaidros describes with obvious approval the activities of his father Thymochares in the Macedonian cause as general under Kassandros' creature, Demetrios of Phaleron (lines 3–19). But the the text goes on to state explicitly that Phaidros himself shared the same political principles with his ancestors: *τὴν αὐτὴν αἵρεσιν ἔχων τοῖς προγόνοις* (lines 19–20); and this is borne out by the subsequent actions of his public career. As hoplite general in the archonships of Kimon and Xenophon (lines 30–52), his policies sufficiently promoted the Macedonian interests so that nine full lines of text, describing Phaidros' actions in those two years, were chiseled from the stone by the vengeful Athenians of 200 B.C. who sought thus to obliterate from the public record all memory of the Antigonid house in their wrath at Philip V.[13] However these lacunae may be filled by modern historians and Phaidros' actions be related to contemporary events, his conduct of affairs was clearly construed by later Athenians as favorable to Macedon, or it would still be possible to read of what he did.

With all this the career of Kallias is in sharpest contrast. He was honored by the nationalist government some 15 years earlier than his brother, as we learn from the plural Board of Administration (*οἱ ἐπὶ τεῖ διοικήσει*) which arranged for his crown and paid for the stele (lines 95, 108). Moreover, his decree is redolent with the rhetoric

[11] For passage of the decree in the second year of an Olympiad, prior to the Great Panathenaia, Beloch, *Gr. Gesch.* IV², ii, pp. 85–87 (with date in 256/5 or 252/1); Dinsmoor, *Archons*, pp. 168–169 (with date in 259/8). Cf. *IG* II², 677, lines 1–3: *[καὶ ἀνανεωσαμένου] τοῦ δήμ[ου τὴ]ν θυσίαν καὶ τ[ὰ ἀγωνίσματα τῶν Πα]ναθηναίων τό τε στάδιον κατ[εσκεύασεν ἐπαξί]ως*. If Dittenberger's restorations are correct, we may infer that the Panathenaic festival was interrupted for some years after the Chremonidean War. It is possible that the renewal of the festival and refurbishing of the stadium by Antigonos' friend, Herakleitos of Athmonon, coincided with the announcement of Phaidros' honors. Both these events would have been eminently appropriate in 254 B.C., the first celebration of the Great Panathenaia after Antigonos' "liberation of Athens" in Ol. 131. 1 = 256/5, Eusebios, *Chron. Can.* II, pp. 120–121 (ed. Schoene), p. 201 (ed. Karst).

[12] For the archonship of Thymochares, *IG* II², 700 + *Hesperia* 7, 1938, p. 110, no. 20; Dinsmoor, *Archons*, pp. 168–169 (there dated 259/8); Pritchett and Meritt, *Chronology*, p. xx (there dated 257/6); Meritt, *Ath. Year*, pp. 140–142 (there dated 258/7). For Antigonos' appointment of archons after the Chremonidean War, *F. Gr. Hist.*, 244, Apollodoros F 44: *κ̣α̣ὶ̣ φρουρὰ[ν εἰς] τὸ Μουσεῖον [τότε] εἰσῆχ-θ[αι ὑπ'] Ἀντιγόνου, [καὶ τὰς] ἀρχὰς [ἀνῃρῆσθ]αι καὶ πνᾶ ἐ̣ν̣[ὶ] βουλεύ[ειν(?) ἐφ]εῖσθαι.*

[13] Livy, XXXI.44.4–6: *rogationem extemplo tulerunt plebesque scivit ut Philippi statuae et imagines omnes nominaque earum, item maiorum eius virile ac muliebre secus omnium tollerentur delerenturque diesque festi, sacra, sacerdotes, quae ipsius maiorumque eius honoris causa instituta essent, omnia profanarentur;... sacerdotes publicos, quotienscumque pro populo Atheniensi sociisque, exercitibus et classibus eorum precarentur, totiens detestari atque exsecrari Philippum, liberos eius regnumque, terrestres navalesque copias, Macedonum genus omne nomenque.* Cf. Ferguson, *HA*, pp. 276–277.

of democracy: Kallias did not shrink from any danger while fighting for the deliverance of the Demos (lines 31–32), and he saw his property confiscated rather than act in any way against the democracy of all Athenians (lines 80–83). Unlike the decree for Phaidros, there is no mention here of Kallias' family and the deeds of his ancestors; there is no reference to their political principles which Phaidros espoused and Kallias rejected. It is to be noted that throughout the 17 years of his career covered by our text, Kallias held no elected nor allotted office in the government of Athens, but he was for all or most of this time a commander of mercenary soldiers in the service of Ptolemy I Soter and Ptolemy II Philadelphos. The decree speaks of the soldiers *τῶν μεθ' αὐτοῦ τεταγμένων ἐν Ἄνδρωι* (line 20), with whom Kallias went to the aid of Athens, *ἀκόλουθα πράττων τεῖ τοῦ βασιλέως Πτολεμαίου πρὸς τὸν δῆμον εὐνοίαι* (lines 22–23); and at the time the decree was passed he is described as being stationed by King Ptolemy in Halikarnassos (line 71). As we shall have occasion to see in more detail shortly, many of the services for which Kallias is here honored specifically concern Athens' relations with the king of Egypt; and his role seems often to have been that of diplomatic intermediary interceding with the king on behalf of Athens and her ambassadors.

Lines 5–9: The decree for Kallias is dated to the archonship of Sosistratos in which Athenodoros, son of Gorgippos of Acharnai, was secretary of the Council. The archon Sosistratos has been known heretofore only from two dedications by the agonothetes of his year, one of which preserves the archon's name, while in the other the name is to be restored (*IG* II², 3081, 3082). A third inscription (*IG* II², 3851) is on the base of an honorary statue of the same agonothetes, Theophanes, son of Dioskourides of Euonymon; but while it can be assigned to the year of Sosistratos, the archon's name does not appear in the text. In the absence of his secretary's name and deme, Sosistratos has been assigned to various otherwise unoccupied years in the early 3rd century. Attempts have been made to restore his name at the beginning of *IG* II², 672 and 670 B, and thus to date his archonship from the context of these documents. He has accordingly been placed in 280/79,[14] but has come more recently to reside in 277/6, there being no other claimant whose title to that year was demonstrable.[15] The discovery of the secretary, Athenodoros of Acharnai, now permits the year of Sosistratos to be fixed precisely. The secretary from Acharnai represents the tribe Oineis (VIII) and must, therefore, occupy the eighth position in a secretary cycle. His year must come before the end of the Chremonidean War since the plural Board of Administration is still in office (lines 95, 108), but it is later than the accession of Ptolemy II Philadelphos (283/2) and the establishment of the Ptolemaia at Alexandria, both of

[14] Restored in *IG* II², 672 by A. C. Johnson, *CP* 9, 1914, pp. 258, 430 (with date in 282/1); followed by Meritt, *Hesperia* 7, 1938, pp. 104, 133 (with date in 280/79); Dinsmoor, *List*, pp. 48–49, 54; Pritchett and Meritt, *Chronology*, p. xviii. Restoration of his name in *IG* II², 670 B was suggested by Meritt, *Ath. Year*, p. 233, note 35.

[15] Proposed by Beloch, *Gr. Gesch.*, IV², ii, p. 72 on the basis of his dating of *IG* II², 672; followed by Dinsmoor, *Archons*, pp. 75–76; *idem*, *Hesperia* 23, 1954, p. 314; Meritt, *Ath. Year*, p. 233; E. Manni, *Historia* 24, 1975, p. 26. But see now Meritt, *Historia* 26, 1977, p. 174.

which events are mentioned in the text (lines 44–45, 55–56). Within this period the only possible position for a secretary from Acharnai (VIII) is in 270/69 to which Sosistratos can accordingly be assigned,[16] next after Pytharatos (271/0) with his secretary from Kephale (VII).

The decree was passed at the principal assembly of the sixth prytany, and the prescript provides the calendric equation: Posideon 18 = Prytany VI 21. This equation is satisfied if Posideon 18 fell on the 166th day of an ordinary year in which Hekatombaion was a full month of 30 days, and the first five prytanies each had 29 days. That 270/69 should prove to be an ordinary year in the festival calendar is appropriate and was to have been expected in view of the intercalary character of Pytharatos' year (271/0) which immediately preceded. Evidence for the calendar of 271/0 comes from the equation: Metageitnion 9 = Prytany II 7 = 39th day,[17] and this alone would have suggested a typical intercalary year in which the prytanies each had 32 days and the year began with a full month. Such a year of 13 months would also normally have ended with 30 days in the last month; and we should then have expected the following year to begin with 29 days in Hekatombaion in order to preserve the usual alternation of full and hollow months. The equation of our inscription will not allow a month of 29 days at the beginning of 270/69, unless we posit a reversal in the alternation of the months so as to place two full months back to back during the first five months of the year.[18]

Two other equations are known, however, from 271/0, and they give evidence of considerable irregularity during the latter part of the year. A total of eight days was intercalated in the festival calendar early in Elaphebolion, the ninth day of that month being itself intercalated four times, presumably in order to postpone the festival of the Dionysia.[19] Another equation has been restored by B. D. Meritt as of Prytany XII: [Σκιροφο]ριῶνος ἕνει καὶ [νέαι προτέραι, μιᾶι καὶ τριακο]στεῖ τῆς πρυτανε[ίας], the same equation which is preserved in *IG* II², 495 for the next-to-last day of 303/2. On

[16] This year has been variously claimed for other archons: Peithidemos, Dinsmoor, *Archons*, pp. 30, 81; Dinsmoor, *List*, pp. 21, 26ff.; Diogeiton, Pritchett and Meritt, *Chronology*, p. xix; Philippides, Dinsmoor, *Hesperia* 23, 1954, p. 314; Meritt, *Ath. Year*, p. 233; Manni, *Historia* 24, 1975, p. 26. Of these Diogeiton, with a secretary from Keiriadai (X) is no longer eligible to follow Pytharatos, with his secretary from Kephale (VII). The secretaries of Peithidemos and Philippides are unknown, but both must now yield 270/69 to Sosistratos. Philippides, the most recent claimant, is known only from a single dedicatory inscription (*IG* II², 2859), and he could be placed equally well in 269/8, which is now no longer occupied since the removal of Philinos from 269/8 to 254/3, Meritt, *Hesperia* 38, 1969, pp. 432f. *IG* II², 672, in which the name of Sosistratos can no longer be restored, is still to be dated in 277/6 although the archon's name for that year is unknown, Meritt, *Historia* 26, 1977, p. 174.

[17] The calendar of 271/0 is known from two inscriptions published by Dinsmoor, *Hesperia* 23, 1954, pp. 284–316; for the equation, p. 288, lines 3–5. Two other texts have been added by Meritt, *Ath. Year*, pp. 192–195, of which the latter, pp. 194–195, should now be dissociated from Pytharatos, cf. Pritchett, *ZPE* 20, 1976, pp. 185–192.

[18] Cf. e.g. the calendar of 306/5: Pritchett, *AJP* 58, 1937, pp. 329–333; Meritt, *Ath. Year*, pp. 138–139; *idem*, *Hesperia* 33, 1964, p. 9; also the arrangement of months proposed by Meritt for 247/6 and 188/7, *Ath. Year*, pp. 137, 156.

[19] *Hesperia* 23, 1954, p. 299, lines 2–5, and cf. pp. 308ff.

the basis of this equation, Meritt has argued that Skirophorion of these two years was planned as a hollow month (29 days) and subsequently made full by repeating the last day (ἕνη καὶ νέα), in order to make the festival calendar coterminous with the prytany year.[20] If this be the case, we may perhaps suppose that the full Hekatombaion of 270/69 was planned when it was thought that Skirophorion of 271/0 would be a hollow month. It may be noted that a similar juxtaposition of full Skirophorion followed by full Hekatombaion probably occurred two years earlier in the summer of 272 B.C., when the ordinary year of Lysitheides (272/1) succeeded the intercalary year of Glaukippos (273/2).[21]

Line 11: The speaker who made the motion, Euchares, son of Euarchos of Konthyle, is known to have served as ἀναγραφεὺς τῶν νόμων in 304/3. He was at that time responsible for the publication of all the laws enacted by the nomothetai of that year, and as a result of his efficient conduct of office, Euchares was praised and crowned by the Boule.[22] It is natural enough that a man who had participated in the revision of the law code after the democratic restoration of 307/6 should likewise find a congenial climate for political activity in the years of the nationalist government. Euchares' involvement in both these periods is closely parallel to that of Demochares of Leukonoe, with whom he must have been nearly contemporary in age, since he was honored for public service a full 34 years before the date of his decree for Kallias. Also like Demochares, Euchares must have been an effective public speaker, if we may judge from the unusually rhetorical style of the present decree.

Lines 12–18: These and the following lines preserve the most detailed and circumstantial account that has yet come to light of Athens' revolt from Demetrios Poliorketes in 286 B.C.[23] We shall turn shortly to consider the proper historical setting

[20] For the text, Meritt, *Ath. Year*, pp. 192–193; for discussion of the same equation in 303/2, *idem*, *Hesperia* 33, 1964, pp. 6–7; cf. *idem*, Ἀρχ. Ἐφ., 1968, pp. 77–80; 1973, pp. 237–245; *AJP* 95, 1974, pp. 268–279. Pritchett, *BCH* 88, 1964, p. 465 has strongly emphasized the degree to which this equation for 271/0 relies upon restoration of the text.

[21] That Skirophorion of 273/2 was a full month at the end of an intercalary year is indicated by *IG* II², 676, lines 3–6 with the equation: Skirophorion 21 = Prytany XII [2]3 = 375th day, W. K. Pritchett and O. Neugebauer, *The Calendars of Athens*, Cambridge, Mass. 1947, p. 70. Inscriptions of the year of Lysitheides (272/1) have been studied by Meritt, *Hesperia* 26, 1957, pp. 54–57. The year was ordinary, and all three equations show exact correspondence between the festival date and the prytany date. The equation of *IG* II², 704: Elaphebolion 26 = Prytany IX 26 = 262nd day (see Pritchett and Meritt, *Chronology*, p. 97, note 29) requires that Elaphebolion be a full month. If the full and hollow months alternated in regular succession, Hekatombaion would likewise have had 30 days at the beginning of the year.

[22] *IG* II², 487. Cf. Kirchner, *PA* 6131. For the revision of the laws after the fall of Demetrios of Phaleron, Ferguson, *HA*, pp. 103–104.

[23] These events have been discussed with varying interpretations and chronologies by Ferguson, *HA*, pp. 144–150 (with date in winter 289/8, dissociated from the archon Diokles); Tarn, *Ant. Gon.*, pp. 92–98, 418–422 (with date in late spring 288, shortly before the archonship of Diokles, there dated 288/7); Beloch, *Gr. Gesch.* IV², i, pp. 231–232; IV², ii, pp. 65–67, 105–106 (with date June–July 288, but before the fall of Demetrios, there placed in late 288). A date in the early summer of 288 has since been adopted by Dinsmoor,

of the new document and the chronology of events which it implies. It is sufficient here to observe the extent to which the new text confirms the evidence provided by other sources for the Athenian uprising. Although Plutarch gave only brief mention to the revolution in his *Life of Demetrios* (46.1–2; Appendix **3**), more detailed information can be pieced together from a passage of Pausanias (I.26.1–2; Appendix **5**) and the honorific decree for the mercenary soldier Strombichos (*IG* II^2, 666, 667; Appendix **7**, **8**). Pausanias reports that the Athenians elected Olympiodoros general. "He led them, old men and young boys alike, against the Macedonians, hoping to succeed in battle more from daring than from strength. When the Macedonians marched out to meet him, he defeated them in battle; they fled to the Mouseion, and he took the place. Athens was thus liberated from the Macedonians." In the decree for Strombichos, the course of the revolution is seen from the point of view of a captain of mercenaries in Demetrios' service, who at the time of the revolt was lieutenant to a certain Spintharos, commandant of Demetrios' garrison on the Mouseion.[24]

> When the Demos took up arms for freedom and asked even the mercenaries to come over on the side of the city, he complied with the Demos for the sake of freedom and put his arms with the city; for he thought that he ought not to oppose the city's best interests, but should rather help to be the author of its deliverance; and he joined with the Demos in besieging the Mouseion (*IG* II^2, 666, lines 9–15).

From these two sources there emerges a clear sequence of events. The Athenian democrats revolted from Demetrios and elected Olympiodoros general, to command whatever forces he could raise against the Macedonian garrison in the city. The insurgents then offered bribes to Strombichos, and he deserted together with a portion of the garrison under his command and fought with the democrats. The remainder of the garrison attempted to crush the revolt, was defeated in battle in the streets of Athens, and forced to seek refuge again in their fort on the Mouseion. Finally, Olympiodoros stormed the Mouseion with the aid of Strombichos and captured the fort itself with the loss of only 13 men, whose graves Pausanias (I.29.13; Appendix **6**) later saw in the Kerameikos, and among whom a certain Leokritos (I.26.2) was first to mount the wall and first to enter the fort.

In the new decree, this celebrated episode is described in a series of temporal clauses in the genitive absolute. The speaker is careful to distinguish with unusual

---

Archons, pp. 57–59; G. Elkeles, *Demetrios der Städtebelagerer* (Diss. Breslau 1941), p. 101 and note 23; P. Lévêque, *Pyrrhos*, pp. 158–161; E. Will, *Monde hellénistique* I, pp. 79–80; C. W. Wehrli, *Antigone et Démétrios*, Geneva 1968, pp. 184–185. A date in 287/6 was accepted by Manni, *Dem. Pol.*, p. 69. A. R. Deprado, *RivFil*, n.s. 31, 1953, pp. 27–42 correctly dated Diokles in 286/5 but placed the revolt during the first 11 days of that archon year. H. Bengtson, *Griechische Geschichte*, Munich 1960, p. 377 and note 5, adopted a date for the revolt in the summer of 287, simultaneous with Demetrios' fall in Macedonia.

[24] The phrase *καταλειφθεὶς ἐν τῶι ἄστει μετὰ Σπινθάρου* (line 8) was construed by Deprado, *RivFil*, n.s. 31, 1953, p. 29 to mean that Strombichos was a prisoner in Spintharos' charge. But the participle derives from *καταλείπω*, not from *καταλαμβάνω*, and means that he was left behind in command. For the same usage applied to a military command, cf. *IG* XII 5, 1004, line 2, quoted footnote 37. For recent discussion of the decree, H. Heinen, *Untersuchungen*, pp. 110ff.

precision the same order of events. The Demos rose up against those who were "holding down the city" and drove the mercenaries out of the city itself, but they still occupied the fort on the Mouseion to which they then retreated. Our text also makes clear distinction between two separate groups of the enemy who tried to put down the nationalist revolt: *τοὺς ἐκ τοῦ ἄστεως στρατιώτας* (lines 13–14), and *τῶν ἐκ τοῦ Πειραέως* (line 16). The former refers to the mercenaries under Spintharos' command who remained loyal to Demetrios, while the latter is to be understood as the Macedonian garrison stationed in the Peiraieus. These troops were probably joined later by those who survived the storming of the Mouseion, and their purpose in ravaging the Attic countryside was undoubtedly to prevent Athens from provisioning herself for the siege with which Demetrios would shortly invest the city.

Another clause in the genitive absolute refers to Demetrios' approach to Athens after the first successful stage of the revolt. It is interesting to note that he came not from the direction of Macedonia, but from the Peloponnese. This evidence serves to bear out Plutarch's statement (*Demetr.* 45.1,3) that Demetrios after his flight from Macedonia went about the cities of Greece as a private man trying to collect his friends and supporters and to secure the loyalty of his garrisons. Although the text speaks generally of the Peloponnese, there need be no doubt that Corinth,[25] as the principal Macedonian garrison in that region, would be the natural place for Demetrios to regroup his forces; and he would have marched thence with his army in his vain attempt to quell the Athenian revolt.

Here, as elsewhere among the documents of the nationalist government, the deposed Antigonid king is referred to without the royal title, although throughout the same inscription the title *βασιλεὺς* is given to both Ptolemy Soter and Ptolemy Philadelphos. Ironically, the Athenians themselves are said to have been the first to address Antigonos Monophthalmos and his son Demetrios as kings, apparently after the battle of Salamis in 306 B.C. In the Athenian inscriptions, the title appears first on the last day of Mounichion in 305 and was used thereafter regularly until the revolution of 286.[26] During the ascendancy of the nationalist regime, from the revolt of Athens to the end of the Chremonidean War, although the preserved inscriptions are many fewer than for the last years of the 4th century, it is a noticeable fact that Antigonos and Demetrios are nowhere called *βασιλεῖς*.[27] All the other kings, on the contrary, both

[25] For Corinth as the principal Antigonid fortress in the Peloponnese, see the full discussion of H. Bengtson, *Strategie* II, pp. 345–362.

[26] Plutarch, *Demetr.* 10.3, first speaks of the Athenians' granting the royal title to Antigonos and Demetrios in connection with the restoration of the democracy in 307/6, but in *Demetr.* 17.5–18.1 and Diodorus, XX.53.2, they are said to have taken the title after the victory at Salamis. For the earliest epigraphical appearance of the title, *IG* II², 471, lines 15–16. It may simply be due to the chance of preservation that the royal title does not appear in earlier inscriptions, but it was evidently a recent innovation in the spring of 305, since *IG* II², 1492, line 99, referring to a date just nine days earlier, mentions Antigonos without title; but the same document uses the royal title under date of Skirophorion 21, 305 B.C., line 121. Cf. Ferguson, *HA*, p. 107, note 4.

[27] Cf. *IG* II², 666, line 8; Appendix **7**; and especially similar to the usage of our text, *IG* II², 657, lines 16–18; 28; Appendix **11**.

living and dead, are consistently referred to by the royal title.[28] It is not here a question that Demetrios was no longer living at the time of our inscription, for Ptolemy Soter had likewise been dead for 13 years before Euchares' decree for Kallias was passed; nor can it be a question that Demetrios was no longer king of Macedon at the time of the revolt here described, since the Athenians had addressed him as king a full decade before he became king of Macedon. The omission of the royal title seems rather to be a sign of deliberate hostility and disrespect on the part of the Athenian nationalists; for a later decree of 252/1,[29] passed by the pro-Macedonian government during the reign of Antigonos Gonatas, refers once again to King Demetrios.

Lines 18–23: Our text here introduces an entirely new dimension into the history of the Athenian revolt; for we are now provided with the astonishing information that a force of Ptolemaic mercenaries, acting on Ptolemy's orders, was fighting in Attica on the side of the Athenian nationalists. What is more, a Ptolemaic military base commanded by Kallias had already been established on the island of Andros prior to the revolt of Athens. Such mercenary garrisons came later to be the basic instrument of Ptolemaic hegemony over the islands of the Aegean. By the time of the Chremonidean War similar bases ringed the Cyclades; and evidence of their presence, the names of some of their commanders, and lists of personnel survive in inscriptions from Thera, Keos, Samos, eastern Crete, and later at Methana in the Peloponnese.[30] This is the first

[28] Lysimachos: *IG* II[2], 657, lines 10, 11, 17, 21, 33, 37; 662 (=*Hesperia* 26, 1957, p. 29=*SEG* XVI, 62), lines 7, 9, 10, 13; 663, lines 3, 5, 8, 18. Seleukos Nikator: *IG* II[2], 672, line 39. Ptolemy Soter: *IG* II[2], 650, lines 11–12; above lines 23, 32, 41. Ptolemy Philadelphos: *IG* II[2], 687, lines 16, 22, 33; above lines 44–45, 48, 51, 55, 66, 68, 71–72, 73–74. Spartokos of Bosporos: *IG* II[2], 653, lines 33, 42 (elsewhere in the text the title is not used). Audoleon of Paionia: *IG* II[2], 654, lines 12, 36–37 (but the title is not used in *IG* II[2], 655, lines 8, 10).

[29] *IG* II[2], 777, line 9, archon Kallimedes. Cf. the same treatment of Kassandros, who as an enemy of both Antigonos Monophthalmos and Athens was mentioned without title by the pro-Antigonid author of the decree for Phaidros of Sphettos, *IG* II[2], 682, lines 13–14, but Ptolemy Soter is called *βασιλεύς*, line 28.

[30] See generally Bengston, *Strategie* III, pp. 183–188 and most recently Bagnall, *Ptolemaic Possessions*, pp. 117–158. The garrison at Thera was evidently established by the time of the Chremonidean War and is well documented in the middle of the 2nd century. Inscriptions of that period preserve the names of many of its officers and men: *IG* XII 3, 327, 466 and 1390, 467 and 1391; 1296 (=*OGIS*, 59, 102, 110, 735; cf. *SEG* I, 343); cf. *Pros. Ptol.* VI, pp. 107–143 *passim*. That Patroklos was honored at Thera in connection with his expedition in the Chremonidean War (*IG* XII 3, 320=*OGIS*, 44) suggests that the base was already established before the middle of the 3rd century. On Ios a Ptolemaic naval squadron, under the command of Zenon, had already been established in the 280's, at about the time of the base on Andros, *IG* XII 5, 1004= *OGIS*, 773. On Keos officers stationed by Ptolemy II are mentioned in *IG* XII 5, 1061, 1066, the former in connection with Patroklos' expedition. The Ptolemaic base on Samos is first mentioned in *IG* XII 7, 506, line 4 (=*SIG*[3], 390) and cannot have been acquired before Lysimachos' death at Kouroupedion in 281 B.C., since the island was formerly in his possession, see below, p. 37 and footnote 92. For a list of mercenaries belonging to the garrison or naval base later in the century, see L. Robert, *Études épigraphiques et philologiques*, Paris 1938, pp. 113ff. The garrison commander Pelops was honored by the city, *SEG* I, 364; cf. Robert, *op. cit.*, p. 116; *Pros. Ptol.* VI, 14618; cf., however, the discussion of Bagnall, *Ptolemaic Possessions*, pp. 80–88. Officers of the garrisons on Crete and at Methana are mentioned in *ICret* III, pp. 81–83, no. 2, lines 4–8 (=*OGIS*, 45), no. 3, lines 4–7 (=*SEG* II, 512), which describe Patroklos as *στρατηγὸς ἐς Κρῆταν* and *IG* XII 3, 466 (=*OGIS*, 102), where there is mention of the oikonomos and grammateus of the mercenaries in

indication that such a garrison was also based on Andros, and its existence there before the revolt of Athens provides the earliest evidence for the expansion of Ptolemaic political and military power into Aegean waters.

The circumstances leading to the establishment of the base on Andros can better be discussed in the context of the events which precipitated the action of the Athenian nationalists, but it is important to stress the location of Kallias' base of operations. As the northernmost of the Cyclades, Andros is one of the islands most conveniently located for access to the harbors on the east coast of Attica. It was there that a foreign expeditionary force coming to the aid of the democracy would naturally seek to land, since the Macedonian garrison in the Peiraieus placed the port of Athens out of reach. Indeed, Kallias' landing in Attica here described bears striking resemblance to the operations of another Ptolemaic commander, Patroklos, who attempted to support the Athenian side in the Chremonidean War. Patroklos staged his campaign from the island of Keos,[31] which is closer to Attica, but further south, opposite Cape Sounion. Andros, on the other hand, although it is somewhat more distant, is more centrally situated with respect to the long reach of the Attic coastline; and the island lies due east of the best natural harbor on the east coast, at Porto Raphti, which later figured likewise in Patroklos' strategy and was defended by his fort on the Koroni peninsula.[32]

The phraseology of the text leaves no doubt about Kallias' position or about the nature of the forces under his command, for Athenian documents frequently express the relation of mercenary troops to their commanding officer in similar terms. Thus a company of mercenaries wishing to praise the Athenian general Thoukritos introduced the decree: *ἔδοξεν τοῖς στρατιώται[ς] τοῖς τεταγμένοις ὑπ[ὸ Τ]ιμ[ο]κράτην* (*IG* II², 1286). The soldiers serving under the peripolarchos Smikithion are similarly described: *ἔταξεν Ἐλευσῖνάδε καὶ τοὺς στρατιώτας τοὺς μεθ' ἑαυτοῦ* (*IG* II², 1193, lines 4–6). In the decree honoring the general Aristophanes, the mercenaries and their commander are carefully distinguished from the Athenians: *το[ῖς ἐν Ἐλευσῖ]νι τεταγμένοις τῶμ πολιτῶν καὶ τοῖς ἐμ Πανάκτωι καὶ ἐπὶ Φυλεῖ καὶ το[ῖς ξένοις τοῖ]ς μετὰ Γνωσίου τεταγμένοις* (*IG* II², 1299, lines 40–42). That Kallias' men were indeed mercenaries is made explicit since the text refers to the wages (*ὀψώνια*) and rations (*σιτομετρήσας*) which he distributed to his thousand picked troops before embarking for Attica. These two elements of remuneration, the day wage paid in currency and the daily allotment of food paid in kind, are often combined to form the salaries of employees in many

Crete, Arsinoe (Methana) in the Peloponnese, and Thera. For a list of Ptolemaic troops at Gortyn, *ICret* IV, 195; cf. also the honors bestowed on Patroklos at Olous in Crete, *ICret* I, pp. 247–248, no. 4, lines 36–37, although there is no mention of the garrison as such.

[31] *IG* XII 5, 1061 shows that Patroklos stationed the Syracusan Hieron on Keos with the title *ἐπιστάτης ἐν Ἀρσινόηι* before setting out for his campaign in Attica. Patroklos' expedition across the Aegean has been discussed in detail by M. Launey, *REA* 47, 1945, pp. 33–45 and Heinen, *Untersuchungen*, pp. 142–152. For Patroklos, *Pros. Ptol.* VI, 15063.

[32] See E. Vanderpool, J. R. McCredie, and A. Steinberg, *Hesperia* 31, 1962, pp. 26–61; *eidem*, 33, 1964, pp. 69–75; McCredie, *Hesperia*, Suppl. XI, *Fortified Military Camps in Attica*, 1966, pp. 1–16. For Patroklos' operations in Attica, *ibid.*, pp. 107–115; Heinen, *Untersuchungen*, pp. 159–167.

classes of work, and the terms employed in our text find frequent parallels among the papyrus documents of Ptolemaic Egypt.[33] Moreover, the pay of mercenary soldiers, as officially defined by treaties between their cities and the employing states, is at times specifically quoted in terms of both wages and rations per day. Although the language differs slightly, the principle is well illustrated in a treaty between Attalos I and several Cretan cities where it is stated: *παρέχ[ο]ντες τῆς ἡμέρας ἑκάστωι ἀνδρὶ δραχμὰν Αἰγιναῖαν, τῶν δ' ἡγεμόνων ἑκάστωι δραχμὰς δύο καὶ κατὰ σῶμα χοίνικα Ἀττ[ικ]ήν, ἐὰν μὴ ἐν πολεμίαι ὦσιν, οὗ ἔσται σῖτον λανβάνειν.*[34] Similarly Polybios makes use of the same juxtaposition of *ὀψώνιον* and *σιτομετρία* when he describes the pay of the Roman army in the 2nd century as composed of both wages in coin and a stated measure of wheat per day.[35]

When Kallias and his mercenaries, serving in the pay of Ptolemy I, came to the aid of Athens (lines 22–23), they were acting in accordance with Ptolemy's policy of good will and friendship toward the Athenian democrats. Once again the language of our decree can be interpreted on the basis of closely similar phraseology elsewhere. The Spartan Hippomedon, who served Ptolemy III as general in charge of the Hellespont and Thrace, received honors from the people of Samothrace because he had gone to the defense of that island and supplied it with armaments and mercenaries: *[ἀκό]λουθα πράττων τεῖ τοῦ βασιλέως αἱρέσει.*[36] This phrase, which appears almost verbatim in the decree for Kallias, makes it clear that in each case the Ptolemaic commanders were the instruments of royal policy and were no doubt acting on orders from the king.

Lines 23–32: The efforts of the Ptolemaic forces to support the revolution are here described, and the decree records two separate engagements in which Kallias' regiment took part. After Olympiodoros' initial success in storming the Mouseion and driving out the Macedonian garrison, the new government faced the critical need to supply the city with food, and above all to harvest the crops in the fields, before Demetrios could reach Attica with the main part of his army and blockade the city. Indeed, Demetrios' troops in the Peiraieus responded at once to this situation (lines 15–16), and resorting to the time-honored tactic of Greek warfare, they began to lay waste the countryside.

33 *P. Cair. Zen.*, 59421, lines 6–7; 59498; 59507, line 5. The payment of Hellenistic mercenaries has been fully discussed by G. T. Griffith, *The Mercenaries of the Hellenistic World*, Cambridge 1935, pp. 274–276; M. Launey, *Recherches sur les armées hellénistiques* II, Paris 1950, pp. 725–735; cf. the useful remarks of P. Ducrey, *BCH* 94, 1970, pp. 653–656.

34 *BCH* 94, 1970, p. 639, lines 21–26. Cf. also the terms of payment in the treaty between Antigonos Doson and Hierapytna, *ICret* III, pp. 24–27, 1 A (=H. H. Schmitt, *Staatsverträge* 502) with the restoration of lines 30–32 proposed by P. Ducrey and H. van Effenterre, *Κρητ. Χρόν.* 21, 1969, p. 297. Two papyri of the 1st century B.C. reflect the same method of payment, partly in cash and partly in kind, W. Kunkel, *Archiv für Papyrusforschung* 8, 1927, pp. 202–205, nos. 8, 9. Here an Egyptian military paymaster requisitions his monthly payroll partly from the *σιτολόγος* of the royal granary, and partly from the *τραπεζίτης* of the royal bank.

35 Polybios, VI.39.12–13: *ὀψώνιον δ' οἱ μὲν πεζοὶ λαμβάνουσι τῆς ἡμέρας δύ' ὀβολούς, οἱ δὲ ταξίαρχοι διπλοῦν, οἱ δ' ἱππεῖς δραχμήν. σιτομετροῦνται δ' οἱ μὲν πεζοὶ πυρῶν Ἀττικοῦ μεδίμνου δύο μέρη μάλιστά πως.*

36 *IG* XII 8, 156, lines 16–17 (=*SIG*^{3}, 502=P. M. Fraser, *Samothrace* 2, I, New York 1960, p. 39).

It was, no doubt, against these raids of the Peiraieus garrison that Kallias deployed his men in order to protect the harvest of the grain (line 25).

In a city which, in the recent past, had been starved into surrender after the siege of 295/4, the urgency of gathering the crops in time of war is readily understandable. The strategic importance of the Attic harvest to the defense of Athens is vividly reflected in other inscriptions in which military officers proudly include among their other feats the fact that they brought in the crops at a critical moment. Thus Kallias' own brother Phaidros reports on his command as hoplite general, in circumstances to which we shall have occasion to return: "And he was responsible for bringing in the grain and the other crops from the countryside" (*IG* II^2, 682, lines 35–36; Appendix **1**). Similarly, during the Chremonidean War the demesmen of Rhamnous praised the general Epichares: *[τούς τε σιτικοὺς καὶ] τ̣οὺς ξυλίνους καρποὺς μέχρι̣ τριάκοντα σταδίων συνεκόμισεν [εἰς τὸ στ]ρατό[πεδον, πύρ]γο⟨υ⟩ς [δὲ ἐν τῆι] χώραι καταστησάμενος κρυπτούς, ἐπὶ τὰς σκο[πιὰς παρεφε]δ̣ρεύων αὐτὸς μ̣ετὰ τ̣ῶν̣ στρατιωτῶν ὅπως ἀσφαλῶς γένηται ἡ [συγκομιδὴ τῶν κ]αρπ̣ῶν τοῖς γεωργοῖς* (*SEG* XXIV, 154, lines 8–11). Indeed, the anxiety of the city as a whole for the success of the harvest in these same years of war is still manifest in the unique sacrifice for the crops in the countryside offered by the eponymous archon, Nikias of Otryne, in 266/5: *ἔθυεν ἐφ' ὑγιείαι καὶ σωτη[ρίαι τῆς βο]υλῆς καὶ τοῦ δήμου τοῦ Ἀθηναίων κα[ὶ τῶν κ]αρπῶν τῶν ἐν τεῖ χώραι* (*IG* II^2, 668, lines 8–10).

Here again the analogous situation of the Chremonidean War serves to illuminate the events of the earlier revolution, and this suggests the extent to which Kallias' timely support was critical to the success of the nationalist cause. But still greater interest attaches to his activities, for they bring to mind at once the involvement in these same events of another Ptolemaic officer, a certain Zenon, who had been stationed in command of a squadron of light cruisers.[37] The Athenian decree in his honor (Appendix **9**) was passed at the time of the revolt, on Hekatombaion 11 of Diokles' archonship; and there is now general agreement that it is the earliest surviving document published by the nationalist government. Although the crucial passage requires restoration, there can be no doubt that Zenon was concerned with supplying grain to the city. His mission has always heretofore been understood to have involved the importation of foreign grain from abroad,[38] and the text of *IG* II^2, 650, lines 16–19 has been restored accordingly: *ἐπιμελεῖται δὲ [καὶ τῆς κομιδῆς το]ῦ σίτου τῶι δήμωι ὅπως ἄ[ν ἀσφαλέστατα δια]κομίζηται συναγωνιζό[μενος τῆι τοῦ δήμ]ου σωτηρίαι*. In the light of the new inscription (lines 25–26), it seems virtually certain that two Ptolemaic commanders, both helping to provide grain for Athens at the same time, took part in

[37] *IG* II^2, 650, lines 11–12: *[καθεστηκ]ὼς ὑπὸ τοῦ βασιλέως Πτολ[εμαίου ἐπὶ τῶν ἀ]φράκτων*; and cf. his activities at about this time in the Cyclades, *IG* XII 5, 1004, lines 2, 4: *καταλειφθεὶς ὑπὸ Βάχχωνος τοῦ νησιάρ[χου]...ἐπὶ τῶν πλοίων τῶν ἀφράκτων*. Cf. *Pros. Ptol.* VI, 15043; Zenon's position in relation to other Ptolemaic officers in the Aegean has been studied by I. L. Merker, *Historia* 19, 1970, pp. 143, 150.

[38] Ferguson, *HA*, pp. 142, 147; Tarn, *JHS* 31, 1911, p. 253; Tarn, *Ant. Gon.*, pp. 92f., 419f.; H. Volkmann, *RE* XXIII, 1959, col. 1627, *s.v.* Ptolemaios I Soter; Bagnall, *Ptolemaic Possessions*, p. 147.

the same operations. Since Kallias is specifically said to have protected the Attic harvest and not the delivery of imported grain, it would seem preferable to restore the decree for Zenon to read: ἐπιμελεῖται δὲ [τῆς συνκομιδῆς το]ῦ σίτου τῶι δήμωι ὅπως ἄ[ν ἀσφαλέστατα εἰσ]κομίζηται.

If these two passages are read together, our picture of Kallias' role in the Athenian revolt comes into sharper focus. Zenon was in charge of gathering the harvest (ἐπιμελεῖται); Kallias defended the operation (προεκάθητο) against attempts by Demetrios' troops from Peiraieus to ravage the crops. It would be natural to suppose that Kallias' troops actually sailed to Attica from Andros on Zenon's cruisers, and the documents even give some indication that Zenon should perhaps be regarded as Kallias' superior officer. The decree for Zenon describes his activities as taking place at the time when the decree was passed. The present tense of the verbs ἐπιμελεῖται and [εἰσ]κομίζηται allows no other interpretation save that Zenon's honors were voted while the harvest was still being gathered, although presumably the task was nearly complete. Kallias, on the other hand, waited a full 16 years before his native city was moved to honor his services at the time of the liberation. The fact that Zenon, and not Kallias, was praised at once in the first flush of success would suggest his seniority in command.

Euchares in drafting the decree was careful to distinguish by the tense of the participles those events which took place while Demetrios was still on the march, παραγιγνομένου ἐκ Πελοποννήσου (line 17), from those which occurred after he had arrived in Attica, παραγενόμενος (line 27). Kallias and his mercenaries saw action a second time after Demetrios had begun to lay siege to Athens, and in his attempt to give battle to the blockading forces, Kallias was himself wounded (line 30). It may be noted once again that this reference to Demetrios' siege of Athens corresponds closely with Plutarch's account of the same events: "He attacked them in a rage and threw a severe siege about the city" (*Demetr.* 46.2). Because of his efforts to break the siege, Kallias is praised for his bravery in combat, which gave no regard to his personal safety, but only to the deliverance of the Demos (lines 31–32). The ringing phrase of our text strikes a familiar note which recurs often in the honorific decrees of the nationalist government. Both Strombichos and Zenon were praised in similar terms[39] for the parts they played in these same events; and other partisans of the democratic cause against the Macedonian domination received similar citations: Audoleon of Paionia, νομίζων εἶναι κοινὴν καὶ αὐτ[ῶ]ι τὴν τῆς πόλεως σωτηρίαν (*IG* II², 654, lines 20–21); and the comic poet, Philippides of Kephale, λέγων καὶ πράττων τὰ συμφέροντα τεῖ τῆς πόλεως σωτηρίαι (*IG* II², 657, lines 32–33). The wording of the text is closely comparable to that used in the much later decree honoring Demainetos of Athmonon: οὔτε κακοπά[θι]αν οὐδεμίαν οὔτε κί[ν]δυνον ὑποστελλόμενος ἀλλὰ καὶ λόγωι κ[α]ὶ ἔργωι τὰ συμφέροντα πράττων τεῖ πατρίδι (*IG* II², 1304, lines 8–10).

Lines 32–40: These lines reveal for the first time something of the diplomatic negotiations as a result of which Demetrios raised the siege of Athens and departed for

[39] *IG* II², 666, lines 13–14 (Appendix **7**); 650, lines 18–19 (Appendix **9**).

Asia. The course of events as outlined in our text will appear at first sight to differ radically from the information which Plutarch had at his disposal. The biographer twice refers to Demetrios' departure for Asia after the Athenian revolt (*Demetr.* 46.1–2; *Pyrrh.* 12.4–5; Appendix **3**, **4**); but these passages are not entirely consistent with each other, and the details are left vague. In both places Plutarch mentions the intervention of Pyrrhos at the request of Athens, but in the former passage he says merely that the Athenians summoned his aid ("Seeing that Demetrios had more strength than they expected, they summoned Pyrrhos to their aid from Macedonia"), and nothing more is said of Pyrrhos' part in the ensuing events. In fact, the impression is clearly conveyed that the philosopher Krates, by the sheer persuasiveness of his personal diplomacy, prevailed upon Demetrios to abandon his siege: "But when Krates the philosopher, a man of great repute and influence, was sent to him by the Demos, Demetrios, persuaded in part by the appeals which the ambassador made in behalf of the Athenians, and in part convinced by what the philosopher showed him to be to his own advantage, raised the siege." Plutarch's account of the same events in *Pyrrhos* 12.4–5 naturally dwells upon the role of his protagonist. There is, thus, no mention of Demetrios' siege or Krates' embassy, but only of Pyrrhos' reception at Athens. It is significant, however, that Pyrrhos is here said to have concluded peace with Demetrios shortly before he sailed for Asia. Although Plutarch says nothing of a formal peace in *Demetrios* 46.2, the correctness of his passing reference here is now confirmed by the inscription, where the phrase τὴν εἰρήνην ὑπὲρ τῆς πόλεως πρὸς Δημήτριον (line 36) must surely refer to the same treaty.

There are conspicuous differences in the two accounts of the peace now available to us. While Plutarch implies that Pyrrhos made peace with Demetrios unilaterally and states explicitly that Krates negotiated the lifting of the siege of Athens, the decree for Kallias makes no reference whatever to this. It, rather, provides the equally explicit and entirely unexpected statement that a treaty between Athens and Demetrios was negotiated by the intercession of a personal envoy from Ptolemy, to whom Kallias was sent to represent the interests of the Athenian nationalists, doubtless because of his personal and professional connections with Ptolemaic officialdom. In order to reconcile this apparent contradiction in our two sources, it will be necessary to place the liberation of Athens within the framework of its contemporary events; and we may accordingly defer more detailed discussion of the peace, its terms, and its signatories until the historical context of the Athenian revolt has been more fully reconstructed. We may here anticipate that discussion only to observe that the diplomatic situation at Athens was plainly far more complex than the picture which Plutarch draws. In all likelihood both Plutarch and the epigraphical text give only a partial account of the negotiations, since the former concerned himself chiefly with the careers of Demetrios and Pyrrhos, while the latter sought only to record the mission of Kallias.

Line 33: Ptolemy's emissary to Athens is named in the text only as Sostratos.

Although the name is by no means uncommon, there is every indication that our man was a personnage of great eminence: he was dispatched personally by the king; he was received in the Peiraieus (line 35) despite control of the port by Demetrios' hostile forces; and he was sufficiently well known so as to be recognizable to the average Athenian without his patronymic and ethnic. Even if formal demonstration is not possible, we can accept with confidence his identification as Sostratos, son of Dexiphanes of Knidos,[40] a man of great wealth and high rank at the court of Alexandria. From the reference to him here, there can at least be no doubt that he is in quite a different class from the mercenary captains Kallias and Zenon.

According to Strabo, Sostratos ranked among the *φίλοι τῶν βασιλέων*, the honorary title which expressed his position in the hierarchy of courtiers and the closeness of his relation to the king.[41] He is said also to have dedicated the famous Pharos which lighted the approaches to the harbor of Alexandria. Lucian purports to quote the dedicatory inscription; and the epigram of Posidippos, composed on the occasion of the dedication, and perhaps commissioned by Sostratos himself, has chanced to survive on papyrus.[42] A later tradition, preserved by Pliny and Lucian, regarded Sostratos as the architect of the lighthouse, rather than its donor, and attributed to him also the construction of buildings in his native Knidos.[43] The mutually exclusive statements of these authors, however, either that Ptolemy magnanimously allowed Sostratos to dedicate the building in his own name (Pliny), or that Sostratos inscribed the king's name on a layer of fugitive plaster, which disintegrated in time to reveal his own name carved beneath (Lucian), hardly inspire much credence. While it is possible that Sostratos took keener interest in the architecture of his buildings than the ordinary donor,

[40] *Pros. Ptol.* VI, 16555. For discussion of his career, see P. Perdrizet, *REA* 1, 1899, pp. 261–272; Dittenberger, *OGIS*, 66, note 1; H. Thiersch, *Pharos, Antike Islam und Occident*, Leipzig and Berlin 1909, pp. 31–34; F. Heichelheim, *RE*, Suppl. VII, 1940, cols. 1221–1222, *s.v.* Sostratos (11 a); P. M. Fraser, *Ptol. Alex.* I, pp. 18–20 with notes.

[41] Strabo, XVII.1.6. For the titles and hierarchy of the court and the position of the *φίλοι* among them, see M. L. Strack, *RhMus* 55, 1900, pp. 168f.; H. Kortenbeutel, *RE* XIX, ii, 1941, cols. 95–103, *s.v.* Philos; Trindl, *Ehrentitel im Ptolemäerreich* (Diss. Munich 1942), pp. 9ff., 44ff.

[42] Strabo, XVII.1.6: *τοῦτον δ' ἀνέθηκε Σώστρατος Κνίδιος, φίλος τῶν βασιλέων, τῆς τῶν πλοϊζομένων σωτηρίας χάριν, ὥς φησιν ἡ ἐπιγραφή*. Cf. the Suda Lexicon *s.v.* *Φάρος* (Φ114, Adler); Eusebios, *Chron. Can.* II, p. 118 (ed. Schoene), p. 200 (ed. Karst) under Ol. 124; Lucian, *Hist. Conscr.* 62: *Σώστρατος Δεξιφάνους Κνίδιος θεοῖς σωτῆρσιν ὑπὲρ τῶν πλοϊζομένων*. For the epigram of Posidippos (preserved on *P. Firmin-Didot*, dated before 161 B.C.), see A. S. F. Gow and D. L. Page, *The Greek Anthology*, *Hellenistic Epigrams*, Cambridge 1965, Posidippos, XI, lines 3099–3109; Page, *Greek Literary Papyri*, Cambridge, Mass. 1950, 104 a, where earlier publications are cited.

[43] Pliny, *Nat. Hist.* XXXVI.83, where he adds that the cost of the Pharos was 800 talents; Lucian, *Hist. Conscr.* 62. Both authors refer elsewhere to buildings of Sostratos at Knidos, which Pliny, *Nat. Hist.* XXVI.12.18 calls a *pensilis ambulatio* and Lucian, *Amor.* 11 calls *στοὰς Σωστράτου*. Sostratos' role in the construction of the Pharos has been much discussed, and the statement that he was its architect generally accepted. Perdrizet, *REA* 1, 1899, pp. 261ff.; Thiersch, *op. cit.* (footnote 40 above), pp. 31ff.; Heichelheim, *RE*, Suppl. VII, cols. 1221–1222. Fraser, *Ptol. Alex.* I, p. 19, II, p. 50, note 111 has argued convincingly that the earlier evidence of Posidippos and Strabo is to be preferred to the later tradition of Pliny and Lucian, and that Sostratos should be regarded not as the architect but only as the dedicant of the lighthouse. Cf. the commentary of Gow, *Hellenistic Epigrams* II (footnote 42 above), pp. 489–490.

his high position at the Ptolemaic court and his activities in the Aegean clearly preclude his being an ordinary architect.

A group of inscriptions at Delphi and Delos gives evidence that Sostratos was active in Greece as a Ptolemaic ambassador in just the years to which our text refers. About 285–280 B.C. he received proxeny status and other honors for unspecified services to the people of both Delphi and Delos.[44] Other benefactions to the cities of Kaunos and Kyrene moved the citizens of those states to erect honorary statues of Sostratos in the sanctuary at Delos, while he himself dedicated a statue of Ptolemy II at Delphi to which he seems to have added a statue of Arsinoe Philadelphos at a later date.[45] At some time in the 270's, Sostratos interceded with Ptolemy on behalf of the Islanders in so signal a manner that a long honorific decree for him was passed by the Island League.[46] This decree awarded him a golden crown, to be made from three thousand Alexandrian drachmas, citizenship and related honors in all the Islands, and a perquisite from the sacrifices to the Ptolemies at Delos to be sent to him at Knidos after every festival. It is greatly to be regretted that we do not know what Sostratos did to deserve such honors, but we may suspect that, like his earlier mission to Athens, it involved a considerable diplomatic achievement. Indeed, the tradition that he was a particularly adroit negotiator lies behind the anecdote of Sextus Empiricus in which Sostratos was dispatched by Ptolemy on a royal embassy to Antigonos. When the latter gave him a hasty and ill-considered response, Sostratos had the wit to quote from the Homeric envoy Iris in the *Iliad*, by which he contrived a graceful compliment for both kings and at the same time a gentle reprimand for Antigonos, who thereupon conceded his request.[47] While the Sostratos of this anecdote has not been universally

[44] Proxeny decrees in honor of Sostratos (285–280 B.C.) and two other Knidians, Pythokles and Archidamos (273/2 B.C.), are inscribed together on a single block from the area of the Knidian Treasury at Delphi, *FD* III, i, 299–301. The names of these three have also been restored in *FD* III, i, 298 (272 B.C.), a decree conferring honors on three men for their announced pledge to restore the statue of Hermes, Protector of the Games, in the Delphic stadium or sanctuary. *IG* XI 4, 563 records a similar proxeny decree of the Delians passed at about the same time as the Delphian decree for Sostratos. The epigraphical evidence has been most recently discussed by Fraser, *Ptol. Alex.* II, pp. 50, note 111, 52, note 121.

[45] *IG* XI 4, 1130, a statue dedicated by the people of Kaunos; *ibid.*, 1190, a statue dedicated by Etearchos, son of Damylos, of Kyrene, both of which probably date 280–270 B.C. The Delphian dedication published by P. Amandry, *BCH* 64–65, 1940–41, pp. 63–64 preserves the words *Σώστρατο*[.] *βασιλισ*[. . . .] separated by an erased line between, so that it is not certain who dedicated a statue of whom. Fraser, *loc. cit.*, note 121 has interpreted the remains as a statue of Sostratos erected by Arsinoe herself; but on the whole it is easier to believe the explanation of Amandry that Sostratos dedicated a statue of Ptolemy alone, to which he later added a statue of Arsinoe after her marriage to her brother, and thus caused the original inscription to be erased and the queen's name to be added, *ca.* 276–271.

[46] *IG* XI 4, 1038. It may be noted that the phrase (lines 12–13) *ἀρετῆς ἕνεκα* [*καὶ εὐν*]*οίας ἧς ἔχων διατελεῖ ἐμ παντὶ καιρῶι εἰς* [*τὸν β*]*ασιλέα Πτολεμαῖον* seems to bear out Sostratos' close relation to the king suggested by Strabo's reference to him as *φίλος τῶν βασιλέων* (XVII.1.6) and by his mission in our inscription.

[47] Sext. Emp., *Adv. Mathem.* I. 276 with a quotation of *Iliad* XV. 201–203. The episode and its date have been frequently discussed: see U. von Wilamowitz, *Antigonos von Karystos*, Berlin 1881, pp. 228–229; Perdrizet, *op. cit.* (footnote 43 above), p. 265; Tarn, *Ant. Gon.*, pp. 386–387. Beloch, *Gr. Gesch.* IV^2, ii, p. 512, following Dittenberger, *OGIS*, 66, note 1, doubts the identification of the Sostratos of this story with the famous Knidian.

identified as the Knidian, the story well illustrates precisely the kind of embassy in which we find him engaged in the decree for Kallias; and there seems to be no good reason for doubting that both episodes refer to the same Ptolemaic diplomat.

Lines 40–43: These and the following lines refer to a policy of the nationalist government to which reference is also made in other contemporary records: that is the efforts of Athens to solicit gifts of money and grain from her friends abroad. Immediately after the conclusion of peace, Kallias sailed with an Athenian embassy dispatched to Ptolemy; and the wording of the text suggests that he served as intermediary between the ambassadors and the king. Although the inscription uses the plural, which implies that Kallias assisted more than one embassy, it seems certain that we should see a reference to the same occasion in another contemporary document. The honorific decree for Demochares of Leukonoe informs us that he took a leading part in the new administration. His was a policy of fiscal retrenchment accompanied by strenuous efforts to raise financial support from abroad in order to bolster the precarious position of the nationalist government. One of his measures, evidently proposed shortly after his recall to Athens on the heels of the revolution, was an embassy to Ptolemy: "He moved that an embassy be sent to Ptolemy in Egypt, and those who were dispatched brought back fifty talents of silver for the Demos."[48]

There is every likelihood that this is the embassy with which Kallias sailed and with which he cooperated in the city's interests. Similar efforts to raise foreign aid as quickly as possible are to be seen in the three embassies led personally by Demochares.[49] As a result of two visits to Lysimachos, with whom he may have enjoyed special influence, and one embassy to Antipatros, Demochares collected a total of 200 talents for the Athenian treasury. Of these the ambassadors to Ptolemy brought back 50 talents, which may have been secured through the good offices of Kallias.

Lines 44–55: The author of the decree here begins a second major episode of Kallias' career, and this is introduced by an indication of chronology. Just as the phrase *γενομένης τῆς ἐπαναστάσεως ὑπὸ τοῦ δήμου* (line 12) served to date the first series of events recorded in the text, so now another clause in the genitive absolute provides the chronological information: *παραλαβόντος τὴν βασιλε[ί]αν Πτολεμαίου τοῦ νεωτέρου βασιλέως*. The next events are dated with reference to the accession of Ptolemy Philadelphos, and probably follow shortly on that event. There may at first sight, however, be some question whether the date intended is the beginning of the co-regency of Philadelphos with his father Soter in 285/4, or the time, after the elapse of two years, at which his sole reign began in 283/2.[50] Our text follows closely the phraseology used

48 The text of the decree (Appendix **10**) is appended to the *Lives of the Ten Orators* and preserved in [Plut.], *Mor.* 851 d–f. The decree was moved by his son Laches in the archonship of Pytharatos (271/0), just a year prior to the decree for Kallias. For the career of Demochares, Kirchner, *PA* 3716; Davies, *APF*, pp. 141–142; and below, pp. 47ff., 80ff.

49 [Plut.], *loc. cit.* Cf. Ferguson, *HA*, pp. 146–147; Tarn, *Ant. Gon.*, pp. 101–102; and below, p. 80.

50 For the co-regency, see Porphyry, in the Armenian Version of Eusebios, *F. Gr. Hist.*, 260, F 2, 2–3; A. E. Samuel, *Ptolemaic Chronology*, Munich 1962, pp. 25–28.

to describe the royal accession in official Ptolemaic documents. Thus we read of the day on which Ptolemy III succeeded to the throne: *καὶ εἰς τὴν πέμπτην καὶ εἰκάδα τοῦ αὐτοῦ μηνός, ἐν ἧι παρέλαβεν τὴν βασιλείαν παρὰ τοῦ πατρός* (*OGIS*, 56, line 6); and the Rosetta Stone of Ptolemy V opens similarly: *βασιλεύοντος τοῦ νέου καὶ παραλαβόντος τὴν βασιλείαν παρὰ τοῦ πατρός* (*OGIS*, 90). These passages refer specifically to the time when the son was officially reckoned to have begun his reign after the death of the father;[51] and there is every reason to believe that the same phrase in the decree for Kallias should indicate the beginning of Philadelphos' sole rule after the death of Soter. Since the death of Ptolemy Soter occurred sometime between the end of December 283 and the summer of 282,[52] the activities of Kallias here recorded should probably be dated in the year 282 B.C., either in the latter part of Euthios' archonship at Athens (283/2), or in the following year of Nikias II (282/1).

It is regrettable that the author of our text, although he devotes 11 lines to the description of Kallias' embassy to Ptolemy II, is so imprecise in recording the circumstances which caused Kallias to be dispatched. Despite the factual vagueness of these lines, a sense of urgency and desperation on the part of the Athenian government nevertheless emerges clearly. The generals called upon Kallias, made the situation clear to him, and begged him to hurry to the king, *ὅ[π]ως ἂν βοήθειά τις γένηται τὴν ταχ[ί]στην εἰς τὸ ἄστυ σίτωι καὶ χρήμασιν* (line 49). This is strong language. The city needed help as quickly as possible, both grain to feed her people and money to replenish her depleted treasury. There can be no doubt that whatever the generals made plain to Kallias (*τὰ κατὰ τὴν πόλιν ἐν οἷς ἦν*, line 47), the situation was not good. Both Kallias and Ptolemy rose handsomely to meet the emergency: the ambassador gained a personal audience with the king in Cyprus, and the king made a gift of 50 talents of silver and 20,000 medimnoi of wheat.

It is likely enough that both money and grain were perennially in short supply in Athens of the early 3rd century.[53] We have already noted the vigorous efforts of Demo-

[51] Cf. Dittenberger's note, *OGIS*, 56, note 17. In literary usage also *παραλαμβάνω* describes the succession to office of a king upon the death of his predecessor, e.g. *F. Gr. Hist.*, 257 a, F 3; Herodotos, II.120; Thucydides, I.9.

[52] According to Porphyry, *F. Gr. Hist.*, 260, F 2, Ptolemy I went as satrap to Egypt one year after the death of Alexander, governed as satrap for 17 years, and ruled as king for 23 years, thus completing a reign of 40 years (322/1–283/2). But Soter lived for two years after bringing his son Philadelphos to the throne as co-regent (285/4); he then died in the course of his 40th year, and in the 2nd year of his son Philadelphos. On Porphyry's reckoning of regnal years, see Jacoby, *F. Gr. Hist.*, II D, Kommentar, p. 856; Samuel, *op. cit.* (footnote 50 above), pp. 4–5. J. Bingen, *Chronique d'Égypte* 35–36, 1943, pp. 138–147, has shown that in the reign of Philadelphos the royal birthday-festival, *τὰ γενέθλια*, marked the anniversary of the accession and the beginning of the regnal year. The second such festival celebrated by Philadelphos, then, provides the date after which Soter died. Samuel, *op. cit.*, p. 29 reckoned this date as Dystros 24 in the Macedonian calendar, which he equated with January 7, 282 B.C. The inscription quoted by Fraser, *Ptol. Alex.* II, p. 382, note 341 now shows that the *γενέθλια* were celebrated 12 days earlier on Dystros 12. The death of Ptolemy Soter must have occurred later than the closing days of 283 B.C., but before the end of the Olympic year, used by Porphyry, in the summer of 282 B.C. Cf. Fraser, *BCH* 78, 1954, p. 56, note 1.

[53] Cf. the discussion of grain shortages at Athens by Jardé, *Céréales*, pp. 43ff. Although he is chiefly concerned with the great famine of the 320's, the effects of this were no doubt projected down into the early

chares to raise funds immediately after the revolution a few years earlier; and other gifts of grain also reached Athens in the spring of 284 B.C., 15,000 medimnoi from King Spartokos of Bosporos and 7,500 medimnoi from King Audoleon of Paionia.[54] The inscription honoring the latter, however, suggests something of the special circumstances which prompted this systematic provisioning of the city. After recording the donation of grain and its delivery to the harbors of Attica, the decree for Audoleon continues (lines 30–35): *ἐπ[α]νγέλλεται δὲ καὶ εἰς τὸ λοιπὸ[ν] παρέξεσθαι χρείας συνεργῶν [ε]ἴς τε τὴν τοῦ Πειραιέως κομιδ[ὴ]ν καὶ τὴν τῆς πόλεως ἐλευθερί[α]ν.* There is here the sharp reminder that the Athenian nationalists had failed to dislodge the Macedonian garrison from the Peiraieus, although as we shall see (below, p. 82) an abortive attempt to do so had already been made a year before Audoleon's gift. The recovery of the harbor city was deemed essential to the survival of the new government, and references to it in the documents of this period show that it was a matter of top priority in the minds of the nationalists. But an attack upon the Peiraieus garrison inevitably meant war with Antigonos and the almost certain risk that the city itself would be speedily besieged and ultimately reduced to surrender. Against this eventuality the only defense was money and food, for the city's ability to withstand a siege depended directly upon the size of her stores.[55]

The far-flung campaign in these years to raise cash and grain from Athens' foreign friends should be understood in this light, not only as a general effort to alleviate depressed economic and fiscal conditions, but more especially as a specific policy to supply the city so that she could move to recover the Peiraieus and survive the consequences. This is made explicit in the honorific decree for Philippides of Kephale (*IG* II^2, 657, lines 33–36; Appendix **11**): "And he begged the king to help with money and grain so that the Demos remains free, and so that it may recover the Peiraieus and the forts as quickly as possible."[56] Although this passage describes Philippides' appeal to Lysimachos immediately after the successful liberation of Athens, it is important to observe the subjunctive mood of the verb (*κομίσηται*, line 35), which shows that Peiraieus and the border forts had not yet been recovered when Philippides was honored for his efforts, on Boedromion 18 of Euthios' archonship (late September,

3rd century, cf. M. I. Rostovtzeff, *SEHHW* I, p. 168. Noteworthy are Lysimachos' gift of 10,000 medimnoi of wheat in 299/8, *IG* II^2, 657, lines 11–13; Demetrios' gift of 100,000 medimnoi in 295/4 after the siege and surrender of Athens, Plutarch, *Demetr.* 34.4; and the successful embassy of Phaidros of Sphettos to Ptolemy Soter for grain and money between 294 and 288, *IG* II^2, 682, lines 28–30.

[54] From Spartokos: *IG* II^2, 653, lines 23–24; from Audoleon: *IG* II^2, 654, lines 25–29. In the latter instance, honors were voted not only for Audoleon who gave the grain but also for his envoy who arranged for its delivery to Athens, *IG* II^2, 655, lines 11–14, where the importance of speed recalls the urgency of our text: *συνήργ[ησ]εν δὲ καὶ [εἰς τὴν] ἐκκομιδὴν τοῦ σίτου [φιλ]οτιμό[τατα ὥστε] τὴν ταχίστην αὐτὸν [παρ]απ[εμφθῆναι τ]ῶι δήμωι.*

[55] During the siege of 295/4, Demetrios took special pains to prevent the grain ships from reaching Athens and thereby reduced the city to starvation, Plut., *Demetr.* 33.3.

[56] Another document of this period (*Hesperia* 30, 1961, p. 211, no. 6) also made reference to the need for recovering the Peiraieus and clearly used phraseology similar to that quoted here, but the text is too fragmentary to reconstruct.

283 B.C.). That policy which Philippides in 286 had urged upon the king pressed now with still greater immediacy upon the orator speaking in his honor in 283; for after three years the need for money and grain in order to recover (ὅπως ... κομίσηται) the Peiraieus was, if anything, more desperate. Viewed against this background, the embassy of Kallias to Ptolemy Philadelphos may perhaps take on more substance, for it can be seen as another manifestation of the same policy. Moreover, we have found reason to date Kallias' journey to Cyprus about 282 B.C., that is to say probably within a year, possibly within a few months, of the time when the decree for Philippides was drafted. Indeed, the passage just quoted shares something of the urgency expressed in the decree for Kallias, but the wording of our text more specifically emphasizes the importance of rapid action.

Little factual information has survived concerning events at Athens in the archonships of Euthios and Nikias II, but the few scraps of evidence available may help to interpret the services of Kallias. The archon Euthios was particularly honored for his conduct of the sacrifices and the procession of the Dionysia; but special interest attaches to the clause of his honorary decree[57] which states (lines 28–31): εἶναι δὲ αὐτῶι καὶ ἄλλο ἀγαθὸν εὑρέσθαι παρὰ τοῦ δήμου ὅτου ἂν δοκεῖ ἄξιος εἶναι ὅταν ὁ Πειραιεὺς καὶ τὸ ἄστυ ἐν τῶι αὐτῶι γένηται. As is not infrequent in decrees of this sort provision is here made for the ex-archon to receive another award from the Demos, but not until the Peiraieus and the city have been re-united.[58] This shows, of course, that the Peiraieus was still in Macedonian hands on Gamelion 9 of Nikias' year (midwinter 282/1) when the decree was passed. It is hard to see why it seemed appropriate to specify the recapture of the Peiraieus as an occasion after which Euthios should receive his reward. But more than that, since there is no discernible connection at all between the Peiraieus and the routine ceremonial duties for which the archon has already been honored and will be again, it seems legitimate to infer that the recovery of the port was uppermost in Athenian minds at just this time. The decree speaks as if there were anticipation of an imminent attack for which plans were being made and supplies collected. Indeed, some support for this suggestion comes from the activities of the hipparchs and phylarchs of this same year. These officers in 282/1 took in hand a reorganization of the cavalry corps, and they were praised especially for their success

[57] Meritt, *Hesperia* 7, 1938, p. 100, no. 18 = Moretti, *Iscr. stor. ell.*, p. 28, no. 14.

[58] For other examples of the formula, but without specification of time as here, see *IG* II², 360, lines 49, 62–63, 75; 686, lines 15–16; 780, line 21; 884, line 20. Moretti, *Iscr. stor. ell.*, p. 30 argues from this phrase that both the Peiraieus and the city were under Macedonian control when this decree was passed, the city having been recaptured sometime between Skirophorion 285/4 and Gamelion 282/1. But this is to misconstrue the phrase ἐν τῶι αὐτῶι γένηται which should mean, when they are together again. A resurgence of the pro-Macedonian government in these years would, however, have caused the democratic administrative institutions to be subverted, as was the case before the liberation of Athens and after the Chremonidean War. Cf. Dinsmoor, *Archons*, p. 65. The plural Board of Administration (οἱ ἐπὶ τῆι διοικήσει) was in office in 285/4 (*IG* II², 654, lines 45, 60), in 283/2 (*ibid.*, 657, lines 68, 71), and in 282/1 when the decree for Euthios was passed (*Hesperia* 7, 1938, no. 18, line 41). In 284/3 there was a special celebration for the liberty of the Demos (*IG* II², 657, lines 43–45). There cannot have been a change of government in any of these years.

in recruiting one hundred men, and so increasing the strength of the cavalry to three hundred.[59] Furthermore, their successors must have continued their efforts at recruiting; for Athens was able to send five hundred horsemen to help defend the pass at Thermopylai against the Gauls in 279 B.C.[60]

In addition to these indications of increased military preparedness in Nikias' year, there is also the suggestion that emotion ran high against the Macedonians at this time. The frequently quoted fragment from a letter of Epikouros written in Euthios' year (283/2) is now completely without context, but it speaks with bitter feeling of "destroying the hated Macedonians";[61] and in 283/2 this can refer only to the garrison in the Peiraieus. Is it possible that an attempt to capture the Peiraieus, otherwise unknown to us, was made in Euthios' archonship? It is just conceivable that the failure of such an attack aroused Epikouros to wrath, gave rise to the military build-up of the following year, and prompted the hasty dispatch of Kallias to bring help from Ptolemy as quickly as possible. Even though these tantalizing bits of information can yield no more than a conjectural reconstruction, it is surely right to regard them as isolated links in the same chain of events, which led shortly to Athens' successful recovery of the Peiraieus a year later in 281/0. In that year, Athens turned again to the hero of the revolution in the city, Olympiodoros; he was elected general and in his term of command accomplished the most brilliant feat of his career, the capture of the Macedonian fort on the Mounychia hill, and thereby the liberation of the Peiraieus.[62]

[59] J. Threpsiades and E. Vanderpool, *Ἀρχ. Δελτ.* 18, 1963, p. 104, lines 7–11 = *SEG* XXI, 525; Moretti, *Iscr. stor. ell.*, no. 16: *προσκατέστησαν ἱπ⟨π⟩εῖς ἑκατὸν [ὅ]πως ἂν ἀναπληρωθέντες οἱ ἱππεῖς εἰς τὸ [δυ]νατὸν ἐπὶ τοῦ παρόντος καὶ γενόμενοι [τ]ριακόσιοι τὰς χρείας παρέχωνται τῆι χώ[ρ]αι.* The editors associated the phrase "as much as possible at present" with the difficulties imposed by the presence of the Macedonian garrison in Peiraieus. It is possible that *IG* II², 3210, the dedication of a crown for the ephebes and kosmetes by the Boule of Nikias' year, should be assigned to Nikias II of 282/1 rather than to Nikias III of Otryne (266/5), as Pritchett and Meritt, *Chronology*, p. xix, because the archon's demotic was not here added as seems to have been regularly the case with Nikias of Otryne (Meritt, *Hesperia* 37, 1968, p. 285). Kirchner earlier assigned the fragment to Nikias I of 296/5. If it can be attributed to 282/1, it may suggest some special activity in the training of the ephebes parallel to the build-up of the cavalry.

[60] Pausanias, X.20.5.

[61] From Philodemos, *περὶ τῶν στωικῶν*, *P. Herc.* 339, col. V: .... *εἶθ' [ὕ]στερον [τοὺς ἐχθίσ]τους ⟨κ⟩ατα[λ]ύειν Μακε[δόνας] ὡς τ[ό]τε ἐπ' Εὐθίου γρά[φει]*, G. Arrighetti, *Epicuro Opere*, Turin 1960, p. 425, no. 103.

[62] For Olympiodoros' recovery of the Peiraieus, Pausanias, I.26.3. The date in 281/0 depends on a combination of evidence. The port must have been in Athenian hands before 279, since Athens sent all her seaworthy triremes to Thermopylai (Pausanias, I.4.3; X.20.5; 22.12). A *terminus post quem* is provided by the fate of Mithres, Lysimachos' minister of finance (see G. de Sanctis, *RivFil*, n.s. 5, 1927, pp. 491–500). A letter of Epikouros (*P. Herc.* 1418, col. XXXIII: C. Diano, *Lettere di Epicuro*, Florence 1946, p. 19, no. XIV = Arrighetti, *Epicuro*, p. 387, no. 42) reports that Mithres, having been captured at Corinth by Krateros, was being held prisoner for ransom in the Peiraieus at the time of writing. At that time, then, Peiraieus was certainly in the control of the Macedonian garrison. The date of Mithres' captivity must be after the death of Lysimachos at Kouroupedion, February-March 281 B.C. (on the date see footnote 71 below). Epikouros had sent letters to his correspondent by a messenger on the staff of Olympiodoros who was at the time general at Athens. There is time for Mithres' imprisonment at Peiraieus in spring and summer of 281. Olympiodoros will have been elected general for 281/0 and presumably captured the Peiraieus in the latter part of his command. For discussion of the evidence, see Tarn, *JHS* 54, 1934, pp. 33–37; Ferguson, *Tribal*

Lines 53–55: It is of great interest to observe that the wheat which Ptolemy Philadelphos gave to Athens was turned over to Athenian agents at Delos, where supplies of Egyptian grain were evidently already stored, awaiting sale on the international market. In the epigraphical records of the Delian sanctuary, there are numerous indications that the island became one of the great centers of the Aegean grain trade during the 3rd century B.C. A decree dating to the first half of the century honors a merchant from Byzantion for selling grain to Delos at an especially favorable price fixed by the city.[63] Numerous other honorific decrees for men not only of Byzantion, but also from other cities of the Hellespont and Bosporos,[64] attest the success of the Delians in cultivating these vital ports along the route by which grain from the Black Sea reached the Aegean market. A later text from the period of Macedonian hegemony honors a grain buyer of Demetrios II whose extended sojourn on the island proved mutually beneficial to the Delians and the king.[65] At about the same time a grain commission from Histiaia managed to complete its purchases at Delos as quickly as possible through the good offices of a Rhodian banker who provided an interest-free loan and thus earned the warm thanks of Histiaia.[66]

This picture of large-scale international commerce is now appreciably augmented by the explicit evidence that the royal monopolies of Egypt had begun to develop Delos as a clearing-house for their grain trade from the earliest years of Ptolemaic control; for the presence on the island of large stores of wheat, which Ptolemy was at liberty to give upon Athens' urgent appeal, can mean nothing else. Ptolemy's efforts at just this time to assure the commercial health and financial solvency of the Delian sanctuary are illustrated by the well-known decree honoring his admiral Philokles of Sidon, who, on the king's orders, had pressured the Island League to repay its loans to Delos.[67] Ptolemy's evident intention to use the Delian market as an outlet for Egyptian grain now helps to explain his clear concern for the temple's financial position. In view of the fact that so many Delian honorific inscriptions and proxeny decrees seem to reflect the island's commercial diplomacy, it may be well to recall that among these is a decree conferring proxeny status and associated honors on Kallias, son of Thymochares the Athenian (*IG* XI 4, 527), the only other extant record of the man

Cycles, p. 72; Meritt, *Hesperia* 4, 1935, pp. 576–578. A date between 274 and 272 was proposed by Beloch, *Gr. Gesch.* IV^2, ii, pp. 45, 607. G. de Sanctis, *RivFil*, n.s. 5, 1927, p. 495; 14, 1936, pp. 144ff. maintained the view that Athens never recovered the Peiraieus after the revolt from Demetrios, and that Olympiodoros captured the port from the tyrant Lachares in 295; followed by Manni, *Dem. Pol.* p. 58; Deprado, *RivFil*, n.s. 31, 1953, p. 38.

[63] *IG* XI 4, 627, and the commentary of F. Durrbach, *Choix*, pp. 57–58. For the Aegean grain market at this period and Delos' place in it, F. Heichelheim, *RE*, Suppl. VI, 1935, cols. 852–856, *s.v.* Sitos; Rostovtzeff, *SEHHW* I, pp. 231–232, 235, 393.

[64] Byzantion: *IG* XI 4, 510, 530, 570, 778, 779, 780; Chalkedon: *ibid.*, 618, 645; Kyzikos: *ibid.*, 562, 1027; Lampsakos: *ibid.*, 571, 708.

[65] *IG* XI 4, 666 = Durrbach, *Choix*, no. 48.

[66] *IG* XI 4, 1055 = Durrbach, *Choix*, no. 50.

[67] *IG* XI 4, 559 = Durrbach, *Choix*, no. 18. For recent discussion of Philokles and his career as Ptolemy's viceroy of the Aegean, see I. L. Merker, *Historia* 19, 1970, pp. 143–150; J. Seibert, *ibid.*, pp. 337–351.

honored in our document. These honors could very well have been voted by the Delians in connection with Kallias' mission to get Ptolemaic aid for Athens.

The Delian evidence also gives some indication of the difficulties in acquiring large quantities of wheat at this particular moment and may also have some bearing on the date of Kallias' mission. The temple accounts for the archonship of Kleostratos at Delos record the purchase of wheat rations for employees of the temple and quote the price paid per medimnos in each month.[68] The price of wheat in this year is seen to have climbed steadily from 4 drachmas, 3 obols in Artemision (April) to 10 drachmas in Bouphonion (September), while in the last three months of the year wheat seems not to have been available on the market at all, and the hieropoioi purchased barley instead at 4 and then 5 drachmas per medimnos. In his study of these statistics, A. Jardé[69] concluded that the extraordinary inflation of this year must have resulted from a major disruption of trade caused by troubled political conditions, which he recognized as the confrontation between Lysimachos and Seleukos culminating in the battle of Kouroupedion. He accordingly placed the battle in the summer of 282 B.C., and thus in the year generally assigned to the archon Kleostratos.[70] Since the battle of Kouroupedion was fought seven months before the assassination of Seleukos, now fixed in August-September 281 B.C.,[71] our interpretation of the rapid rise in the price of wheat at Delos will have to be adjusted accordingly.

The statement of our text that 20,000 medimnoi of Ptolemaic wheat were measured out to Athenian agents from Delos cannot easily be squared with the obvious inflation and apparent scarcity of wheat on Delos recorded in the accounts of Kleostratos. It is especially difficult to believe that both documents refer to the same year; and yet the embassy of Kallias is dated to the period after the death of Ptolemy Soter, and thus at the earliest in 282 B.C. Now if the Delian accounts are correctly interpreted to mean

[68] *IG* XI 2, 158 A, lines 37–50; for discussion of the prices there recorded, F. Heichelheim, *Wirtschaftliche Schwankungen der Zeit von Alexander bis Augustus*, Jena 1930, pp. 51ff.; Jardé, *Céréales*, pp. 166ff.

[69] *Op. cit.*, pp. 170–173.

[70] Evidence for the order and date of the Delian archons comes from the annual accounts of the hieropoioi which are dated by the names of the archons, often with reference to their immediate predecessors. Especially important are the long lists of sacred phialai dedicated annually from various royal foundations, and listed in order by the names of the archons in whose years they were dedicated (*IG* XI 2, 226, lines 8ff.; 287, lines 91ff.). These lists enabled the construction of an unbroken sequence of 77 archons in fixed order (group II), covering the first three quarters of the 3rd century from Lysixenos to Anektos, of which Kleostratos is the 20th name. See T. Homolle, *Les archives de l'intendance sacrée à Délos*, Paris 1887, pp. 58–70; Durrbach, *BCH* 40, 1916, pp. 300–308; Beloch, *Gr. Gesch.* IV², ii, pp. 97–101. The absolute dates of the entire sequence depend on the dates of the royal foundations, donated in the archonship preceding the dedication of the first phiale. The death of Philetairos of Pergamon in 263 or 262 provides the *terminus ante quem* for his foundation, while the accession of Ptolemy III Euergetes (246 B.C.) gives the *terminus post quem* for his. Within these controling dates, the series can run either from 301 to 225 or 300 to 224. The earlier dates were adopted by Homolle and Durrbach, followed by Beloch and others, and place the archon Kleostratos in 282 B.C.

[71] On the date of the battle, Justin, XVIII.2.4. The Babylonian king list published by A. J. Sachs and D. J. Wiseman, *Iraq* 16, 1954, pp. 202–212, places the death of Seleukos in the 6th month of Year 31 of the Seleucid era, after a reign of 25 years beginning in Year 7. Cf. A. Aymard, *REA* 57, 1955, pp. 102–112; H. Bengtson, *Historia* 4, 1955, pp. 113–114; Heinen, *Untersuchungen*, pp. 20–24.

that no wheat was available at Delos after September of Kleostratos' year, then Philadelphos' gift to Athens must have been made before that time at the latest, provided that the accepted date for Kleostratos in 282 is, in fact, correct. On the whole, it seems more satisfactory to suppose that the crisis on the wheat market in Kleostratos' year did indeed reflect the dislocations of Kouroupedion, as Jardé suggested, and that both the battle and the archon should be dated one year later in 281, as proposed by Dinsmoor.[72] The evidence of the decree for Kallias may now be adduced in support of Dinsmoor's dating of the Delian archons.

When the accounts of Kleostratos are dated in 281, the rapid inflation in the price of wheat can once again be understood to reflect the tumultuous events of that year. It is not the battle of Kouroupedion itself which so disturbed the grain market, but rather its aftermath. Jardé[73] attributed the shortage of grain in the Aegean to the closing of the Bosporos to shipping from the Black Sea, and this may well be right. With the battle now dated in February–March 281 B.C., the first major rise in wheat prices, in Thargelion (May), will be seen to have occurred at just the time when Seleukos' forces were trying to win over the cities of northwestern Asia Minor, an unsuccessful attempt which brought about the defensive alliance of Herakleia, Byzantion, Chalkedon, and Mithradates of Pontos. The highest price of wheat is recorded in Bouphonion (September), a date which coincides precisely with Seleukos' crossing of the Hellespont and his assassination near Lysimacheia at the hands of Ptolemy Keraunos.[74] This precipitated the crisis; and in the turmoil of that autumn, which saw Keraunos on the throne of Macedon, a war for the succession between him and Antigonos Gonatas, and the latter's defeat at sea,[75] it will cause no surprise if the grain ships from the Black Sea failed to reach the Aegean, with the result that there was no wheat on the market at Delos during the last three months of the year. When Kallias' embassy and Philadelphos' gift of wheat to Athens are viewed against this background of contemporary events, it seems desirable to suppose that the 20,000 medimnoi of Ptolemaic grain were measured out from the stores at Delos before the crisis on the Delian market, and thus before May 281.[76]

[72] *Archons*, pp. 495–498, 503. Dinsmoor adopted the lower dating of group II of the Delian archons, from Lysixenos (300) to Anektos (224), a possibility admitted by Durrbach, *BCH* 40, 1916, pp. 306–307, 342, although he preferred the earlier dating. Cf. footnote 70 above. Dinsmoor argued that the donation of the first Ptolemaia at Delos, one year before Hypsokles, when the first phiale was dedicated, should be contemporary with Ptolemy's donation of land to Miletos in 279/8, after the peace with Antiochos I in 279 (A. Rehm, *Milet*, I, *Das Delphinion*, Berlin 1914, p. 259, no. 123, lines 38–40; p. 300, no. 139, lines 3, 30–31; Tarn, *Hermes* 65, 1930, pp. 446–454). The synchronism is accomplished by dating Hypsokles in 278, and so post-dating the entire series by one year.

[73] *Céréales*, pp. 170–173.

[74] For the alliance of the northern cities, Memnon, *F. Gr. Hist.*, 434, F 7, 2; the murder of Seleukos, *ibid.*, F 8, 1–7; Justin, XVII.2. The months from Kouroupedion to the death of Seleukos have been studied extensively by Heinen, *Untersuchungen*, pp. 37–53; cf. Will, *Monde hellénistique* I, pp. 86–87, 120.

[75] See Heinen, *Untersuchungen*, pp. 61–68.

[76] A reference to this transaction may possibly be preserved in the Delian accounts for the year next after Kleostratos, but unfortunately Durrbach's restoration of the critical words is only one of several possibilities, even if the most likely. *IG* XI 2, 159, lines 53–54: Ἀρτίμαι καὶ Δεινί[αι οὗ ὁ Πτολεμαϊ]κὸς

Lines 55–64: Reference is here made to the first celebration by Ptolemy Philadelphos of the great festival of the Ptolemaia at Alexandria in honor of his father Soter. The present passage relates at once to the well-known decree of the Island League which records its acceptance of Ptolemy's invitation to recognize and participate in the same festival.[77] Indeed, the wording of our text, even in this passing reference to the occasion, bears resemblance to the language of that decree (lines 20–22): *καὶ θυσίαμ ποιεῖ τῶι πατρ[ὶ] καὶ ἀγῶνα τίθησιν ἰσολύμπιογ γυμνικὸγ καὶ μουσικὸν καὶ ἱππικόν.* The provisions of the decree of the Islanders help to elucidate further what is merely alluded to in the Athenian document. Ptolemy's invitation was conveyed in a letter from Philokles, King of the Sidonians, and Bakchon, the nesiarch of the League, calling on the constituent cities to send representatives to a meeting at Samos which would deliberate concerning the festival. After rehearsing in courteous and diplomatic fashion the many good services of Ptolemy Soter and of his son, both to the Islanders and to other Greeks, the delegates voted to recognize the games as isolympic, that is quadrennial, to approve the sacrifice for Soter, and to send a sacred embassy to the celebration in perpetuity, as the king had requested. In addition to the divine honors thus proclaimed for Soter, the Islanders bestowed a gold crown on Philadelphos and appointed three theoroi to perform the sacrifices and present the crown at Alexandria.

Our text makes mention of the same elements, except that specific reference to a gold crown conferred upon Philadelphos is here lacking, and we may infer that the form of the invitation to Athens and of its acceptance was closely analogous to that recorded by the Island League. As in the latter case, Philokles may perhaps have presented the invitation personally, for certainly a Ptolemaic embassy will have journeyed to Athens.[78] It is even possible that the fragmentary Athenian decree in honor of Philokles and the inscribed base for his honorary statue might have been connected in some way with

---

σῖτος ἔκειτο κλεῖδας ποιήσασι καὶ ἐπιθεῖσι. It is tempting to think that reference to the place "where the Ptolemaic grain used to lie" may reflect its shipment to Athens. Why keys needed to be prepared after the dispatch of the grain is not apparent.

[77] *IG* XII 7, 506 = *SIG*³, 390.

[78] It was standard practice for theoroi to travel from city to city announcing local festivals and soliciting decrees of acceptance in response to the invitation. See in general the discussion of P. Boesch, *Θεωρός*, Berlin 1908, pp. 28ff. A series of such decrees from all over the Greek world has survived in response to the announcement of the Asklepieia in Kos, R. Herzog and G. Klaffenbach, *Asylieurkunden aus Kos* (*Abhand. Akad. Berlin*, 1952, no. 1). They regularly open with a phrase like: *ἐπειδὴ παραγεγένηνται θεωροὶ παρὰ τῆς Κώιων πόλεως ἐπαγγέλλοντες τὰ Ἀσκληπίεια καὶ τοὺς ἀγῶνας* (*ibid.*, p. 15, no. 6). A similar series of responding decrees relates to the Leukophryena at Magnesia, O. Kern, *Die Inschriften von Magnesia am Maeander*, Berlin 1900, nos. 16–87. Cf. the Athenian decree (*ibid.*, no. 37, lines 6–11): *ἐπειδὴ Μάγνητες οἱ ἐπὶ Μαιάνδρωι οἰκεῖοι καὶ φίλοι τοῦ δήμου τοῦ Ἀθηναίων ὄντες ψηφισάμενοι θυσίαν καὶ ἀγῶνα στεφανίτην ἰσοπύθιον μουσικὸν καὶ ἱππικὸν καὶ γυμνικὸν συντελεῖν τεῖ ἀρχηγέτιδι τῆς πόλεως αὐτῶν Ἀρτέμιδι Λευκοφρυηνῆι ἀφεστάλκασιν θεωρούς.* Cf. also the Hadra vase inscribed for a Delphian ambassador who died in Alexandria: *Σωτίων Κλέωνος Δελφὸς θεωρὸς τὰ Σωτήρια ἐπαγγέλλων*, H. Braunert, *JdaI* 65–66, 1950–51, p. 237, no. 26; B. F. Cook, *Inscribed Hadra Vases in the Metropolitan Museum*, New York 1966, p. 25, no. 10. Cf. also the Chian answer to the announcement of the Delphian Soteria, *SIG*³, 402, lines 4–5.

this occasion.[79] Like the Islanders, the Athenian Demos clearly recognized the establishment of the sacrifices and games for Ptolemy Soter and agreed to send a theoria. Kallias, because of his long association with Ptolemaic Egypt, was chosen to lead the sacred embassy as architheoros; and the mention of other theoroi elected with him (lines 64, 69) shows that he was accompanied also by colleagues, who are likely to have been two in number on the analogy of the three-man delegation dispatched by the Islanders.[80]

Something of the duties of these sacred ambassadors emerges from several sources. The architheoros is described as manager and spokesman for the delegation[81] and was no doubt often chosen in the hope that he would defray the expenses of the embassy from his own resources. Although the Demos had appropriated a sum of money for the theoria, Kallias declined to accept it and paid himself for the sacrifices in honor of the king whom once he had served. The exact amount of Kallias' donation for the theoria is no longer legible at the right end of line 60. The figure has been restored as 50 minas (5,000 drachmas) since that best fits the available space, but both 80 and 90 are also possible epigraphically, although the sums of money involved seem rather too high. The other numerals ending in tau alpha are of inappropriate length, 30 and 60 being a little short, 40 and 70 too long. A close parallel both for the sum of money and for the duties which Kallias was called upon to perform is found in the decree honoring Boulagoras of Samos, who led the Samian theoria to the Ptolemaia in Alexandria either in 247/6 or 243/2. On that occasion Boulagoras contributed "not much less than 6,000 drachmas"; and the decree specifies that his gift paid for crowns for Ptolemy III and Berenike, sacrifices for their parents and grandparents, and the traveling expenses for the embassy which would deliver the crowns and perform the sacrifices.[82] The same duties were assigned to the theoria elected by the Island League for the first Ptolemaia. Their decree stipulates that the theoroi were to sacrifice in behalf of the League to Ptolemy Soter and to present the crown to the king, provision also being made for the cost of the latter and for the traveling expenses of the theoroi.[83]

[79] E. Schweigert, *Hesperia* 9, 1940, p. 353, no. 48, and the statue base, *IG* II[2], 3425. Schweigert associated the honors for Philokles with the liberation from Demetrios, but since Sostratos is now known to have been the chief Ptolemaic envoy in these negotiations, another occasion should be sought for Philokles' honors at Athens.

[80] *SIG*[3], 390, line 54 (footnote 83 below). The Koan theorias were normally composed of three, occasionally of only two, men, Herzog and Klaffenbach, *op. cit.*, (footnote 78 above), pp. 28–30, as also were those from Magnesia, Boesch, *op. cit.* (footnote 78 above), pp. 31–33.

[81] Polybios, XXVIII. 19. 3 speaks of an Athenian architheoros: *ἡ δ' ἄλλη* (*sc. θεωρία*) *περὶ μυστηρίων, ὑπὲρ ἧς Κλεόστρατος ἐποιεῖτο τὸν χρηματισμὸν καὶ τοὺς λόγους.*

[82] *SEG* I, 366, lines 28–36: *ἐπειδὴ εἰς μὲν τοὺς στεφάνους αὐτῶν καὶ τὰς θυσίας, ἃς ἔδει συντελέσαι τοὺς θεωροὺς ἐν Ἀλεξανδρείαι, περιορισμένα ὑπῆρχεν χρήματα, εἰς δὲ τὰ ἐφόδια τῶι ἀρχιθεωρῶι καὶ τοῖς θεωροῖς, ὑφ' ὧν ἔδει τοὺς στεφάνους ἀποκομισθῆναι καὶ συντελεσθῆναι τὰς θυσίας οὐχ ὑπῆρχεν οὐδ' ἦν, ὅθεν ἐπὶ τοῦ παρόντος ποριsθήσεται, βουλόμενος μηθὲν ὑπολ(ει)φθῆναι τῶν προεψηφισμένων τιμίων τῶι βασιλεῖ καὶ τῆι βασιλίσσηι καὶ τοῖς γονεῦσιν καὶ προγόνοις αὐτῶν ὑπέσχετο τὸ εἰς ταῦτα ἀργύριον αὐτὸς προχρήσειν ἐκ τοῦ ἰδίου οὐ πολλῶι ἔλασσον ὂν δραχμῶν ἐ̣ξ[α]κισχιλίων.*

[83] *SIG*[3], 390, lines 53–57: *ἑλέσθαι [δ]ὲ τοὺς συνέδρους καὶ θεωροὺς τρεῖς, οἵτινες ἀφ[ικ]όμενοι εἰς Ἀλεξάνδρειαν θύσουσίν τε ὑπὲρ τοῦ [κ]οινοῦ τῶν Νησιωτῶν Πτολεμαίωι Σωτῆρι καὶ [τὸν σ]τέφανον ἀποδώσουσιν τῶι βασιλεῖ.*

The references in our text [τὴν μὲν θεωρία]ν ἀγαγὼν ἐκ τῶν ἰδίων (lines 61–62) and [τῆς δὲ] θυσίας ἐπιμεληθεὶς ὑπὲρ τῆς πόλεω[ς] (lines 62–63) leave no doubt that Kallias conducted the same ceremonies as the Islanders and paid the same expenses as Boulagoras. Similar invitations were no doubt extended to all parts of the Ptolemaic dominions and to Greek cities all over the eastern Mediterranean,[84] so that the embassies of Kallias and the Islanders will have been joined in Alexandria by numerous other sacred delegations. A few of these theoroi have become known to us because they chanced to die in the course of the festivals which they attended; and their ashes were buried in special vases which bear their names and often the date of death.[85]

Lines 64–66: Once again a clause in the genitive absolute provides a chronological reference, or in this case more specifically a synchronism. For τότε (line 64) refers back to the description of the theoria which precedes; and the clause should be understood to say what the Demos was about to do at the time of the Ptolemaia which justified Kallias' appeal to Ptolemy recorded in the following lines. Unfortunately the precise meaning and syntax of the clause depend upon the restoration of the words at the right end of lines 64 and 65. In the first instance there is space for no more than five letters, and the missing word, ending in nu (line 65), can hardly be anything but an adverb qualifying the participle and infinitive of the next line. The restoration [πρῶτο]ν not only fits the space perfectly and is recommended by the similar precise reference to the "first" Ptolemaia (line 55), but it also explains the words at the end of line 65, which are best construed as a temporal clause: ἀ[φ'] ο[ὗ τ]ὸ ἄστυ ἐκεκόμιστο. The Demos was about to celebrate the Panathenaia for the first time after it had recovered the city.[86]

If this restoration be accepted, the text will then be seen to provide chronological information which bears both upon the date of founding of the Ptolemaia and upon the history of the Panathenaia, but information which is not entirely without problems in its interpretation. The phrase τὸ ἄστυ ἐκεκόμιστο has a precise meaning in the documents of this period, and it refers specifically to the liberation from Macedon in 286 B.C.[87] Our text then seems to say that when Ptolemy Philadelphos first established

[84] A fragmentary decree of the Amphictyonic Council of Delphi accepts the invitation to the Ptolemaia in terms closely analogous to those in the decree of the Islanders; see Fraser, *BCH* 78, 1954, pp. 49–62 = *SEG* XIII, 351. The text was revised with the addition of another fragment by J. Bousquet, *BCH* 82, 1958, pp. 77–82 = *SEG* XVIII, 241. The decree is dated in 266/5 (or possibly 270/69) and is thus later than the foundation of the festival. See below, p. 37.

[85] For theoroi and other ambassadors in Egypt, see Braunert, *JdaI* 65–66, 1950–51, pp. 231–263; those named on Hadra vases have been studied by B. F. Cook, *op. cit.* (footnote 78 above); *idem*, *Brooklyn Museum Annual* 10, 1968–69, pp. 114–138. Architheoroi are known from Phokaia, Dyme, and Akarnania (Cook, *op. cit.*, pp. 20ff., nos. 3, 7, 16 = Braunert, pp. 234ff., nos. 16, 23); theoroi are recorded from Crete and Boiotia (Cook, nos. 1, 8 = Braunert, nos. 10, 24). The festivals which they attended are not usually mentioned. Cf. also theoroi from Delphi, *FD* III, iv, 161, line 4, and from the Island League, *IG* XI 4, 1037, line 4. For a convenient list, see *Pros. Ptol.* VI, pp. 74–76.

[86] The restoration of these lines was suggested to me by C. Habicht, but he is in no way responsible for the manner in which the wording of the text has here been defended.

[87] Cf. *IG* II^2, 653, lines 21–22 (285/4): ὅτι ὁ δῆμος κεκόμιστ[αι τὸ ἄστυ]; 654, lines 17–18 (285/4):

the Ptolemaia at Alexandria, the Athenians were preparing for the first celebration of the Panathenaia after the revolt from Demetrios Poliorketes. The phrase *τὰ Παναθήναια τεῖ Ἀρχηγέτι[δι]* is unusual in that this epithet for Athena Polias rarely occurs in Attic inscriptions.[88] Moreover, the festival in question should be the penteteric festival of the Great Panathenaia, even though the text does not specify *τὰ Παναθήναια τὰ μεγάλα*; for preparations were under way to present the peplos to Athena, a ceremony which seems to have been performed, at least in this period, only once every four years.[89] Since the Great Panathenaia fell in the third year of the Olympiad, the festival should have been celebrated on Hekatombaion 28 of 286 B.C. In that year, however, the festival coincided with the later stages of the revolution. On Hekatombaion 11, the crops were

---

κομισαμένου [τ]οῦ δήμ[ο]υ τὸ ἄστυ. As in these cases, the verb in line 66 is middle and not passive; *τοῦ δήμου* (line 64) as subject of the preceding genitive absolute should be understood also as subject of *ἐκεκόμιστο*. The expression is somewhat elliptical as in line 14, where also *τοῦ δήμου* is to be understood as the subject of *ἐγβαλόντος*.

[88] Cf. *IG* II², 674=*Agora* XV, 78, line 16 (273/2): *τὰ Χαλκεῖα θύσωσιν τῆ⟨ι⟩ Ἀθηνᾶι τεῖ Ἀρχη[γέτιδι τ]ῆς πόλεως*; *IG* II², 3175, 3199, 3474; *SEG* XXI, 789; *Hesperia* 30, 1961, p. 231, no. 30. The proposal of F. Sokolowski, *Lois sacrées des cités grecques*, Paris 1969, no. 33, lines 9–10, to restore *Ἀρ[χηγέτιδος]* in the law on the Lesser Panathenaia, where *IG* II², 334 has *ἀρ[χαίωι νεῶι]* seems unlikely and does not solve the difficulty of this passage as he claims, pp. 66.

[89] The ancient evidence for the dedication of the peplos is contradictory; some sources speak of it as quadrennial and others as annual, collected and fully quoted by A. Michaelis, *Der Parthenon*, Leipzig 1871, p. 328. See especially Plato, *Euthyphr.* 6 c: *καὶ δὴ καὶ τοῖς μεγάλοις Παναθηναίοις ὁ πέπλος . . . ἀνάγεται εἰς τὴν ἀκρόπολιν*; Harpokration, quoting Isaios (=Suda, *Π*1006, Adler) *s.v. πέπλος· περὶ τοῦ πέπλου τοῦ ἀναγομένου τῇ Ἀθηνᾷ τοῖς μεγάλοις Παναθηναίοις*; Schol. Euripides, *Hec.* 467: *τοῦτον* (*sc. τὸν πέπλον*) *δὲ ἀνιέρουν διὰ πενταετηρίδος ἐν τοῖς Παναθηναίοις*; cf. Schol. Aristophanes, *Knights* 566; Plautus, *Mercator* 64ff.; [Vergil], *Ciris* 21ff. But another scholiast on Aristoph., *Knights* 566 states: *ἐπεσκευάζετο οὖν ὁ πέπλος καθ' ἕκαστον ἐνιαυτόν*. A scholiast on Plato, *Republic* 327 a distinguishes between the peplos dedicated at the Great Panathenaia and a different peplos dedicated at the Lesser Panathenaia; and Lutatius on Statius, *Theb.* X. 56 compromises on a triennial peplos. Diodorus Siculus, XX.46.2, quotes the decree of Stratokles in honor of Antigonos and Demetrios (307/6), of which one of the provisions is *καὶ συντελεῖν αὐτοῖς κατ' ἐνιαυτὸν ἀγῶνας καὶ πομπὴν καὶ θυσίαν, ἐνυφαινόντων αὐτοὺς εἰς τὸν τῆς Ἀθηνᾶς πέπλον κατ' ἐνιαυτόν*.

On the basis of this evidence, it has been argued that the peplos was only dedicated at the penteteric festival until the end of the 4th century, but was offered annually thenceforward until the Imperial period, so A. Mommsen, *Feste der Stadt Athen*, Leipzig 1898, pp. 112–113; Pfuhl, *de pompis*, pp. 7–8; Dinsmoor, *Archons*, pp. 242–244. Others have argued that the peplos was always limited to the Great Panathenaia, Deubner, *Attische Feste*, pp. 29–31; L. Ziehen, *RE* XVIII B, 1949, col. 460, *s.v.* Panathenaia. Deubner has shown that the Platonic scholia (*Rep.* 327 a) have confused the Plynteria and Lesser Panathenaia; and editors of Diodorus, notably Wesseling and Fischer, have excised the second *κατ' ἐνιαυτὸν* of the MSS as an erroneous duplication of the first. Even if the MSS reading were allowed to stand, the decree of Stratokles cannot be used as evidence for annual dedication of the peplos. Stratokles was assailed by the comic poet Philippides for bringing the vengeance of the gods on Athens by this decree (Plut., *Demetr.* 12), because the peplos and its mast and spar were destroyed by a storm at the Great Panathenaia of 302 B.C. (Dittenberger, *SIG*³, 374, note 6). At the request of Philippides, a new mast and spar were donated by Lysimachos (*IG* II², 657, lines 14–16; Appendix **11**); but the order of events in the decree shows that Philippides' request was made before the battle of Ipsos (301 B.C.), although the new mast and spar were not delivered until 299/8. Lysimachos' donation was thus made in preparation for the Great Panathenaia of 298 B.C., and no peplos can have been dedicated between 302/1 and 299/8. See Ferguson, *Klio* 5, 1905, p. 163, note 2; Ferguson, *HA*, p. 123. At the time of our inscription, then, the peplos was still being presented only at the penteteric festival.

still being gathered in anticipation of Demetrios' arrival in Attica, and the siege of Athens had not yet begun.[90] In the crisis of the revolt, it will cause no surprise if the Great Panathenaia were omitted altogether in that year. Had we no independent evidence at our disposal, it would then be natural to think that Euchares' decree referred to the next subsequent celebration of the penteteric festival in the summer of 282 B.C.

There are, however, serious objections to accepting this simple and obvious interpretation of the text; and these concern the foundation date for the Ptolemaia at Alexandria. That date has been much discussed, but it still depends largely upon the decree of the Island League to which reference has already been made. The decree was voted by the delegates of the League meeting at Samos under the chairmanship of Ptolemaic officials; and that island must have passed under Ptolemaic control before such a meeting can have taken place.[91] But as late as 282 B.C., Samos was still in the possession of Lysimachos, as is shown by the fact that in or about that year the king awarded to the Samians a tract of land on the mainland opposite, which had long been the subject of dispute between the islanders and the people of Priene.[92] Since there is no reason to think that Lysimachos lost Samos to Ptolemy between 282 and his death the following year, it is then the battle of Kouroupedion in 281 which forms a fixed *terminus post quem* for the Ptolemaic acquisition of Samos, for the meeting and the decree of the Islanders, and for the founding of the Ptolemaia. The new text now fixes the first Ptolemaia at Alexandria in a year immediately preceding the Great Panathenaia at Athens, and in all probability the first celebration of that festival after the liberation of the city. Since the establishment of the Ptolemaia must be dated after 281, the Panathenaia here mentioned (line 65) should be the festival of 278, in which case the first Ptolemaia will have been celebrated at Alexandria in the preceding year 279/8. The present passage thus provides strong support for the traditional dating of the Ptolemaia to coincide with the exact penteteric anniversary of the death of Ptolemy Soter.[93]

[90] *IG* II^2, 650, lines 16–19; cf. p. 20 above.

[91] *SIG*^{3}, 390, lines 1–4.

[92] Lysimachos' award of the Batinetis to Samos is recorded in *OGIS*, 13 = C. B. Welles, *Royal Correspondence in the Hellenistic Period*, New Haven 1934, pp. 46ff., no. 7. The same decision is mentioned in the later Prienian account of the boundary dispute, which also provides the date, F. Hiller von Gaertringen, *Inschriften von Priene*, Berlin 1906, no. 37, lines 125ff.: *ποτὶ δὲ τὸν Λυσίμαχον ἀ[ποστ]εῖλαι ὑπὲ[ρ τ]οῦ Βατινήτο[υ ἐπὶ στε]φαναφόρου τοῦ θεοῦ τοῦ μετὰ Νίκανδρον, ὅς ἐστι ἀπὸ Λύκου πεντε[και]δέκατος.* In the eponymous stephanephorate of Lykos, the tyrant Hieron, who had installed himself for three years in the turmoil after the battle of Ipsos, was overthrown (*ibid.*, lines 80–83, 111). Lykos' date should thus be *ca.* 297, and the year next after Nikandros (15th after Lykos) should fall *ca.* 282. See T. Lenschau, *LeipzStud* 12, 1890, pp. 199–200; Fraser, *BCH* 78, 1954, p. 55, note 2.

[93] For discussion of the date of *SIG*^{3}, 390 and of the founding of the Ptolemaia, see Fraser, *op. cit.*, pp. 55–62; the date of the Delphian decree there published, which responds to Ptolemy's invitation, has been shown to be 266/5 (or less probably 270/69) by J. Bousquet, *BCH* 82, 1958, pp. 77–82; but this does not affect the foundation of the festival itself in 279/8, see Fraser, *HTR* 54, 1961, pp. 141–145. That the festival marked the penteteric anniversary of the death of Ptolemy Soter was suggested by H. von Prott, *RhMus* 53, 1898, pp. 460–476, and has been generally accepted, see E. R. Bevan, *History of Egypt under the*

If, however, our decree does indeed refer to the first Great Panathenaia after the revolt of Athens, then a date in 278 is not easy to reconcile with other Athenian evidence. It becomes necessary to postulate that the festival was omitted entirely in 282, for only in this way can the Panathenaia of 278 be described as the first after the Demos had recovered the city. The difficulty arises because the year 282/1 (archon Nikias II) is one of only two known instances in the first half of the 3rd century when two agonothetai were appointed to manage the Athenian festivals, this task being normally assigned at this period to a single agonothetes. According to *IG* II², 682, line 53 Phaidros of Sphettos was elected agonothetes in Nikias' year, while Glaukon of Aithalidai is named agonothetes of Nikias' year in *IG* II², 3079, line 2.[94] A similar double agonothesia also seems assured for 266/5 (archon Nikias III of Otryne) which was likewise a Panathenaic year; and on that occasion one of the two was specifically designated [ἀγωνοθέτης Παναθη]ναίων.[95] It thus seems hardly conceivable that in 282/1 two agonothetai were elected and yet the Great Panathenaia were not celebrated, unless there were compelling circumstances of which no explicit evidence has survived. The problem appears stubbornly intractable, and yet on the whole it seems preferable to think that [πρῶτο]ν is correctly restored at the end of line 64, and that for some reason the Panathenaia were, in fact, omitted in 282 B.C.

A possible explanation may be seen in the crisis alluded to in lines 46–50 of our text, which we have found reason to date in 282 B.C., and as a result of which Kallias hurried to bring financial aid to Athens from Ptolemy Philadelphos. Whatever other difficulties the city may have faced at that moment, there can be no doubt that the treasury was short of funds. It may be that at the last minute, after the election of the agonothetai, the city simply had insufficient funds to stage the festival. Similar difficulties had arisen in the past over the financing of the Panathenaia, partly because the festival fell in the first prytany of the year when the city's revenues had not yet come in.[96] Demosthenes (XXIV.26–29) refers to such a financial crisis in 353/2, which was discovered only 17 days before the festival and gave rise to a special meeting of the nomothetai. About 335 this problem was treated again in a law of the nomothetai which designated specific revenues from specific sacred land to finance the Lesser

---

Ptolemaic Dynasty, London 1927, p. 127; Tarn, *Ant. Gon.*, p. 104, note 29; Beloch, *Gr. Gesch.* IV², ii, p. 327.

[94] The dating is complicated by the fact that in this period there were three archons named Nikias, in 296/5, in 282/1, and in 266/5, the last being distinguished by the regular use of his demotic, Nikias Otryneus, see Threpsiades and Vanderpool, Ἀρχ. Δελτ. 18, 1963, p. 105. The last is now excluded since the agonothetai of his year are known, Meritt, *Hesperia* 37, 1968, pp. 284–285, no. 21. To place Phaidros' agonothesia in 296/5 (with Kirchner, commentary on *IG* II², 3079) violates the chronological order of *IG* II², 682; but 296/5 is too early for Glaukon, who was still active in the 240's, Kirchner, *PA* 3019. It is, therefore, difficult to avoid the conclusion that there were two agonothetai in 282/1, as proposed by Ferguson, *Klio* 5, 1905, p. 165; 8, 1908, pp. 345ff. For recent discussion of the career of Glaukon, see R. Étienne and M. Piérart, *BCH* 99, 1975, pp. 57–58; J. Pouilloux, *Mélanges Claire Préaux*, 1976, pp. 377–378.

[95] *Hesperia* 37, 1968, p. 284, no. 21, line 3; and cf. the same title in *IG* II², 1705, line 2.

[96] See D. M. Lewis, *Hesperia* 28, 1959, pp. 246–247, and cf. L. Robert, *Hellenica* XI–XII, Limoges 1960, pp. 189ff.

Panathenaia, [ὅπως ἂν τῆι] Ἀθηνᾶι ἡ θυσία ὡς καλλίστ[η ἧι Παναθηναίοις τοῖς μ]ικροῖς καὶ πρόσοδος ὡς πλεί[στη γένηται ἱεροποιο]ῖς.[97] But even such legislation did not solve the problem altogether; and when the state's income proved insufficient for the Great Panathenaia of 142 B.C., the crisis was averted only by the personal munificence of the agonothetes, Miltiades of Marathon: τῶν μὲν ἀποτετα[γμένω]ν προσόδων μὴ συνεκποιουσῶν, ἐ[λλειπόντω]ν δὲ πλειόνων χρημ[άτων σ]κῆψιν οὐδεμίαν ποιησάμενος [προσήν]εγκεν παρ' ἑαυτοῦ [χρήματ]α ἄτοκα, οὐκ ὀλίγα δὲ καὶ ἐκ τῶν ἰδί[ων προαν]ήλωσεν πρὸς τὸ μὴ [ἀποστ]ερῆσαι τὸν δῆμον μηθενὸς τῶν π[ρὸς τὴν ἀγ]ωνοθεσίαν [ἀ]νηκόν[των].[98] In view of the fiscal stringency of the late 280's, and of 282 in particular, it is easy to believe that a similar lack of funds caused the festival to be omitted in that year. Moreover, the agonothetai do not seem to have come forward, as did Miltiades, with generous financial contributions or interest-free loans. Glaukon's dedication (*IG* II^2, 3079) shows that he managed the Dionysia, which means that the Panathenaia would have fallen to Phaidros. Now the decree for Phaidros describes his agonothesia in the most routinely formulaic language, but if he had paid for the Panathenaia, it would hardly have failed to say so.[99] Behind the hackneyed phrases of his decree, there may lurk the fact that the Panathenaia were not celebrated in his year for lack of funds.

Lines 66–70: In his capacity as Athenian architheoros to the first Ptolemaia, Kallias took advantage of his visit to Alexandria to ask Ptolemy Philadelphos for a gift to Athens which was appropriately in the same religious spirit as his own contribution (lines 61–62) toward the celebration of the Ptolemaia. He suggested and Ptolemy agreed to donate the ὅπλα which had to be prepared for the conveyance of the peplos of Athena at the forthcoming Panathenaia. The expression of our text seems elliptical in that it is by no means made clear why ὅπλα should have to be got ready εἰς τὸν πέπλον, nor indeed what precisely these ὅπλα were, no doubt because all these things were well known to every Athenian. The decree praising the contributions of Miltiades of Marathon to the Panathenaia of 142 B.C. is here helpful once again: [ἔδωκ]εν δὲ καὶ ὅπλα στύπ[πινα καὶ] τὰ λοιπὰ τὰ ἐλλείποντα πρ[ὸς τὴν κομιδὴ]ν τοῦ πέπλου (*IG* II^2, 968, lines 48–49). The meaning of ὅπλα in this sense is also usefully defined by Erotianus, the grammarian of the 1st century after Christ (103.33, ed. Nachmanson), *s.v.* ὅπλα· Βακχεῖός φησι τὰ στύππινα σχοινία, οὐκ εὖ. ἔστι γὰρ κοινῶς τὰ ἐν τῇ νηΐ διακρατοῦντα ὀρθὸν τὸν ἱστὸν σχοινία. From this it becomes apparent that the ὅπλα made of tow (στύππινα) which Miltiades gave in 142 B.C., and likewise those donated earlier

[97] *Hesperia* 28, 1959, p. 239, lines 5–7; the upper part of the stele which also carried the decree concerning the organization of the festival, *IG* II^2, 334.

[98] *IG* II^2, 968, lines 42–47. The mention here of the "appointed revenues" shows the correctness of Lewis' surmise, *loc. cit.* (footnote 96 above), that a special law, parallel to that published by him, designated sources of revenue also for the Great Panathenaia.

[99] *IG* II^2, 682, lines 53–56 (Appendix **1**). By contrast, the decree for Miltiades, just quoted, devotes 15 lines to his management of the Panathenaia. Cf. the agonothesia of Philippides (284/3), *IG* II^2, 657, lines 39–40, 46–47 (Appendix **11**); the decree honoring Eurykleides of Kephisia (after 229), *IG* II^2, 834, lines 4–7: καὶ ἀγωνοθέτης ὑπακούσα[ς ἀνήλω]σεν ἑπτὰ τάλαντα.

by Ptolemy, were heavy ropes used like the shrouds and stays of a ship's mast to keep it in an upright position. One is reminded at once of yet another donation to the Panathenaia of 298 B.C. made by Lysimachos at the request of Philippides of Kephale: "And he discussed (*sc.* with the king) the matter of the yard and mast, which were delivered in Euktemon's archonship, that they might be given to the goddess at the Panathenaia for the peplos" (*IG* II^2, 657, lines 14–16, Appendix **11**). What Ptolemy gave in 278 is evidently to be interpreted as a new set of ropes to support the mast and yard, given by Lysimachos just twenty years earlier, upon which the peplos was spread like the sail of a ship.[100]

The present passage takes its place beside the very few existing references to the conveyance of the peplos that are earlier than the reign of Hadrian; and the addition of a third epigraphical reference from the Hellenistic period now enables us to bring into sharp focus a curious feature which they share in common. The ropes and the mast and yard are all said to be given *εἰς τὸν πέπλον*, or *πρ[ὸς τὴν κομιδὴ]ν τοῦ πέπλου*, or simply *τῶι πέπλωι*; but there is no mention of the vehicle on which the mast must have been carried in the procession, and most particularly there is no mention of the Panathenaic ship, which dominates all descriptions of the festival after Herodes Atticus' extravagant spectacle in A.D. 139.[101] The omission of all reference to the ship in the early sources was observed long ago by E. Pfuhl,[102] who then drew the conclusion that the ship was not introduced until later times, and in the Classical period the peplos was carried on a simple wagon. On the other hand, Deubner[103] has convincingly demonstrated the close analogy between the conveyance of the peplos, hung upon its mast and yard, and the wheeled processional float, fitted out to resemble a ship, on which the image of Dionysos moved each year through the streets of Athens at the Anthesteria. If, as is generally believed, the ritual of the Panathenaia in this respect took its inspiration from the much older Dionysiac rite, this favors a high antiquity for the Panathenaic ship, which should then date, as Deubner saw, from the first dedication of the peplos. To those who have followed this view, it has then seemed natural to infer the existence of the ship from Lysimachos' gift of the mast and yard, and from the fragment of Strattis describing the peplos hoisted like a sail on its mast.[104]

[100] Cf. Photios, *s.v. ἱστὸς καὶ κεραία· ὁ μὲν ἱστὸς τὸ ἐπίμηκες ξύλον ἄνω τεταμένον, κεραία δὲ τὰ πλάγια, ὥστε γενέσθαι γράμμα τὸ Τ· διετείνετο δὲ πολλάκις ὁ τῆς Ἀθηνᾶς πέπλος τοιοῦτο σχῆμα ξύλων καὶ ἐπόμπευσαν*. References to the Panathenaic ship are conveniently collected by Michaelis, *op. cit.* (footnote 89 above), p. 329.

[101] Herodes' agonothesia and the splendid ship-float which he had built for the festival are described by Philostratos, *Vit. Soph.* II.1.5; cf. P. Graindor, *Hérode Atticus*, Cairo 1930, p. 65; and for the dating of the festival in this period, L. Moretti, *Iscrizioni agonistiche greche*, Rome 1953, pp. 202–203. This was presumably the same vessel seen by Pausanias, I.29.1. Either it or a successor appeared at later celebrations of the festival, *IG* II^2, 3198 (A.D. 262/3 or 266/7); 3818 (5th century); it was described by Himerios, *Orat.* III.12–16; Heliodoros, *Aethiop.* I.10; mentioned by Schol. Aristoph., *Peace* 418; *Knights* 566; Schol. Aristid., *Orat.* I.197.8 (III, p. 342, Dindorf); Suda, *s.v. πέπλος* (*Π*1006, Adler).

[102] *de pompis*, p. 10.

[103] *Attische Feste*, p. 33, and cf. pp. 102–106.

[104] Cf. e.g. L. Ziehen, *RE* XVIII B, 1949, col. 461: "*Auch die Urkunde* IG *II*^{2} *657, nach der König Lysimachos für den Peplos der P(anathenaia) des J. 299/8 den ἱστὸς und die κεραία stiftete, und Phot. s. ἱστὸς*

As long as the early sources consisted only of the single reference in *IG* II², 657 and the two poetic passages of Strattis and the pseudo-Vergilian *Ciris* (lines 21–26), such an inference appeared to pose no difficulty. But now that no fewer than three Hellenistic inscriptions are seen to refer in the same elliptical manner to contributions "for the peplos", the question presents itself with greater urgency: if the mast, yard, and ropes of the inscriptions were in fact fittings for the Panathenaic ship, is it not more natural to say that they were donated "for the ship" than "for the peplos"?[105] What is still more surprising is the nature of the donations themselves. Lysimachos, who sent to Athens 10,000 medimnoi of wheat and later 130 silver talents,[106] contented himself with a gift of three pieces of timber for the goddess Athena; and Ptolemy, who had earlier donated 20,000 medimnoi of wheat and 50 silver talents (lines 52–53), and whose appetite for splendor in the staging of festivals is vividly attested in the great Pompe described by Kallixeinos,[107] gave only a few ropes to help celebrate the Panathenaia. Surely one might have expected these wealthy monarchs to contribute the entire ship itself. Moreover, it is strange that Miltiades of Marathon, who as agonothetes is said to have paid virtually all the expenses of the festival, should single out for mention "the ropes of tow and everything else that was lacking for the conveyance of the peplos." Clearly if Miltiades had paid for a ship, he would not so describe it, and the inference seems equally obvious that the kings were not asked to do so. Their contributions "for the peplos" were no doubt considered to have more symbolic significance than actual monetary value. They were dedications more than donations.

Whatever the form of the vehicle which carried the peplos at this time, it was evidently not built anew at each celebration of the festival, but was rather stored somewhere with other sacred paraphernalia and merely repaired and the missing parts replaced in preparation for the Great Panathenaia. In this respect, the presentation of the peplos finds a close analogy in the Dionysia at Delos, where a great phallus was fashioned for each celebration of the festival, in this case annual rather than quadrennial, but it was transported on a cart which was stored in the sanctuary and repaired as needed.[108] From time to time, the hieropoioi paid for nails and wood for the cart, and the wages of a workman who repaired *τὴν ἅμαξαν ἧι ἄγεται τὸ ἄγαλμα τοῦ Διονύσου*.[109] In the archonship of Charilas (268 B.C.), they handed it on to their successors

---

καὶ κεραία...können, wenn hier auch das Wort Schiff selbst nicht steht, doch der unbefangenen Auslegung nur als Beweis für sein Vorhandensein gelten." The peplos is first compared to a sail in Strattis, fr. 30 (*ca.* 400 B.C.): *τὸν πέπλον δὲ τοῦτον ἕλκουσ' ὀνεύοντες τοπείοις ἄνδρες ἀναρίθμητοι εἰς ἄκρον ὥσπερ ἱστίον τὸν ἱστόν*, J. M. Edmonds, *Frag. Att. Com.* I, p. 822.

105 Cf. *IG* II², 3198, lines 7–10 (A.D. 262/3 or 266/7): *τὸ ἀκρ[οστό]λιον τῇ πόλ[ει τῆς Π]αναθηναίδ[ος σκά]φης.*

106 *IG* II², 657, line 12; [Plut.], *Mor.* 851 e.

107 Athenaios, V.196–203.

108 Evidence for the annual preparation of the phallus and its conveyance in the Dionysiac procession has been collected by R. Vallois, *BCH* 46, 1922, pp. 94–112; cf. M. P. Nilsson, *Griechische Feste*, Leipzig 1906, pp. 280–282.

109 *IG* XI 2, 161 A, lines 89–91; nails for the cart, *ibid.*, 158 A, lines 70–71; wood, *ibid.*, 287 A, lines 51–52.

along with the treasures and other objects stored in the Oikos of the Andrians: *ἅμαξαν τῶι ἀγάλματι τοῦ Διονύσου παρέδομεν.*[110] This car of Dionysos at Delos can be traced in the records of the sanctuary for more than a century and a quarter; and its longevity suggests by analogy that the peplos of Athena may well have been transported on a vehicle of great antiquity, which had become a traditional part of the festival and was refitted from time to time as the need arose.[111] This would explain some of the peculiarities of the epigraphical references.

If, however, we follow Farnell and Pfuhl[112] in thinking that such a vehicle was at first a simple cart to carry the mast of the peplos and only later assumed the form of a ship, the problem is then greatly compounded. On this view, the transformation from cart to ship cannot then have taken place until after 142 B.C., the date of Miltiades' agonothesia, and probably not until after the Augustan period, since the poet of the *Ciris* speaks of *currus* (line 26) and not *navis*. Indeed, if this line of argument is pushed to its logical conclusion, there is no reason to believe that the Panathenaic ship was introduced into the festival before it is first mentioned in the Hadrianic period, when Herodes Atticus was agonothetes. But it seems most improbable that so violent a change in ritual would be tolerated in a festival which had nearly seven centuries of tradition behind it. Indeed, the tenacious conservatism of the Panathenaia is best illustrated by the prize amphoras, which retained their traditional iconography and their archaic black-figure technique as late as the 4th century after Christ.[113] Moreover, it is impossible to explain why at so late a date the peplos should suddenly be borne for the first time by ship when the festival has no other associations with the sea. It is equally difficult to understand why, several centuries before the introduction of the ship, Lysimachos should have sent a ship's mast and yardarm to be mounted on a wagon; for the κεραία καὶ ἱστὸς of *IG* II², 657, line 14 are technical naval terms, unlike the ὅπλα of our text,[114] and they should be taken to mean that these parts were removed

[110] *IG* XI 2, 203 B, lines 98–99. Along with the cart, the inventory lists also a ὅπλον στύππινον which may possibly have been used to draw the cart in the procession. It was evidently drawn by men and not animals, cf. *IDélos*, 442 A, lines 198–199: ἐργάταις τοῖς τὴν ἅμαξαν ἀγαγοῦσιν καὶ ἀπαγαγοῦσιν.

[111] That such a car existed in Athens is suggested by the very fragmentary decree *IG* II², 673 (278/7) where there is mention of [ἅμαξαν τ]ετράκυκλον (line 18). The reference τῆς φαλλαγ[ωγίας] (line 7) suggests that the decree regulated the procession of the Dionysia; Nilsson, *JdaI* 31, 1916, pp. 315f. A close parallel at Athens for such a venerable sacred vehicle was the ship of Theseus, which existed down to the time of Demetrios of Phaleron and was so often repaired that philosophers debated whether it was still the same ship, Plut., *Theseus* 23.1; *Mor.* 786 f; Plato, *Phaedo* 58 a–b.

[112] *Cults of the Greek States* I, Oxford 1896, p. 297; Pfuhl, *de pompis*, p. 10.

[113] For Panathenaic amphoras of the Roman period in the black-figure technique, see G. R. Edwards, *Hesperia* 26, 1957, pp. 320–349, especially nos. 12, 13, 24, 25. Another black-figured Panathenaic (Agora Inv. P 26600) was found in a dated context of the 4th century after Christ, see H. A. Thompson, *Hesperia* 29, 1960, p. 366, pl. 80:d. Although the figures are rather more reddish brown than black, their details are still indicated by incision. For the shape, cf. the relief amphoras at the top of *IG* II², 2245 (A.D. 262/3 or 266/7), Graindor, *Album d'inscriptions attiques d'époque impériale*, Paris 1924, pl. LXXXII; cf. also J. Frel, *Panathenaic Prize Amphoras*, Athens 1973, p. 33, figs. 32–33.

[114] The official lists of gear belonging to the Athenian triremes of the 4th century B.C. always include ἱστὸς and κεραία but never ὅπλα, the general term for ropes there used being always τοπεῖα, *IG* II², 1624, lines 105–124; 1627, lines 436–472; 1628, lines 576–608; 1629, lines 1050–1085; 1631, lines 257–278. For

from an actual ship and sent to Athens. But this surely implies the association of ship and peplos at that time; for if the vehicle were a simple wagon, the peplos might just as well be fastened to ordinary wooden beams (ξύλα). The mast and yard were not necessary and not even appropriate without the naval association.

But the question still arises why, if the ship existed in the Hellenistic period, do all three inscriptions so explicitly fail to mention it. We can here, unfortunately, do no more than speculate, but a possible explanation may perhaps be found in the suggestion, put forward long ago by Frickenhaus, that the same processional vehicle, shaped like a ship on wheels, was used to carry the image of Dionysos at the Anthesteria and the peplos of Athena at the Panathenaia.[115] Several black-figured vases show a four-wheeled wagon decorated to look like a ship, in which Dionysos rides in procession,[116] and these attest the existence of the ship-car as early as the 6th century B.C. The details of this vehicle bear close resemblance to the only surviving representation of the Panathenaic ship, on the festival calendar frieze, now built into the old Metropolitan church at Athens. Even though the relief of the ship is heavily defaced by a Christian cross, it was clearly depicted as a four-wheeled wagon to which the bow, stern, and rudder of a ship were attached in the same manner as the ship-car of the vases.[117] If these can be interpreted as representations of the same processional float, which may have survived for a long period like the Dionysiac car at Delos, though often repaired and even heavily restored over the years, we can then perhaps understand why our inscriptions do not mention it specifically. What made this vehicle the ship of Dionysos was the image of the god placed in it for the procession, and on that occasion the ship carried no mast or sail, which are lacking in all of the vase-paintings. The same vehicle became the Panathenaic ship when it was rigged with mast, yard, and ropes, and then of course carried the peplos as its sail. It is precisely this equipment, the mast, yard, and ropes,

---

discussion of the technical terminology, see L. Casson, *Ships and Seamanship in the Ancient World*, Princeton 1971, pp. 229–233, 259–263. ὅπλα could be used of great cables, as well as ropes generally; and Herodotos, VII.25,36; IX.115,121, invariably uses it to describe the cables of Xerxes' bridge over the Hellespont.

[115] A. Frickenhaus, *JdaI* 27, 1912, p. 73, where, however, he attempted to associate the ship-car procession with the City Dionysia instead of the Anthesteria, *ibid.*, pp. 67–72. See the conclusive discussion in favor of the latter festival by Deubner, *JdaI* 42, 1927, pp. 172–192; Deubner, *Attische Feste*, pp. 102ff.; and cf. M. P. Nilsson, *Geschichte der griechischen Religion*, 3rd ed., Munich 1967, pp. 572, 582–584; A. Pickard-Cambridge, *The Dramatic Festivals of Athens*, 2nd ed., Oxford 1968, p. 12.

[116] Skyphos, Bologna 130: *CVA*, Bologna 2[Italy 7] III H *e*, 43 [342]; C. H. E. Haspels, *Attic Black-figured Lekythoi*, Paris 1936, p. 253, no. 15. Skyphos, London B 79: Farnell, *op. cit.* (footnote 112 above), V, pl. 42; Pickard-Cambridge, *Dithyramb Tragedy and Comedy*, Oxford 1927, figs. 5–6; Haspels, *op. cit.*, p. 250, no. 30. Skyphos fragment, Athens, Acropolis 1281 a: B. Graef and E. Langlotz, *Die antiken Vasen von der Akropolis zu Athen* I, Berlin 1925, pl. 74; Haspels, *op. cit.*, p. 250, no. 29. The best general discussion of the vases is Frickenhaus, *op. cit.*, pp. 61–67, and Beilage 1; cf. Deubner, *Attische Feste*, pls. 11:1, 14:2.

[117] Deubner, *Attische Feste*, pp. 248ff.; pl. 39:32. Although opinions have ranged widely concerning the date of this monument, from 3rd century B.C. to 3rd century after Christ, it should represent the vehicle used for the conveyance of the peplos before the ship of Herodes Atticus. For on the relief, the most prominent feature of the ship-car is its large front wheels, whereas the ship of Herodes caused particular wonder because its wheels and means of locomotion were somehow concealed beneath the float. Philostratos, *Vit. Soph.* II. 1.5: δραμεῖν δὲ τὴν ναῦν οὐχ ὑποζυγίων ἀγόντων, ἀλλ' ὑπογείοις μηχαναῖς ἐπολισθάνουσαν.

which is omitted from the Dionysiac car, but was specifically required for the conveyance of the peplos, was dedicated for that purpose by Lysimachos, Ptolemy, and Miltiades of Marathon, and is accordingly mentioned in the inscriptions.

Lines 70–72: The text here records the position of Kallias at the time the decree in his honor was passed by the Athenian assembly (270/69). He was now stationed in Halikarnassos where he had been assigned by Ptolemy Philadelphos, whom he still served as a mercenary commander, as we learn from the mention (lines 76–77) of *τῶν στρατ[ιωτῶν τῶν ἐκεῖ τεταγ]μένων μεθ' αὐτοῦ*. Whether Kallias had remained continuously in the Ptolemaic service from the time when we first hear of his commanding mercenaries in Attica in 286 is not altogether clear. The phrase *ἐπιδημήσας ε[ἰ]ς τὸ ἄστυ* (line 45) suggests that he was living in Athens as a private citizen at the beginning of Philadelphos' sole reign in 283/2. Like others of his countrymen whose politics were strongly democratic and nationalistic, he may well have returned to his native city after the liberation from Macedon. If so, it seems most likely that he was still resident in Athens and not in the king's service when he undertook to lead the Athenian theoria to the first Ptolemaia in 279/8. But there is no way of determining at what time and for what reason he rejoined Ptolemy's mercenary forces. On these points our text is silent. In fact there is a noticeable gap in Kallias' career, as here recorded, between his activities of 279/8 and mention of his post at Halikarnassos in 270/69. Perhaps for all or most of this period he was once again an officer of the crown. The wording of lines 69–70, where the theoroi are said to have brought the ropes for the peplos to Athens at once, seems almost to imply that Kallias himself did not accompany his colleagues on their return journey from Alexandria.

Halikarnassos, together with the other Karian cities of Miletos and Myndos, is known to have belonged to the Ptolemaic dominions in the years after 280, when Philokles of Sidon, acting as viceroy, could direct that judges from those cities serve as arbitrators at Samos.[118] Like Miletos, it was probably ceded to Ptolemy by Antiochos I in the peace treaty of 279 which brought an end to the so-called "Carian War".[119] It is thus at least possible that Kallias received his appointment to Halikarnassos in 279/8 in connection with his visit to Alexandria for the Ptolemaia, and he may have remained at this post thenceforward until the time of the Athenian decree. This would account for the silence of our text concerning nine years of his career.

[118] *SEG* I, 363, lines 3–4 = M. Schede, *AthMitt* 44, 1919, pp. 21–23, no. 9.

[119] The peace is mentioned in a later decree of Miletos answering a letter from Ptolemy II, Rehm, *Milet* I, iii (footnote 72 above), p. 300, no. 139, lines 27ff.: *διαδεξάμενός τε τὴμ βασιλείαν ὁ υἱὸς αὐτοῦ βασιλεὺς Πτολεμαῖος .... χώραν τε ἐπιδιδοὺς καὶ τὴν εἰρήνην παρασκευάζων τῶι δήμωι*. The date is fixed by mention of the same gift of land in the list of eponymous stephanephoroi, against the incumbent of 279/8, *ibid*., p. 259, no. 123, line 38: *ἐπὶ τούτου ἐδόθη ἡ χώρα τῶι δήμωι ὑπὸ τοῦ βασιλέως Πτολεμαίου*. The short duration of the conflict, which evidently arose in the confusion after the death of Seleukos, is indicated by the fact that Antiochos I was himself named stephanephoros at Miletos in the previous year 280/79, *ibid*., line 37. See W. Otto, *Beiträge zur Seleukidengeschichte* (*Abhand. Akad. Berlin* 34, 1, 1928), pp. 17ff.; Tarn, *Hermes* 65, 1930, pp. 446ff., especially p. 451. The "Carian War" is his term. Cf. Will, *Monde hellénistique* I, pp. 121–123.

Neither the official title nor the exact nature of his position in Halikarnassos is expressly stated; but since there were mercenary soldiers under his command, he is most likely to have been the commandant of a local garrison. Although this is the first evidence to attest the existence of such a garrison at Halikarnassos, there can be no doubt about the Egyptian military presence in the district of Karia; for sometime during the period 270 to 259, a Samian decree conferred honors on a Macedonian, Aristolaos, who bore the title *στρατηγὸς ἐπὶ Καρίας*.[120] This officer was plainly the military governor of the district who held a command comparable to that of his contemporary Patroklos, *στρατηγὸς ἐς Κρήταν*, or Hippomedon, *στρατ[ηγὸς τοῦ Ἑλ]λησπόντου καὶ τῶν ἐπὶ Θράικης τόπων*, during the reign of Ptolemy III.[121] No doubt the garrison commanders of individual cities came under the jurisdiction of these high-ranking officers; and in fact when our decree was passed, it is not impossible that Aristolaos himself was Kallias' immediate superior. Such a relation between local commandant and territorial commander is well illustrated at just this time on the island of Keos, where an inscription honors Hieron of Syracuse *τεταγμένος ὑπὸ τὸμ βασιλ̣[έα] Πτολεμαῖον παραγεγενημένος εἰς τὴν νῆσον μετὰ τοῦ στρατηγοῦ Πατρόκλου κ̣αθεστηκὼς ἐπιστάτης ἐν Ἀρσινόηι* (*IG* XII 5, 1061, lines 2–4). An official description of Kallias' position, which was doubtless of little interest to the Athenian orator, would probably have been closely similar to Hieron's.

It is tempting to think that some trace of Kallias' sojourn may survive at Halikarnassos itself in the tantalizing fragment of an honorific decree, which has been dated to the period 281 to 266.[122] Although the inscription is too broken to recover any sense of the text, there is mention of both Athens and a King Ptolemy, who is certainly Philadelphos. Since it appears that the Demos of Halikarnassos will publish the honors, while the prytaneis are to arrange that they be published in Athens as well, the decree probably honors an Athenian who used his influence with Ptolemy for the benefit of Halikarnassos. The situation agrees well with what we now know of Kallias, and we may suggest the possibility that he was himself the honorand of the Halikarnassian decree, just as other Ptolemaic officers were at times honored by the cities in which they were stationed.

Lines 72–74: From his post in Halikarnassos, Kallias was able to use his influence in Alexandria to assist Athenian embassies and theorias sent to King Ptolemy. The present tense of the verb *διατελεῖ* makes it clear that Athens was still calling upon his good offices at the time when the decree was voted, or had done so very recently. The theorias are undoubtedly those which Athens sent to the second and third celebrations of the Ptolemaia in Alexandria, in 275/4 and 271/0 respectively; and the latter

[120] C. Habicht, *AthMitt* 72, 1957, pp. 218–223, no. 57. For discussion of Ptolemaic relations with Karia, see Bagnall, *Ptolemaic Possessions*, pp. 89–102.

[121] Patroklos: *ICret* III, pp. 81–83, no. 2, lines 4–8; no. 3, lines 4–7; see *Pros. Ptol.* VI, 15063. Hippomedon: *IG* XII 8, 156, lines 3–4 (= *SIG*³, 502 = P. M. Fraser, *Samothrace* 2, I, New York 1960, p. 39); see *Pros. Ptol.* VI, 14605.

[122] F. J. Frost, *Anatolian Studies* 21, 1971, pp. 167–172.

of these festivals, it may be noted, occurred less than a year before the passage of the decree for Kallias. The *πρεσβείας* of our text ought likewise to refer to equally current events, and we may well consider in what diplomatic negotiations between Athens and Ptolemy II Kallias can have served as intermediary in, or shortly before, 270/69.

Both the mention of embassies and the date call to mind a much-discussed passage in the celebrated decree of Chremonides, recording the alliance between Athens and Sparta which led to the Chremonidean War: *ὅ τε βασιλεὺς Πτολεμαῖος ἀκολούθως τεῖ τῶν προγόνων καὶ τεῖ τῆς ἀδελφῆς προ[α]ιρέσει φανερός ἐστιν σπουδάζων ὑπὲρ τῆς κοινῆς τ[ῶν] Ἑλλήνων ἐλευθερίας· καὶ ὁ δῆμος ὁ Ἀθηναίων συμμαχίαν ποιησάμενος πρὸς αὐτόν.*[123] There is here the explicit statement, first, that Ptolemy's foreign policy, which sought to encourage an uprising of the Greek cities against Antigonos Gonatas under the diplomatic tag of "common freedom", had been developed earlier by his father Soter[124] and had been urged more recently by his sister and queen, Arsinoe II. Secondly, there is specific reference to an alliance between Athens and Ptolemy concluded prior to the decree of Chremonides. Whatever role Arsinoe may have played in the implementation of this policy, there can be no doubt that her death in July, 270 B.C.[125] must have affected negotiations between Egypt and the Greek cities. At the very least, a procession of Greek ambassadors is likely to have journeyed to Alexandria, if only to inquire to what extent the passing of the queen might lead to changes in Ptolemy's Greek policy. It should now be noted that the date of our decree, Posideon 18, 270/69, falls barely six months after the death of Arsinoe. Some of the Athenian embassies here mentioned may then have been dispatched in these months to ascertain the status of Athens' negotiations with Egypt, and the *συμμαχία* of Chremonides' decree may be viewed as the fruit of their efforts. This is made the more likely inasmuch as Kallias, whose aid they sought, is first cited in our text for helping to restore to Athens in 286 what might well be described as the *κοινὴ τῶν Ἑλλήνων ἐλευθερία* in the name of Ptolemy Soter.

The assistance which Kallias continued to provide to Athenian ambassadors is described in vague and formulaic terms by comparison with the unusually fulsome detail used in describing his other services. This might be thought to indicate simply that Kallias did not help the ambassadors very much; for if he had been instrumental in negotiating the alliance with Ptolemy, we should have expected a more explicit statement. In view of the fact, however, that the Demos chose this moment to lavish upon him many of its highest honors, an alternative explanation recommends itself. It is equally possible that negotiations were in progress at the date of the decree, but

[123] Schmitt, *Staatsverträge* III, no. 476, lines 16–19 = *IG* II², 687 = *SIG*³, 434–435. For discussion of the passage and the decree, see Ferguson, *HA*, pp. 169f., 175ff.; Tarn, *Ant. Gon.*, pp. 293–297; Beloch, *Gr. Gesch.* IV², i, pp. 587f.; ii, pp. 502f.; F. Sartori, "Cremonide: un dissidio fra politica e filosofia," *Miscellanea di studi alessandrini in mem. di A. Rostagni*, Turin 1963, pp. 117–151, especially 126, 145ff.; Will, *Monde hellénistique* I, pp. 196–200; Heinen, *Untersuchungen*, pp. 132–137.

[124] For the policy and propaganda of Ptolemy Soter concerning the freedom of the Greek cities, see J. Seibert, *Untersuchungen zur Geschichte Ptolemaios' I.*, Munich 1969, pp. 180–189.

[125] For the date, see Fraser, *Ptol. Alex.* II, p. 937, note 415.

that the alliance had not yet been formally concluded, in which case the decree for Kallias provides a *terminus post quem*, and the alliance is to be placed between 270/69 and the date of Chremonides' decree.[126]

Lines 79–80: The closing lines of the citation provide an interesting glimpse at an earlier episode in Kallias' life, and one which undoubtedly affected the whole of his subsequent career. There is reference here to a time at which "the Demos was destroyed" and to an oligarchy with which Kallias would evidently have nothing to do. The spirit of nationalist democracy unmistakably fires these sentiments, and it places Kallias in the company of two other men prominent in public life after the liberation of Athens: Demochares of Leukonoe and Philippides of Kephale. The extant decrees for these men provide instructive comparisons for the present passage. The citation of Demochares' services concludes: "He endured exile for the sake of the democracy, he had no part of any oligarchy, he held no public office of any kind after the democracy had been subverted; and he was the only Athenian of those active in politics in his time who never plotted to change the country to any form of constitution other than democracy. By his policies he ensured the safety of judicial decisions, the laws, the courts, and private property for all Athenians, and he never acted in opposition to the democracy either by word or deed" ([Plut.], *Mor.* 851 f, Appendix **10**). Much less fulsome but in a closely similar vein are the words which end the citation for Philippides: "And he never did anything in opposition to democracy either by word or deed" (*IG* II², 657, lines 48–50, Appendix **11**). Here speaks the voice of those Athenians who adhered so stubbornly to their partisan views of democratic government and national autonomy that they preferred to endure exile rather than make any accommodation either with the extremists on one side who bought the appearance of democracy at the price of obeisance to Demetrios Poliorketes, or with the oligarchs on the other who sacrificed the democratic institutions for a short measure of illusory autonomy.

In the case of Demochares, the circumstances of his exile are explicitly set forth. The decree drafted by his son Laches enumerates his many services as administrator, military organizer, and diplomat during the Four Years' War (307/6–304/3),[127] in

[126] The year of the archon Peithidemos, in which the Chremonidean War began, remains one of the cruces of Athenian chronology in the first half of the 3rd century. The best discussion of the problem is that of Heinen, *Untersuchungen*, pp. 102–110, who adopts the date 268/7, before the archons Menekles (267/6) and Nikias III of Otryne (266/5). Meritt has consistently preferred a date for Peithidemos after Nikias of Otryne, Pritchett and Merritt, *Chronology*, pp. 29–30, 33–35; *Ath. Year*, p. 233, and thus now in 265/4. This is less attractive in view of the specific evidence that Athens was at war during the archonships of Menekles and Nikias (*IG* II², 665, lines 7–12; 666, line 18; 667, lines 6–7).

[127] The ancient term τετραετὴς πόλεμος is used in Laches' decree, [Plut.], *Mor.* 851 e. Numerous testimonia document Athens' vigorous preparations for war and siege in these years: repair of the city walls and collection of arms, artillery, and ammunition in 307/6 and 306/5 (*IG* II², 463 + *Hesperia* 9, 1940, p. 66, no. 9; 468; 505, lines 30ff.; 554); gifts of armor, grain, timber for 100 triremes from Demetrios and Antigonos (Plut., *Demetr.* 10.1; 17.1; Dio. Sic., XX.46.4); gift of money from Antigonos, Mounichion 305 (*IG* II², 1492, lines 97ff.); arrival of ship timber, Skirophorion 305 (*ibid.*, lines 118ff.); collection of money on motion of Demochares (*ibid.*, lines 124ff.); Kassandros' attack on Athens in 306/5 (*IG* II², 467, lines 22–23;

return for which ungrateful Athens rewarded him with banishment: "In return for these services he was driven into exile by those who destroyed the democracy; and when he was recalled by the Demos in the archonship of Diokles...." Plutarch (*Demetr.* 24.4–5) reports his exile as the result of a bitter controversy between the anti-Demetrian democrats and Stratokles of Diomeia, Demetrios' strongest supporter and most servile flatterer in Athens. Incensed at the king's practice of governing by royal letter, the Demos had decreed that no letters from Demetrios should be brought before the assembly. Thereupon Stratokles, in response to royal expressions of outrage, had succeeded in having the decree annulled and replaced by another which provided that whatsoever Demetrios might order be deemed just to men and righteous to the gods. Those who introduced and supported the former decree and who opposed the latter were then punished with execution or exile, and among them was Demochares. The incident is to be dated in 303/2 when Demetrios was absent from Athens campaigning in the Peloponnese.[128] On Skirophorion 29 of 303, Stratokles is known to have read such a letter from the king to the assembly and thereby secured passage of a decree of citizenship for Demetrios' friend Eupolis and honors for the royal messengers.[129] The opposition possibly arose on this very occasion, but in any event not earlier, and certainly before the following Mounichion of 302,[130] when Demetrios returned to Athens for his infamous initiation into the Eleusinian Mysteries, by which time Stratokles had again sufficiently cowed the assembly so that he was able to manipulate both the calendar and the sacred traditions of Eleusis.

The reference in our text to the time at which "the Demos was destroyed" is surely to be equated with the incident described in the same words, as a result of which Demochares refused to accept any public office, and was also driven into exile "by those who destroyed the Demos." Exactly what it was that Kallias could never abide at this same time, there seems to be no way of reconstructing except by guesswork (lines 78–79), but his response to the situation was clearly similar to Demochares'.

469, lines 8–10; 470, lines 11–13; Pausanias, I.26.3); Demetrios' campaign against Kassandros in 304 (Dio. Sic., XX.100.5–6; Plut., *Demetr.* 23.1–2). See Ferguson, *HA*, pp. 112–118; M. Fortina, *Cassandro, re di Macedonia*, Turin, etc. 1965, pp. 91ff., 97–99.

[128] For the date of Demochares' exile, see Ferguson, *Klio* 5, 1905, pp. 174–175 and note 4; Ferguson, *HA*, p. 122. Plutarch's date for the exile, in the context of the events of 303 B.C., has not always been accepted, and attempts have been made to remove the incident to the years about 292 B.C.: G. de Sanctis in Beloch's *Studi di storia antica* II, 1893, pp. 30ff.; *RivFil*, n.s. 14, 1936, pp. 131ff.; Beloch, *Gr. Gesch.* IV^2, i, p. 221 and note 1; ii, p. 447; Manni, *Dem. Pol.*, pp. 89ff. These have been answered and the evidence reviewed by L. C. Smith, *Historia* 11, 1962, pp. 114–118. For Demetrios' campaign in the Peloponnese, Plut., *Demetr.* 25.1; Dio. Sic., XX.102–103, in the archonship of Leostratos (303/2); Ferguson, *Hesperia* 17, 1948, pp. 120–123.

[129] *IG* II^2, 486, lines 11–13: *[περὶ ὧν ὁ βασιλ]εὺς ἐπέστειλεν τεῖ [βουλεῖ καὶ τῶι δήμωι ἀπο]φαίνων φίλον ε[ἶναι Εὔπολιν]*. Passed at the same assembly was another decree moved by Stratokles, *Hesperia* 7, 1938, p. 297, no. 22 which begins, lines 12–15: *ὅπως ἂν τ[ιμῶνται οἱ ἀπὸ Δη]μητρίου τοῦ βασιλ[έως ἐξαποστελλό]μενοι πρὸς τὴν πόλ[ιν]*.

[130] Cf. Ferguson, *Hesperia* 17, 1948, p. 121, note 27; pp. 123–124. For Demetrios' initiation, Plut., *Demetr.* 26; Dio. Sic., XX.110.1 who places the incident in the archonship of Nikokles (302/1) instead of Leostratos (303/2).

Moreover, the curious statement that he allowed his property "to be given as a contribution" (*δόσιν δοθῆναι*) under the oligarchy should in all likelihood be interpreted as a euphemism for confiscation and therefore implies that he, too, either went or was driven into exile. It was, perhaps, at this time in the years about the turn of the century, and as a result of the political convulsions at Athens, that Kallias first went to seek his fortune in the service of Ptolemy. This would explain why the decree begins his career at the time of the revolution, for like Demochares he may only then have returned to Attica. He was probably too young for high political office under the restored democracy of 307/6,[131] and the expression of mere partisanship at that time was no recommendation for the public honors conferred by our decree. His early years are therefore omitted.

If it be thought strange that there is not a more specific statement of Kallias' exile, glorying in it as does the decree for Demochares, the career of Philippides affords a precise parallel, and it is possible that in both cases the exile was self-imposed.[132] Although the comic poet is nowhere said specifically to have been in exile, the decree makes it obvious that he was away from Athens for most if not all of the period from 301 to 286. He is said to have gone abroad (*ἀποδημήσας*, line 10) to King Lysimachos, to whom he applied before the battle of Ipsos (*πρότερόν τε διαλεχθεὶς*, lines 10–11) for the gifts which were sent to Athens in 299/8. He was with Lysimachos in Asia at the time of Ipsos and just afterwards (301), for he buried the Athenian casualties in the battle at his own expense (lines 18–20) and arranged for the release and return of Athenian prisoners of war (lines 20–28). He was with Lysimachos also at the time of the liberation of Athens (286), when he appealed to the king to send aid to the new nationalist government (lines 31–36). During the 14 intervening years, his only activity worthy of mention in an honorary decree was to continue to be helpful to those Athenians who met up with him from time to time. It is surely correct to infer that he was abroad the entire time, and in this respect his career is strikingly similar to that which we have sketched for Kallias.

It has been observed that "the destruction of the Demos", which Demochares blamed for his exile, is a curiously ambiguous description for Stratokles and his party of extreme pro-Demetrian democrats, since in Athenian political parlance the phrase *καταλύειν τὸν δῆμον* is normally applied to the work of tyrants and oligarchs. Laches' use of the phrase thirty years after the fact to describe his father's enemies would, it has been thought, convey the erroneous impression that he was exiled by

[131] Kallias' brother Phaidros dated the beginning of his public career with election to the board of generals in 296/5, at which time he should have been in his mid-thirties, hence the birth-year *ca.* 330 B.C. proposed for both brothers by Davies, *APF*, p. 526. Kallias was probably slightly younger (footnote 5 above) and will thus have been only in his early twenties at the time of the Four Years' War.

[132] Cf. Smith, *Historia* 11, 1962, p. 115. For discussion of the honorific decree, *IG* II^2, 657 (Appendix **11**), Ferguson, *Klio* 5, 1905, p. 163 and note 2; Ferguson, *HA*, pp. 124, 126, 144. Tarn, *Ant. Gon.*, pp. 94f. and note 12 takes the silence of the decree to mean that Philippides was not exiled and remained in Athens whence he was merely sent as ambassador. But the decree does not so describe him, and in lines 37–38 careful distinction is made between Philippides and the Athenian ambassadors. Cf. also A. Körte, *RE* XIX, 1938, col. 2204, *s.v.* Philippides (7).

oligarchs who had been able to subvert the democracy because of Stratokles' irresponsible actions.[133] Possibly there is some ambiguity in the wording of Laches' decree, but in Euchares' decree for Kallias the same terminology is juxtaposed in such a way as to make it clear that "the destruction of the Demos" is not the same thing as the oligarchy. The present passage states that Kallias could never submit to one thing when the democracy was subverted ([κ]αταλελυμένου τοῦ δήμου), but he even allowed something else to happen ἐν τεῖ ὀλιαρχίαι.[134] Even Athenians with the shortest memories for history were not likely to think that the orator of our decree intended these phrases to be synonymous. "The destroyers of the Demos" to which the decrees for both Demochares and Kallias make reference should be identified as Stratokles and his friends, the toadies of Demetrios; and what is more, there is evidence that they were so called even before the oligarchy came into power. In the celebrated lines quoted by Plutarch, Philippides criticized Stratokles in a play probably produced in 301 B.C.[135] The poet attacked his manipulation of festivals and calendar, his lodging of Demetrios in the Parthenon, and granting of divine honors to a man, unholy acts, which had caused the crops to be blighted and the peplos to be torn asunder by a storm. The poet's indictment of Stratokles ends with the significant line: *ταῦτα καταλύει δῆμον, οὐ κωμωδία* and it sounds as if the stage has borrowed a current slogan from the bema.

To suppose that Philippides and Demochares were at that time worried only about the possibility of an oligarchy is to misconstrue the very explicit associations of the phrase *καταλύειν τὸν δῆμον*, which to the Athenian ear would at once conjure up the spector of the "tyrant". Indeed, the notion and probably the phrase itself had been contained in legislation against tyranny from the time of Solon, and even of Drakon.[136] The decree framed by Demophantos in 410/9, and modeled on this earlier legislation, begins: *ἐάν τις δημοκρατίαν καταλύῃ τὴν Ἀθήνησιν, ἢ ἀρχήν τινα ἄρχῃ καταλελυμένης τῆς δημοκρατίας, πολέμιος ἔστω* (Andokides, I.96). More significant for our present purpose is the later version of the law against tyranny, promulgated by Eukrates in 336 B.C., which provides: *ἐάν τις ἐπαναστῆι τῶι δήμωι ἐπὶ τυραννίδι ἢ τὴν τυραννίδα συνκαταστήσηι ἢ τὸν δῆμον τὸν Ἀθηναίων ἢ τὴν δημοκρατίαν τὴν Ἀθήνησιν καταλύσηι . . . μὴ ἐξεῖναι δὲ τῶν βουλευτῶν τῶν τῆς βουλῆς τῆς ἐξ Ἀρείου Πάγου καταλελυ⟨μ⟩ένου τοῦ δήμου ἢ τῆς δημοκρατίας τῆς Ἀθήνησιν ἀνιέναι εἰς Ἄρειον Πάγον.*[137] This law has been convincingly interpreted as a product of the anti-Macedonian activity just after the defeat at Chaironeia, an attempt to forestall the possibility that the rulers of Macedon might establish a tyranny at Athens through the agency of their Athenian

[133] So Ferguson, *Klio* 5, 1905, pp. 174–175. P. Treves, *Athenaeum*, n.s. 10, 1932, pp. 190–191 sought to attribute the "subversion of the democracy", and with it Demochares' exile, to the appointive second archonship of Olympiodoros (293/2); Manni, *Dem. Pol.*, pp. 89–92 argued for 294. But the "subversion of the democracy" must come before the oligarchy as is seen by the reference in our text.

[134] For the same phrase applied to the oligarchy of 321–318 B.C., *IG* II^2, 448, line 61. Note, too, the same spelling of the word with gamma omitted.

[135] Plut., *Demetr.* 12.4; 26.3 = Philippides, fr. 25, Edmonds, *Frag. Att. Com.*, III A, p. 178. For the date, Ferguson, *op. cit.* (footnote 133 above), p. 163, note 2; Ferguson, *HA*, p. 123 and note 2.

[136] See the full discussion by M. Ostwald, *TAPA* 86, 1955, pp. 103–128.

[137] *Hesperia* 21, 1952, p. 355, no. 5, lines 7–15.

sympathizers. Moreover, two exactly contemporary speeches have been shown to reflect the same fear of tyranny which gave rise to the law of Eukrates, and both are explicit in calling the Macedonian kings "tyrants".[138]

In one of these, the fragmentary speech of Hypereides, *Against Philippides*, the issue concerns the bestowing of public honors on a number of Macedonians; and Philippides was indicted for proposing to crown the proedroi who, bowing to Macedonian pressure, had illegally allowed the honorary decrees to pass the assembly.[139] It is people like these, says the orator, who cater to the interests of tyrants and bring slavery upon the city; and instead of being democrats as they claim, they are subservient to tyrants so that they can give orders to the Demos.[140] The response to such activity in 336 B.C. was a law aimed at preventing the *κατάλυσις τοῦ δήμου*; and it was no doubt exactly that which the anti-Demetrian democrats of the next generation also feared, as they watched Stratokles and his friends prostrating themselves and the government of Athens before Demetrios, his parasites, and his courtesans. The words of Hypereides, directed at Philippides in 336, might also describe perfectly the regime of Stratokles between 303 and 301. He, too, had lavished public honors upon the king and his retinue; even our imperfect record preserves no less than nine decrees of Stratokles bestowing honors upon Demetrios' friends.[141] His apparent absolute control of the assembly in these years put him in the classic position from which tyrants had historically arisen in Greece. Moreover, his was a regime which had punished Athenian citizens with death and exile because they had balked at the king's peremptory letters and ventured to dissent on the question whether he should be declared infallible by solemn decree. To Athenian democrats of any period such actions would betoken the subversion of the democracy. Especially in an age as fervently anti-Macedonian as that to which the decrees here in question belong, it is natural that Laches should describe his father's enemies as *οἱ καταλύσαντες τὸν δῆμον*, and his insistence upon Demochares' refusal to hold public office (*οὐδὲ ἀρχὴν οὐδεμίαν ἠρχότι καταλελυκότος τοῦ δήμου*) forms a precise verbal reminiscence drawn from the phraseology of Athenian laws against tyranny.[142]

[138] Hypereides, *in Phil.* 8,10 and fr. 1; [Demosthenes], XVII.4,12, 29. For the historical context of Eukrates' law, Ostwald, *op. cit.* (footnote 136 above), pp. 123–125.

[139] G. Colin, *Hypéride: Discours*, Paris 1946, pp. 87–89. The Philippides against whom Hypereides speaks is, of course, not to be confused with the homonymous comic poet discussed above. See Kirchner, *PA* 14351.

[140] Hypereides, *in Phil.*, fr. 1 (ed. Colin): . . . . *ἐν] ἐλευθέρᾳ πό[λει τὰ τ]οῖς τυράννοις [συμφέρο]ντα πράττοντ[ες, καὶ αὐτὴ]ν εἰς δουλεία[ν ἐμβάλλοντες . . . .*; *ibid.*, 10: *διὰ τί γὰρ ἂν τούτου φείσαισθε; πότερα διότι δημοτικός ἐστιν; ἀλλὰ ἴστ' αὐτὸν τοῖς μὲν τυράννοις δουλεύειν προελόμενον, τῷ δὲ δήμῳ προστάττειν ἀξιοῦντα.*

[141] In addition to Plut., *Demetr.* 10.3–11.1; Dio. Sic. XX.46.1–2; *IG* II², 471, 486, 492, 495, 496 + 507, 559 + 568, 560, 561; *Hesperia* 7, 1938, p. 297, no. 22. Of seven other known honorary decrees moved by Stratokles, *IG* II², 469 and 503 are also likely to honor friends of the king; eight decrees of Stratokles are of unknown subject matter. To the list assembled by Dinsmoor, *Archons*, pp. 13–14, should be added *Hesperia*, *loc. cit.*; *Hesperia* 1, 1932, p. 45; 11, 1942, p. 241, no. 46.

[142] There is no suggestion in the sources that legal action against Stratokles was attempted by Demochares and his followers; but the suggestion that he was subverting the democracy was undoubtedly an

Lines 81–83: Mention of the oligarchy in the decree for Kallias alludes to one of the darkest and least documented episodes of Athenian history. The use here of the definite article is worth emphasizing, for it signifies that during the active career of Kallias, between the democratic restoration of 307/6 and the Chremonidean War, there was only one period which an Athenian orator could describe as oligarchy. Once again there is a parallel in the decree for Demochares which states that he "took part in no oligarchy" (οὐδεμιᾶς ὀλιγαρχίας), but the positive statement in our text of something which happened "in *the* oligarchy" is welcome confirmation.

During the decade after the battle of Ipsos in 301, there is an unusual dearth of documentary evidence bearing on the institutions of Athenian government. That the moderates who controlled the government in these years instituted some changes is best seen in the reorganization of Athenian financial administration. In this period the funds used to pay for the publication of inscriptions and for such public honors as the erection of statues were no longer disbursed by civilian administrators, the treasurer of the assembly (ταμίας τοῦ δήμου) or the Superintendent of Administration (ὁ ἐπὶ τῇ διοικήσει), but now by the paymaster of the mercenary soldiers and officials associated with military and naval finance, the exetastes and the trittyarchs.[143] But the same decrees which show the emergence of these new officials demonstrate equally that there was no far-reaching change in the basic democratic forms of government; for the secretaries of the Council continued to rotate annually in unbroken tribal order between 301/0 and 295/4. The mere re-alignment of administrative duties would seem insufficient cause for an orator speaking 25 years later to describe the regime as "the oligarchy".

That this period witnessed considerable civil disturbance there can be no doubt. Although the exact order, duration, and chronology of the events has been subject to various interpretations, the sources speak of the rise of Lachares to a position of prominence in the assembly, of stasis among the Athenian generals, of the secession of the Peiraieus, and of Lachares' tyranny.[144] But there is no suggestion that any of

important element in the political rhetoric of these years. The democrats of the late 4th century and the nationalists of the early 3rd cannot have known the text of Eukrates' law since it had been repealed and the stele pulled down before 322 B.C., Meritt, *Hesperia* 21, 1952, p. 359. However, the law on εἰσαγγελία, in force at the time and quoted by Hypereides, *pro Eux.* 7–8, was applicable ἐάν τις τὸν δῆμον τὸν Ἀθηναίων καταλύῃ ἢ συνίῃ ποι ἐπὶ καταλύσει τοῦ δήμου. Furthermore, the old decree of Demophantos, quoted above, still stood in the Bouleuterion in 331/0, when Lykourgos had it read into his speech *Against Leokrates* (124, 127). The reference to its text in Laches' decree suggests that it was still there two generations later.

[143] See Ferguson, *Klio* 5, 1905, pp. 171f.; *CP* 24, 1929, pp. 16f.; Dinsmoor, *Archons*, p. 64. The exetastes and the trittyarchs appear in a number of decrees of this period: *IG* II², 641; 643 + *Hesperia* 9, 1940, p. 80, no. 13 (see now J. S. Traill, *Hesperia*, Suppl. XIV, 1975, p. 130); *IG* II², 646, 648, 1270; *Hesperia* 11, 1942, p. 278, no. 53; 13, 1944, p. 242, no. 7; 29, 1960, p. 8, no. 9 (restored).

[144] The principal source for the history of these events is *P. Oxy.* XVII, 2082 = *F. Gr. Hist.*, 257 a, which records Lachares' command of the mercenaries, stasis among the generals, and the secession of Peiraieus, evidently very shortly before the death of Kassandros, there dated in 298/7. For Lachares' prominence in the assembly and subsequent tyranny, Pausanias, I.25.7; 29.10; Plut., *Demetr.* 33; Polyainos, IV.7.5. Modern discussion has followed two lines of interpretation. Ferguson, *CP* 24, 1929, pp. 1–20, dated Lachares' *coup d'état* in 300 B.C. and saw his fall from power in the change of government in Elaphebolion 295 (*IG* II², 644, 645, 682, lines 21–23); followed by Dinsmoor, *List*, p. 31 and note 46; G. Elkeles, *op. cit.*

this should be connected with oligarchy. On the contrary, Lachares command of the mercenary soldiers (*ὁ τῶν ξένων ἡγούμενος*) and Pausanias' reference to him as a popular leader (*προεστηκότα τοῦ δήμου*, I.25.7) imply precisely the opposite, that he rose to power as a soldier and a demagogue. Certainly the tyranny of Lachares can in no way be equated with the oligarchy of our text.

The oligarchy mentioned here in the decree for Kallias is evidently to be identified with the period immediately following Athens' capitulation to Demetrios Poliorketes in 295/4.[145] There are several indications that the new government put in office at that time by Demetrios, and supported by his garrisons, espoused a major dislocation of traditional democratic forms, which anti-Macedonian democrats would have called oligarchy. The extant decrees of this period show that the two most characteristic institutions of Athenian democracy, the cyclical rotation of the secretaries of the Council and the election of archons by allotment, were both abolished. The secretary, who regularly appeared in the prescripts of decrees as a part of the formula of date, was replaced by a registrar (*ἀναγραφεύς*) in 294/3 and 293/2.[146] Moreover, these were not chosen in conformity with the tribal order of rotation, but form a clear break in the cycle; for the secretary of 295/4 represented Aiantis (XI),[147] while the registrars of the next two years represented Demetrias (II) and Aiantis (XI) respectively. Although no decrees are preserved from 292/1, the period of the registrars evidently extended into that year also, because the secretary cycle which resumed in 291/0 began with a secretary from Aiantis (XI), the same tribe which had commenced the new secretary cycle after the democratic restoration in 307/6.[148] The registrar is to be recognized as an official of oligarchic government, for the only analogy to his appearance in these years falls in the period of the extreme oligarchy between 322 and 318. The parallel is close indeed. As in 294, Athens had fallen under Macedonian domination in 322, and a garrison had then been stationed in the Peiraieus. The decrees of the next three

(footnote 23 above), p. 91; Meritt, *Hesperia* 11, 1942, pp. 278ff.; *idem*, *Ath. Year*, p. 178; Wehrli, *op. cit.* (footnote 23 above), p. 164. G. de Sanctis, *RivFil*, n.s. 14, 1936, pp. 253–273 interpreted the change of government in Elaphebolion 295 as Lachares' *coup d'état* and placed his fall and the capitulation of Athens to Demetrios a few days before the passage of *IG* II^2, 646 in Elaphebolion 294. This chronology, followed here, was also adopted by F. Jacoby, *F. Gr. Hist.*, II D, p. 849, Commentary on 257 a, F 1–2; Manni, *Dem. Pol.*, p. 48; Deprado, *RivFil*, n.s. 32, 1954, pp. 290–302; Bengtson, *Griech. Gesch.*^{2}, p. 376; Will, *Monde hellénistique* I, pp. 75, 78; H. Berve, *Die Tyrannis bei den Griechen* I, Munich 1967, p. 388. The events of these years will be examined anew in a forthcoming study by C. Habicht, to whom I am indebted for showing me the manuscript of his article, which advances convincing arguments in favor of the chronology of Lachares' career adopted here.

[145] This interpretation of the oligarchy and the following discussion owe much to the views of Habicht, which he has kindly shared with me in several stimulating conversations, and which will form part of a forthcoming study of his.

[146] The *ἀναγραφεὺς* Thra.... of Phyle is attested for 294/3 in *IG* II^2, 378 + *Hesperia* 4, 1935, pp. 173–174 (cf. *Hesperia* 7, 1938, p. 99). Epikouros of Rhamnous was registrar in Olympiodoros' second archonship 293/2: *IG* II^2, 389 (cf. Dinsmoor, *Archons*, p. 21); 649 + Dinsmoor, *Archons*, pp. 7–8; *Hesperia* 7, 1938, p. 97, no. 17. The basic discussion of the registrars is Dinsmoor, *op. cit.*, pp. 16–28.

[147] *IG* II^2, 647, lines 3–4; Traill, *op. cit.* (footnote 143 above), p. 130, lines 2–3 (restored).

[148] See Meritt, *Hesperia* 26, 1957, p. 54.

years were dated by reference to the registrars whose appointments interrupted the regular rotation of the secretary cycle.[149] The government which held office in these years was specifically described in a decree of 318/7 as *οἱ ἐν τεῖ ὀλιαρχίαι πολιτευόμεν[οι]* (*IG* II², 448, line 61). In view of this it is easy to understand how Athenians of the nationalist democracy could refer to the period after 295/4 as the oligarchy.

A still more striking indication of the nature of the regime is the abolition of allotment for the election of archons. That Demetrios appointed the archons in these years is implied by Plutarch who says that "he established the archons which were most acceptable to the Demos." The same inference is to be drawn from a later passage which states that after the liberation "they voted to elect archons again as had been their ancestral custom."[150] Evidently prior to the liberation the archons were chosen in some other manner, that is by royal appointment. The epigraphical record bears out this drastic break with traditional usage, for it shows that Olympiodoros held the archonship in two successive years, 294/3 and 293/2, and one decree is specifically dated *[ἐπὶ Ὀλυμπ]ιοδώρου ἄρχοντος δεύτε[ρον ἔτος]*.[151] Furthermore in Olympiodoros' second year as eponymous archon, the king was Philippides, son of Philomelos, of Paiania, a wealthy and distinguished elder statesman of oligarchic background.[152] That the random chance of allotment should fall in one year upon two of the most prominent men in Athens is hardly to be imagined, and the conclusion seems inescapable that the archons were designated by the Macedonian king, a practice which was also adopted later by his son, Antigonos Gonatas, in the years after Athens' defeat in the Chremonidean War.[153]

Having established at Athens a coalition government under oligarchic forms, in which oligarchs like Philippides of Paiania, military leaders like Olympiodoros, and pro-Macedonian democrats like Stratokles could take part, Demetrios then reinstated the exiled Athenian oligarchs, many of whom like Deinarchos had been abroad since 307/6; and these returned to Attica in the archonship of Philippos (292/1). Although the return of the exiles was attended by portents so ominous that the seer Philochoros was consulted on their interpretations, he reports no change in the constitutional forms at

[149] The documents attesting the appearance of the registrars in 321/0, 320/19, and 319/8 are conveniently assembled by Meritt, *Ath. Year*, pp. 112–125. For the establishment of Antipatros' garrison on Boedromion 20, 322 B.C., Plut., *Phokion* 28; Dio. Sic., XVIII.18.4–5. Cf. Ferguson, *HA*, pp. 20–28 for discussion of the oligarchy.

[150] Plut., *Demetr.* 34.4: *κατέστησεν ἀρχὰς αἳ μάλιστα τῷ δήμῳ προσφιλεῖς ἦσαν*; 46.1: *ἄρχοντας αἱρεῖσθαι πάλιν, ὥσπερ ἦν πάτριον, ψηφισάμενοι.* The first passage should not be understood to mean that Demetrios acquiesced in the form of constitution most pleasing to Athenians, but rather that he chose to be archons the most acceptable men, and chief among them the popular general Olympiodoros.

[151] Dinsmoor, *Archons*, p. 21, line 1; for other references to Olympiodoros as archon, footnote 145 above.

[152] Kirchner, *PA* 14361; Dinsmoor, *Archons*, pp. 14f.; P. Treves, *RE* XIX, 1938, cols. 2201f.; *s.vv.* Philippides (4), (5), (6); D. M. Lewis, *BSA* 50, 1955, pp. 17–18; Davies, *APF*, pp. 549–550. His career is chiefly known from Stratokles' decree in his honor *IG* II², 649 + Dinsmoor, *Archons*, pp. 7–8. That he was king at the time of the decree appears from lines 25–26. He is described as *ὀλιγαρχικὸς* by Demosthenes (XXI.208,215).

[153] *F. Gr. Hist.*, 244, Apollodoros, F 44; see footnote 12 above.

this time.[154] The government established two years earlier by Demetrios evidently continued in office without major disturbance. It was at this moment, however, that the anti-Macedonian democrats like Demochares, Kallias, and Philippides of Kephale chose to remain in exile rather than participate in an oligarchic regime under Macedonian domination. The oblique reference in our text to the confiscation of Kallias' property or infringement of his property rights during the oligarchy is quite possibly to be associated with the return of the oligarchic exiles in 292/1. In its efforts to resettle the exiles without political upheaval, the government may well have made free with the properties of anti-Macedonian democrats who remained abroad. It is perhaps in this context that we should understand the loss which Kallias preferred to suffer rather than "act in any way contrary either to the laws or the democracy of all Athenians." In this connection it is especially interesting that Demochares' policies are said so emphatically to have protected the judicial process and the properties of all Athenians. The inference is clear that others had done the reverse, and this was undoubtedly the oligarchy.

Lines 89–101: In these lines the Boule presented to the Demos its motion to reward Kallias with an expression of praise and a golden crown, which was to be publicly announced at the forthcoming celebration of the Great Dionysia in Elaphebolion of 269 B.C., some three months after passage of the decree. As was standard at this period, the crown was to be presented in conformity with the law (*κατὰ τὸν νόμον*), to which reference is first made in 303/2 and regularly thereafter.[155] Prior to that date, and for the last time in 306/5 (*IG* II[2], 467, line 27), the cost of the crown was specified in the formula, normally a thousand drachmas for honors of the order voted for Kallias.[156] During the period of nationalist democracy, the expense of such public honors and the task of arranging for them fell to the Board of Administration (*οἱ ἐπὶ τῇ διοικήσει*), which is also assigned these duties in *IG* II[2], 653, line 39; 654, line 45; 657, line 68, just as they invariably met the cost of publishing the decrees at this time.

In addition to the crown, Kallias was to receive a seat of honor at all the festivals, and a bronze statue of him was to be erected in the Agora. These two awards place him in the select company of Athens' leading generals, statesmen, and most distinguished benefactors. In the mid-4th century, Athenian orators could comment on how sparing the Demos was in bestowing such privileges. Demosthenes says that Konon was the

[154] For the return of the exiles in the archonship of Philippos, Dionys. Hal., *Deinarchos* 9; for the date 292/1, Dinsmoor, *Archons*, pp. 39–44. For the portents which signaled the return of the exiles and their interpretation by Philochoros, *F. Gr. Hist.*, 328, F 67 = Dionys. Hal., *Deinarch.* 3: *φυγάδων κάθοδον ἔφαμεν προσημαίνειν ἀμφότερα, καὶ ταύτην οὐκ ἐκ μεταβολῆς πραγμάτων ἐσομένην ἀλλ' ἐν τῆι καθεστώσηι πολιτείαι.*

[155] The earliest dated appearances are in *IG* II[2], 492, line 28; 495, line 21. The officials crowned in *IG* II[2], 488, line 3 held office in the archonship of Pherekles (304/3). The decree thus probably belongs in 303/2 but might conceivably have been passed at the end of 304/3.

[156] Dinsmoor, *Archons*, p. 8, line 41 (*IG* II[2], 649) has restored the cost of three hundred drachmas in a decree of 293/2, which, however, has other anachronistic elements. If the figure is correct, the law of 303/2 may have stipulated a reduction in the cost of crowns.

first to receive a bronze statue,[157] and just a century before our decree, Iphikrates was for the first time granted the full range of honors voted for the tyrannicides, Harmodios and Aristogeiton.[158] In 330 B.C. Lykourgos (*Leokrates* 51) could still boast that other cities put statues of athletes in the agora but Athens set up generals. Although the assembly seems to have been far readier to award such honors in the early Hellenistic period, nevertheless prior to the decree for Kallias our literary and epigraphical sources yield evidence of relatively few men, exclusive of reigning kings, to whom the city had granted bronze statues during lifetime.[159] In this connection a peculiarity of the present decree may be noticed. By far the greater part of the bronze statues awarded before Kallias' carried with them also a grant of sitesis in the Prytaneion which is here omitted.

As in a number of other instances, provision is made (lines 99–101) for election of an *ad hoc* committee of three to oversee the making of the statue and its installation in the Agora. There is no specific statement from what source the committee would draw its funds, but in the absence of such provision it is reasonable to conclude that the Board of Administration would defray the cost of the statue as it did for the crown and the stele. In one case at the end of the 4th century, their predecessor, the Superintendent of Administration, was instructed to work with the committee and to disburse the amount of three thousand drachmas for the statue (*IG* II^2, 555, lines 14, 18–19, 27–29). In the year of Lachares' fall (295/4), from which two examples happen to survive, the committee of three was still financed by the exetastes and the trittyarchs, but there is no specification of the amount to be spent (*IG* II^2, 646, lines 40–46; 648, lines 5–10). Sometimes the work of the committee was increased if its members had to travel abroad as ambassadors in order to announce the award of honors and deliver the decree to a foreigner in his own country (*IG* II^2, 653, lines 43–47), or as in one case to erect the statue on foreign soil (*IG* II^2, 555, lines 20–25). In only two instances do we have information about the personnel of the committees: that elected to make the statue of Phaidros of Sphettos (*IG* II^2, 682, lines 98–101) and that charged with preparation of a crown and a tomb for the philosopher Zenon (Diogenes Laertius, VII.12). On the committee for Phaidros it is interesting to find his son Thymochares listed first, together with another fellow demesman. The first man chosen for Zenon's committee was the orator of the decree. It is doubtless the merest coincidence that Menon of Acharnai happened to be elected to both these committees.

Lines 98–99: Reference is here made to an official who is directed to assign a front seat to Kallias at all the ἀγῶνες which the city puts on. The all-inclusive wording of this

[157] After the battle of Knidos, 394 B.C., Demosthenes, XX.70. Pausanias saw two statues of Konon and his son Timotheos, one in the Agora (I.3.2), and the other on the Acropolis (I.24.3; and cf. *IG* II^2, 3774 for the inscribed base of the latter).

[158] In 371/0, Dionys. Hal., *Lysias* 12; [Lysias] fr. 36–43; Demosthenes, XXIII.130,136; Schol., XXI.62.

[159] A convenient list of those who had honorary statues in the Agora has been collected by R. E. Wycherley, *The Athenian Agora*, III, *Literary and Epigraphical Testimonia*, Princeton 1957, pp. 207–217. Cf. the remarks of H. A. Thompson and R. E. Wycherley, *The Athenian Agora*, XIV, *The Agora of Athens*, Princeton 1972, pp. 158–159.

standard formula means that he will have a seat of honor in the theater for all the dramatic contests and in the stadium for all the games. The privilege also seems to have entitled those upon whom it was bestowed to the same precedence in the Council, the assembly, or any other gathering;[160] and provision is here made for Kallias' seat to be reserved beside those of others who held the right of proedria. The official charged with this duty is the *ἀρχιτέκτων ἐπὶ τὰ ἱερά*, the superintendent in charge of sanctuaries, who appears here for the first time in this function with his full title. Moreover, we learn that he was an elected official (*χειρο⟨το⟩νούμεν[ο]ν*), a fact which heretofore had not been demonstrable before 185/4, when the architect who assigned theater seats is once again described as elected.[161] The *ἀρχιτέκτων ἐπὶ τὰ ἱερὰ* is thus closely similar to the *ἀρχιτέκτονες ἐπὶ τὰς ναῦς* who according to Aristotle (*Ath. Pol.* 46.1) were elected by the Demos, as was also the architect in charge of repairing the long walls in 307/6 (*IG* II², 463, line 6). All other references to the assignment of proedria speak of this official simply as *ὁ ἀρχιτέκτων* without further qualification.[162] This has led some to suppose that he was a different official from the architect in charge of sanctuaries, who is not otherwise attested before the late 3rd century B.C.[163] In the light of the present passage, it now seems certain that we have to do with one elected official, who performed various duties in different sanctuaries, and who properly took charge of seating in the theater because the theater was a part of the sanctuary of Dionysos and came therefore under his jurisdiction in all its aspects.

In the early 4th century, the management of the theater at Peiraieus had been let to a group of four paid contractors, called *οἱ πριάμενοι τὸν θέατρον*, who were specifically instructed to arrange proedria for anyone granted the privilege by the deme and duly registered by the demarch.[164] By the end of the century, however, the same duties at Peiraieus had passed into the hands of the architect, and in 307/6 we find him designated to reserve seats at the Rural Dionysia for some ambassadors from Kolophon (*IG* II², 456, line 32). In the Theater of Dionysos at Athens, the first reference to the architect performing this function is in 346. Demosthenes (XVIII.28) had then moved that Philip's ambassadors receive proedria at the Dionysia, and he spoke of the privilege in very nearly the same formula which appears in inscriptions from the late 4th century to the early 2nd.[165] A number of these documents instruct the architect now to reserve

[160] Schol. Aristophanes, *Knights* 575: *ἐξῆν δὲ τοῖς τῆς τιμῆς ταύτης τυχοῦσι καὶ ἐν βουλευτηρίῳ καὶ ἐν ἐκκλησίᾳ καὶ ἐν θεάτροις καὶ ἐν ἄλλῳ παντὶ συλλόγῳ τοὺς προλαμβάνοντας, οἵτινες ἦσαν, ἐξεγείραντας αὐτοὺς εἰς τὸν ἐκείνων τόπον καθίσαι.*

[161] *IG* II², 900, line 12. An alternate but less explicit formula also appears, *Hesperia* 23, 1954, p. 300, line 42 (= *SEG* XIV, 65): *καὶ [τ]ὸ[ν] ἀρχιτέκτον[α τ]ὸν ἀεὶ καθιστάμενον καταν[μ]ειν αὐτοῖς τὴ[ν θέα]ν* (271/0); cf. *IG* II², 792, line 8 (*ca.* 230 B.C.).

[162] In addition to the references, footnote 161 above, *IG* II², 456, line 32 (307/6); 466, line 52 (307/6); 500, line 33 (302/1); 512, line 7 (late 4th century); 567, line 22 (late 4th century). For discussion of the architect, U. Kahrstedt, *Magistratur*, pp. 310–312; Pickard-Cambridge, *op. cit.* (footnote 115 above), p. 266, where a distinction should now be made between the elected *ἀρχιτέκτων*, the custodian of sanctuaries, and the lessees who collected the price of admission; Rhodes, *Athenian Boule*, pp. 125–126.

[163] Rhodes, *loc. cit.*

[164] *IG* II², 1176, lines 3–9 + *Hesperia* 29, 1960, p. 1, no. 1.

[165] See above, footnotes 161, 162.

seats at a single performance for foreign ambassadors, now to assign permanent seats of honor at all festivals for worthy Athenian officials and individual benefactors. Another group of inscriptions of the late 3rd and 2nd centuries illustrates a different aspect of the architect's office, and in these he is regularly given his full title ἀρχιτέκτων ἐπὶ τὰ ἱερά as in the decree for Kallias.[166] Upon application from the priest of the Hero Doctor, the Boule appointed a committee to supervise the making of a new oinochoe, to be fashioned from old dedications melted down for the purpose. Here we find the architect, the priest, and the general ἐπὶ τὴν παρασκευὴν serving *ex officiis* with a group of three men from the Council and two from the Areopagus.[167] This committee administered the cataloguing of the old plate in the shrine and the preparation of the new dedication in the name of the Council. The architect as general custodian of sanctuaries is known to have supervised a similar operation on at least four occasions, and at another time he attended to the repair of buildings in a sanctuary, when once again he served *ex officio* as specialized administrator on a committee of the Council.[168]

Lines 101–104: The privileges awarded to Kallias by the Demos were granted with the proviso that he successfully sustain judicial scrutiny of his qualifications to receive them. As in normal procedure, the thesmothetai were to introduce the δοκιμασία after passage of a certain number of days prescribed by law. The process of δοκιμασία before a dikastic court of 501 jurors[169] came to be applied to public honors awarded by decree of the assembly only in the latter part of the 4th century. Even then, only a few scattered examples can be cited among the numerous honorific decrees of the late 4th century; and in all these, among the other honors, Athenian citizenship is conferred upon a foreigner.[170] In the 3rd century, the practice became normal in grants of citizenship and was frequently required also when the privilege of owning Athenian real estate was awarded to a foreign proxenos or other benefactor.[171] This is understandable and had as its purpose to verify whether a candidate for these privileges met

[166] *IG* II², 839, line 29 (221/0); 840, lines 13, 22–23 (late 3rd century); 841, lines 14–15 (early 2nd century); 842, line 2 (mid-2nd century); *Hesperia* 16, 1947, p. 165, no. 64, line 7. See Rhodes, *Athenian Boule*, pp. 95–96, 126.

[167] *IG* II², 839, lines 25–30.

[168] See footnote 166 above.

[169] The number of jurors is frequently specified in the formula from the latter part of the 3rd century onward, e.g. *IG* II², 850, line 18; 851, line 16.

[170] The earliest extant example of dokimasia in an honorific inscription is *IG* II², 398 (320/19). Other instances of its use in the late 4th century are: *IG* II², 496 + 507, 538; *Hesperia* 10, 1941, p. 55, no. 19 where the text is too fragmentary to be sure that citizenship is involved. The restoration of the formula in *IG* II², 336 (334/3) is very doubtful. All these decrees confer citizenship. But in the last quarter of the 4th century, there are many more citizenship decrees which do not require dokimasia, e.g.: *IG* II², 391–395, 448, 495, 508, 511, 553. See U. Kahrstedt, *Staatsgebiet*, pp. 81–82; A. R. W. Harrison, *The Law of Athens* II, Oxford 1971, pp. 200–207. The decrees granting citizenship have been most recently studied by M. J. Osborne, *BSA* 67, 1972, pp. 129–158; *idem*, *Ancient Society* 5, 1974, pp. 83–104; 7, 1976, pp. 107–125.

[171] For dokimasia in grants of enktesis, see J. Pečírka, *The Formula for the Grant of Enktesis in Attic Inscriptions*, Prague 1966, pp. 140ff., 143, note 7.

the prescribed legal qualifications, just as Athenian candidates for public offices and magistracies had always been required to prove before a court that they were qualified to hold them.[172] However, provision of dokimasia in the award of public honors to a native Athenian is quite exceptional and calls for comment.

Among the considerable body of extant Athenian honorary decrees, there are only two in addition to the present text which provide similar dokimasia for Athenians. To the decree for Phaidros of Sphettos is appended a special amendment moved by the orator of the decree itself: "All other provisions concerning the honors which Phaidros has requested shall be enacted according to the former decree which Lyandros moved, and in addition the thesmothetai shall introduce the scrutiny of his award in court according to the law" (*IG* II², 682, lines 93–98, Appendix **1**). From this it is evident, first, that Phaidros had personally requested the honors, and second, that debate in the assembly had brought out some provision of the law, applicable to Phaidros' request, which required a dokimasia in certain instances. Thus the orator rectified his oversight by an amendment from the floor. H. Francotte[173] has explained the anomaly by reference to the statement in the decree that Phaidros had already previously been crowned for all his services by the Boule and the Demos. He has suggested that the law required a dokimasia if further honors were sought for the same services. While this explanation may be correct, it does not agree fully with the evidence of the second decree providing dokimasia for honors to an Athenian. A decree of 196/5 honors the politician Kephisodoros after a career of thirty years in politics.[174] Upon enumerating his many services, the preamble concludes: *καὶ διὰ ταῦτα πάντα δίκαι[ον ἀποφαί]νων ἑαυτὸν τυχεῖν τιμῆς κατὰ τὸν νόμον αἰτεῖ[ται νῦν δοῦν]αι ἑαυτοῦ τὸν δῆμον εἰκόνα χαλκῆν*, etc. (lines 31–33). This passage has in common with the decree for Phaidros the fact that the award was requested by the candidate himself;[175] but there is here no suggestion that he had ever been honored previously for the same services. In fact, the wording seems almost to preclude that.

Comparison of these two cases with that of Kallias reveals no obvious common denominator, for Euchares' decree includes no specific statement that Kallias had either asked for the honors or had been previously crowned for his services. Striking, too, is the mention of the heliaia in the dokimasia formula (line 103), where all other examples use the word dikasterion. Since the heliaia appears nowhere else in this context, there

[172] Kahrstedt, *Magistratur*, pp. 59–63; Harrison, *op. cit.* (footnote 170 above), pp. 201–203; Rhodes, *Athenian Boule*, pp. 171–178.

[173] *La Musée Belge* 4, 1900, pp. 109–111; cf. also A. Wilhelm, *AthMitt* 39, 1914, pp. 259f.

[174] *Hesperia* 5, 1936, pp. 419ff., no. 15.

[175] As emphasized by Francotte, *loc. cit.* (footnote 173 above), there had always to be an *αἴτησις* before the Boule in order for honors to be voted, but the petition did not necessarily have to originate with the candidate himself. In *IG* II², 657, lines 54–55, there is no indication that Philippides requested the honors as did Phaidros. In [Plut.], *Mor.* 851 d–f (Appendix **10**), it is the *αἴτησις* of honors for Demochares which has survived, not properly speaking the decree: "Laches, son of Demochares of Leukonoe petitions the Boule and the Demos of the Athenians for the award of honors to Demochares, son of Laches of Leukonoe." Sometimes there was provision for the petition to be published as well as the decree, *IG* II², Add. 637, line 4.

is no way of knowing what significance we should attach to it. It is just possible that Euchares intended Kallias' dokimasia to be presented before the entire body of available jurors who formed the heliastic courts, but if so, a more precise formulation of this notion would have been welcome. We may more readily see this as one more example of Euchares' evident predilection for the avoidance of formulaic language. All three instances of dokimasia for Athenians were doubtless unusual cases, perhaps in different ways. They may have been controversial. Certainly, Lyandros in drafting his original decree for Phaidros had not thought it necessary and only added the dokimasia after the probouleuma had come before the assembly. Just conceivably, the inclusion of dokimasia might have had the effect of forestalling the possibility that the motion would be attacked in a *γράφη παρανόμων*, as Aischines had attacked Ktesiphon's motion of a golden crown for Demosthenes, in what is the most celebrated action for and against public honors that has come down to us. The judicial scrutiny would bring the case before the courts as a matter of routine, but in circumstances which might possibly be more favorable to the candidate. The orators of the decrees for Kallias and Kephisodoros were merely more cautious parliamentarians than Lyandros. If Ktesiphon had also been more cautious in drafting his famous decree, Demosthenes might have got his crown six years before, and Greek literature would be immeasurably the poorer.

CHAPTER III

THE REVOLUTION OF 286 B.C.

The foregoing discussion of the text of Euchares' decree makes it absolutely clear that Kallias' principal services to Athens were bound up with the liberation of the city from Macedonian domination. To his part in these events Euchares devoted no less than 32 lines in support of his motion that Kallias deserved the public honors therein decreed. It is to these same events that we should now return in order to place the revolt of Athens in the context of contemporary history and to reconsider the ancient evidence, now so greatly enriched by the new inscription.

The reign of Demetrios Poliorketes as king of Macedonia has suffered badly in the received tradition of ancient history because of the almost total loss of all contemporary historical writings. Only in the biographies which Plutarch culled from these sources, nearly four centuries after the events, has there survived any narrative account of those turbulent years in the early 3rd century B.C. Although Plutarch's narrative provides only a secondary source at best, a mixture well larded with moralizing comment and seasoned with personal anecdote, nevertheless the closing chapters of the *Life of Demetrios* (43–53) give a detailed and circumstantial treatment of the final years of Demetrios' life, from his massive preparations for the conquest of Asia to his death in captivity imposed upon him by Seleukos. For a few brief chapters the *Life of Pyrrhos* (7–12) offers a parallel account of the same events, at just that point where, for a short time, the lives of the two men became tangled with each other and their careers collided; and it is at this point of collision that there occurred the events at Athens to which the biographer gave only passing mention.

The magnitude of Demetrios' armaments, the size of his forces, and still more the enormous and innovative warships, with the construction of which the shipyards teemed at Peiraieus, Corinth, Chalkis, and Pella, all this struck alarm in the other kings and drove Seleukos, Ptolemy, and Lysimachos to form a mutual alliance against Demetrios.[176] By urgent appeals the allies persuaded Pyrrhos to join them; and before Demetrios had completed preparations for his expedition, they executed a concerted attack upon his dominions in Macedonia and Greece. Ptolemy sailed for Greece with a great fleet, his aim being to induce rebellion in the Greek cities, while at the same time Lysimachos invaded upper Macedonia from Thrace and ravaged the country.

[176] The sources for the events here summarized are Plut., *Demetr.* 44; *Pyrrh.* 11; Pompeius Trogus, XVI Prologue; Justin, XVI.2.1–2; Pausanias, I.10.2; Polyainos, IV.12.2. For discussion see Tarn, *Ant. Gon.*, pp. 91–92, 96–97; Beloch, *Gr. Gesch.* IV^2, i, pp. 229f.; C. F. Edson, *HSCP* 45, 1934, pp. 236–246; Manni, *Dem. Pol.*, pp. 56–57; Wehrli, *op. cit.* (footnote 23 above), pp. 181–185; and especially Lévêque, *Pyrrhos*, pp. 153–158. See Chronological Table, pp. 98–100.

Leaving his son Antigonos to hold down Greece, Demetrios hurried to meet Lysimachos' attack and massed his forces in the vicinity of Amphipolis. Thereupon Pyrrhos invaded Macedonia from the west, took up a position at Beroia, and sent out his generals to subdue the undefended country in Demetrios' rear.

Plutarch goes on to relate how Demetrios abandoned his position at Amphipolis because of desertions among his troops at the news of Pyrrhos' invasion, and how he encamped instead against Pyrrhos at Beroia, thinking that Macedonians would stand more loyally against the Epeirote than against a Macedonian who had fought with Alexander. But the high praises of Pyrrhos, sung by the people of Beroia, and the agitations of his agents turned the desertions from Demetrios' camp into open mutiny.[177] Demetrios fled from his own camp, leaving Pyrrhos and Lysimachos to divide Macedonia between them; he took refuge at Kassandreia and thence departed for Greece, where he toured the cities as a private citizen trying to hold the loyalty of his commanders and to gather about him his friends and supporters (*Demetr.* 45). After he had begun to reassemble his forces, the course of his progress took him to Thebes, where he restored the ancestral constitution, and thence to the Peloponnese, as we learn from the decree for Kallias (line 17), where he undoubtedly established his headquarters at Corinth. According to Plutarch's narrative, it was at this moment that Athens revolted (*Demetr.* 46.1; Appendix **3**).

The evidence of the Athenian decrees for Kallias, Strombichos, and Zenon, taken together with Pausanias' testimony on the career of Olympiodoros, has enabled us to form some impression of the course of events at Athens.[178] The partisans of Athenian nationalism seized the moment of Demetrios' fall from power in Macedonia to raise the banner of revolt against his forces which were holding down the city. Olympiodoros was elected general to lead the assault on Demetrios' garrison, whose strength was effectively diminished when the democrats induced one of its officers, Strombichos, to desert the Macedonian cause and to bring over a body of mercenaries to fight on the Athenian side. The remainder of the garrison, led by the commandant, Spintharos, attempted to put down the revolt by force of arms. They were beaten in pitched battle and driven back to their fort on the Mouseion hill, whereupon the triumphant revolutionaries took the fort by storm and proclaimed the liberation of the Demos. This was the signal for the intervention of a Ptolemaic force, commanded by Zenon and Kallias, who reached Attica from their base on Andros with a squadron of light cruisers and a thousand picked mercenaries. These took in hand at once the harvest of the crops, for the garrison troops in the Peiraieus had begun to ravage the countryside at the first onset of the revolution. With the help of the Egyptian troops, much of the grain crop was carried into the city, and the Ptolemaic commanders had joined forces with Olympiodoros and Strombichos when Athens closed her gates to meet the Besieger of Cities.

[177] Plutarch's two accounts of the mutiny at Beroia differ. *Pyrrh.* 11.4 has the mutiny result from carefully arranged agitation. *Demetr.* 44.5–6 mentions only the Macedonians' discontent with Demetrios' rule. See H. C. Girard, *Essai sur la composition des Vies de Plutarque*, Paris 1945, pp. 62–65.

[178] See above, pp. 14–17, 19–21, commentary on lines 12–18, 23–32.

The date of the revolution at Athens has been much debated,[179] for it has long been recognized—and would now, one ventures to suppose, be generally accepted—that the chronology of the events is closely bound up with the date of the archon Diokles. There are several indications that in his year of office the nationalist party had already seized power. Most striking is the action of the Athenian assembly in voting public honors for the Egyptian commander Zenon, on Hekatombaion 11 of Diokles' year. His presence in Attica with Egyptian warships and his efforts to provision the city for the sake of "the deliverance of the Demos" have been taken to indicate his involvement in the revolt from Demetrios.[180] It is now necessary to emphasize once again the strong probability of his association with Kallias of Sphettos, as has been argued above.[181] Both men were mercenary captains in Ptolemy's service, operating in Attica to secure the grain supply, and both were subsequently honored for the role they played in the "deliverance of the Demos." That they collaborated in the same campaign can scarcely be doubted. But their association, if it be accepted, constitutes virtually formal proof for the date of the Athenian uprising; for on the one hand, Kallias is said specifically (lines 12, 16–17) to have campaigned in Attica during the revolution of the Demos from Demetrios, while on the other hand, the decree for Zenon shows, by the present tense of the verbs (lines 14, 16), that the same campaign was still in progress on the 11th day of Diokles' archonship.

Confirmation that the nationalists governed Athens in Diokles' year comes from the familiar decree for Demochares of Leukonoe. We have already seen, in the closing lines of Laches' citation for his father, an explicit statement of Demochares' fervor and singleness of purpose in the cause of nationalist democracy.[182] He had not ventured to return from exile to his native city at the time of the general amnesty and recall of exiles, in the archonship of Philippos (292/1),[183] but Laches' decree states that he was recalled by the Demos in the archonship of Diokles and took part in the financial administration of the new government. The change is at once manifest in Athens' foreign relations with the enemies of Demetrios Poliorketes. Not only did she enjoy the good will of Ptolemy, as the decree for Kallias informs us (line 23), but her successful appeals for aid addressed to Pyrrhos and Lysimachos, the latter by Demochares personally, make clear the cordial state of her relations with the kings of the coalition against Demetrios.[184] Moreover, there is evidence that in Diokles' archonship Athens

[179] For bibliography, see footnote 23 above.

[180] Tarn, *Ant. Gon.*, pp. 419–420; Dinsmoor, *Archons*, pp. 57–59; Deprado, *RivFil*, n.s. 31, 1953, pp. 28–29.

[181] See above, pp. 20–21.

[182] [Plut.], *Mor.* 851 f; Appendix **10**.

[183] See footnote 154 above.

[184] Pyrrhos: Plut., *Demetr.* 46.1; *Pyrrh.* 12.4. Lysimachos: [Plut.], *Mor.* 851 e; Appendix **10**. There is little evidence for Athens' relations with Seleukos, but what there is suggests cordiality. He restored their autonomy to the Athenian cleruchs on Lemnos, and probably also Imbros, and Skyros, after the battle of Kouroupedion, on the appeal of the Athenian ambassador Komeas (*IG* II², 672, lines 40–41 and cf. Ferguson, *HA*, pp. 155f.). This suggests earlier good relations. Either at that time, or earlier as suggested below, p. 76, the Athenians awarded him an honorary statue (Pausanias, I.16.1). At some time, too, Seleukos sent

was also on good terms with the Delphic Amphictyony and with the Aitolians, who in 290 B.C. had prevented Demetrios from celebrating the Pythia at Delphi and whose country he subsequently ravaged.[185] At home the evidence for change is less marked but nonetheless apparent: one copy of a decree honoring Artemidoros of Perinthos requires, by the stoichedon order of the inscription, the restoration of the plural Board of Administration as the officials responsible for disbursing the cost of publication.[186] This shows that in Diokles' archonship, to which the document belongs, the characteristic institutions of democratic administration were already in force; and the same conclusion is to be drawn from the upsurge of activity in the assembly at just this time. No less than ten decrees of the assembly have survived from the years of Diokles and his immediate successor Diotimos, whereas only four decrees are known from the previous five archonships.[187] This phenomenon finds striking analogy during the years of the restored democracy after 307/6, and in the 280's it is doubtless an equally reliable indicator that the democratic government was once again in power.

On the basis of the evidence here reviewed, the archonship of Diokles, which saw the return of Demochares and honors bestowed on a Ptolemaic commander, can be accepted with virtual certainty as the first year of the nationalist democracy after the liberation of Athens. The date of Diokles' archonship is now fixed in 286/5

---

to Athens a collection of books purported to have been looted from the city by Xerxes' army (Aulus Gellius, *Attic Nights* VII.17); and his gift of a tiger, presumably captured in India, caused a great sensation (Philemon, 47; Alexis, 204; Antiphanes the Younger, 6 in Edmonds, *Frag. Att. Com.* II, pp. 472, 630; III A, p. 24). The most likely occasion is just after the revolt from Demetrios, but one trusts that these were only the luxurious trimmings accompanying more substantial gifts of which there is no longer any record.

[185] For the Pythia of 290 B.C. and the expedition against Aitolia, Plut., *Demetr.* 40.4; 41.1; *Pyrrh.* 7.3. By contrast with the period just after the revolt, the Aitolians had evidently raided Attica itself shortly before 290 B.C. and abducted Athenian citizens, see Athenaios, VI.253 e–f=*F. Gr. Hist.*, 76, Duris of Samos F 13. Good relations with Delphi and the Aitolians after the revolt are indicated by *IG* II², 652, lines 5–9 which relate an incident in the archonship of Diokles. The inscription was attributed to Diokles III (215/4) by Dinsmoor, *Archons*, pp. 214f. because mention of the Aitolian general Charixenos (line 9) seemed to preclude a date as early as the 280's. But the early date under Diokles II (then dated 288/7) was retained by G. Klaffenbach, see commentary on *IG* IX² 1, 5, who identified the general of *IG* II², 652 as Charixenos of Trichonion; cf. also *IG* IX² 1, 14, 54; Pritchett and Meritt, *Chronology*, pp. xvii, 105, note 49. The honorand of this decree, Aischron, son of Proxenos, like others of this period, probably "shared in the struggle for the deliverance of the Demos" (lines 3–4); and subsequently in Diokles' year, he and Charixenos brought about the release of some Athenians apparently captured by bandits in the country near Delphi. It was the Amphictyonic Council which reported his help to Athens. It would fit with what we know of Olympiodoros (Pausanias, I.26.3) if he had sought the help of the Aitolians after the revolt from Macedon, as he had earlier against Kassandros in 306 B.C. In fact, it has been suggested that the Aitolians may even have joined formally in the coalition against Demetrios, R. Flacelière, *Les Aitoliens à Delphes*, Paris 1937, pp. 78–79. The captured Athenians were possibly one of the many embassies of Diokles' year, concerning which see below.

[186] *IG* II², 663, line 37; Appendix **13**; on Artemidoros, see below, p. 76.

[187] Diokles: *IG* II², 650, 651, 652, 662–663+*Hesperia* 26, 1957, p. 29, no. 2; *Hesperia* 8, 1939, p. 42, no. 10. Diotimos: *IG* II², 653, 654, 655; *Hesperia* 9, 1940, p. 83, no. 14; the building contract *IG* II², 1682 implies a decree of the assembly. Extant decrees from the previous archonships are Charinos (291/0), *Hesperia* 26, 1957, p. 53, no. 10; Telokles (290/89), *IG* II², 2797 implying a decree of the assembly; Aristonymos (289/8), *IG* II², 669, 671.

by reference to the annual rotation in tribal order of the secretaries of the Council. Diokles, with his secretary from Halai Araphenides, belonging to Aigeis (IV), must occupy the fourth position in a secretary cycle; and the block of four interconnected archons immediately following him fill the fifth through the eighth years of the same cycle, which must also antedate the death of Epikouros in whose letters several of these archons are mentioned. Since Pytharatos and his predecessor fall in the seventh and sixth years of a cycle, and Pytharatos was archon in 271/0 when Epikouros died, Diokles and his successors must be placed in the next previous cycle, of which the fourth through the eighth years date from 286/5 to 282/1.[188]

The fact that the plural Board of Administration was already in office during Diokles' year (*IG* II^2, 663, line 37) suggests that the revolt began early enough in the spring to allow time for the election and allotment of democratic officials who entered office together with the archon Diokles in mid-summer.[189] This is now fully confirmed by the evidence of the decree for Kallias (line 25) that the revolt occurred before the grain harvest, which would normally take place in Thargelion (May–June).[190] Kallias learned of the revolt and of the expulsion of the Macedonian garrison, and on receipt of the news he set out for Attica, where he found the grain still uncut in the fields. The inference is plain that the revolt of Athens should be dated in the late spring of 286 B.C., but in the Attic year next before Diokles, when his immediate predecessor was still archon. Now, the change of government would have occurred at once on the heels of the revolution, and we should naturally expect it to have disrupted the institutions and officers of state. When Lachares seized power as tyrant in the spring of 295 B.C., a new Council was chosen for the remainder of the year and took office on or about Elaphebolion 14 with prytanies of no more than eight or nine days in length. A new board of generals was also elected for the "later" part of that year, as it was officially designated against the archon's name in the surviving decrees.[191] That the same radical changes and re-election of officials also attended the liberation from Macedon is the clear implication of Pausanias (I.26.1), who says that the democratic insurgents elected Olympiodoros general. He had not been general during the earlier part of the year but was chosen at the time of the revolt.

At this point we must turn to consider two episodes in the career of Kallias' brother, Phaidros of Sphettos. In the famous honorary decree for Phaidros (*IG* II^2, 682; Appendix **1**), the major offices to which he was elected are dated by archons; and it is a natural assumption, but one which has not always been made, that here as in

[188] See Dinsmoor, *Hesperia* 23, 1954, pp. 284–316; Deprado, *RivFil*, n.s. 31, 1953, pp. 21–31; Meritt, *Ath. Year*, p. 233; Samuel, *Greek and Roman Chronology*, Munich 1972, p. 213; Manni, *Historia* 24, 1975, p. 26; Meritt, *Historia* 26, 1977, p. 172.

[189] Deprado, *loc. cit.*, attempted to compress all of the events of the revolution into the first 11 days of Diokles' year, but this is now shown to be incorrect.

[190] On the date of the harvest, beginning in mid-May and ending in mid-June, see Jardé, *Céréales*, p. 45, note 2.

[191] For the archon and Council, *IG* II^2, 644, 645; for the election of new generals, *IG* II^2, 682, lines 22–23; Ferguson, *CP* 24, 1929, pp. 6–10; De Sanctis, *RivFil*, n.s. 14, 1936, pp. 253ff. On the date when the new Council took office, Dinsmoor, *Archons*, pp. 389–390; Meritt, *Ath. Year*, pp. 178–179.

other decrees describing men's careers the archons appear strictly in chronological order. Phaidros was elected hoplite general on two occasions, in the archonship of Kimon (line 31) and subsequently in the archonship of Xenophon (line 45); and these are bracketed in the decree by two archons both of whom were named Nikias (lines 21, 53). Although Kimon and Xenophon are attested nowhere else, the two Nikiai are readily recognizable: the first is the archon of 296/5, in whose year Lachares seized the tyranny, as is confirmed by the fact that Phaidros was elected general ἐπὶ τὴν παρασκευὴν *twice* in one year; the second is the archon of 282/1 because his name is not qualified by the demotic Otryneus which seems to have been used regularly to distinguish Nikias III of 266/5 from his homonymous predecessors.[192] The two archons Kimon and Xenophon, together with Phaidros' two terms as hoplite general, must then be dated in the years between 296/5 and 282/1, and that means before the archonship of Diokles (286/5), there being no years available between Diokles and Nikias II. But there is the further consideration that, between Nikias I (296/5) and Kimon, Phaidros was elected general ἐπὶ τὴν χώραν several times (πλεονάκις) and three times ἐπὶ τοὺς ξένους. Evidently, then, Kimon and Xenophon must have followed Nikias I by at least four years, but possibly by a minimum of seven, in each of which Phaidros was elected to the board of generals.[193]

The decree describes Phaidros' conduct of office in the archonship of Xenophon as follows: "Elected hoplite general first by the Demos in the year of Xenophon's archonship, he continued to act in every way in accordance with the laws and the decrees of the Boule and the Demos" (lines 44–47). Immediately following this passage five and one quarter lines of text have been excised from the stone. These presumably enumerated Phaidros' real services during the year, for the fact that Athens' highest military officer always acted according to the law is not cause for special praise, but rather to be expected. The extensive scholarly discussion of this passage has focused on the meaning of the word πρῶτος. Why should Phaidros' election as hoplite general in Xenophon's year be so specifically characterized as "first"? Among the various answers to this question devised by modern historians, that which seems to accord best with the evidence now available was proposed long ago by Tarn.[194] He argued that Phaidros

[192] Meritt, *Hesperia* 37, 1968, p. 285.

[193] It has sometimes been assumed, e.g. by Dinsmoor, *Archons*, pp. 70–71, that Phaidros' three commands ἐπὶ τοὺς ξένους were generalships distinct from those ἐπὶ τὴν χώραν thus indicating a total of at least seven commands. The wording of the text: ἐπὶ τὴν χώραν χειροτονηθεὶς πλεονάκις καὶ ἐπὶ τοὺς ξένους γενόμενος τρίς (lines 24–25), is better understood to mean that he was elected general ἐπὶ τὴν χώραν several times, and in three of those terms he was designated to command the mercenaries. See Ferguson, *CP* 2, 1907, pp. 308–309; Ferguson, *Tribal Cycles*, pp. 69–70; W. Schwahn, *RE*, Suppl. VI, 1935, col. 1091, *s.v.* Strategos. But it is impossible to believe with the latter that πλεονάκις and τρὶς are identical. It must surely mean more than three, otherwise there is no point in making the distinction. Thus a minimum of four years come between Nikias I and Kimon.

[194] *Ant. Gon.*, p. 422. Scholars have generally adopted one of three interpretations of the passage to which widely differing dates have been applied: 1) the explanation of Tarn here adopted in the text, accepted by Johnson, *CP* 9, 1914, pp. 249–250; Dinsmoor, *Archons*, p. 77, with a date in 274/3; Dinsmoor, *List*, pp. 51–52, with a date before Diokles (then 288/7); and by implication, *idem*, *Hesperia* 23, 1954, p. 314 (287/6); Meritt, *Ath. Year*, p. 232. 2) πρῶτος means the first general elected *after* some change of govern-

was so designated because he was the first of two hoplite generals elected in the same year. During his tenure of office, there was a change of government which brought about the selection of new generals and civic officials. The analogy to 296/5 is exact, except that in that year Phaidros was re-elected after the *coup d'état* of Lachares (lines 22–23), whereas in the archonship of Xenophon he was deposed and another was chosen in his place. On the internal evidence of Phaidros' own career, we have seen that Xenophon, following Kimon, should be dated a number of years after Nikias I (296/5) and thus close to Diokles (286/5); and we need not hesitate to identify the change of government in Xenophon's year with the revolt of Athens in the year immediately preceding Diokles. This agrees well also with the statement of Pausanias (I.26.1) that Olympiodoros was elected general at the time of the revolution, and thus in an irregular election. It was no doubt he who replaced Phaidros as hoplite general in the latter part of Xenophon's archonship (287/6).

Phaidros, for all his moderate politics, shows his pro-Macedonian sympathies, if only in the fact that he was a regular member of the government during the years of Macedonian domination from 295/4 to 287/6. If, indeed, he was hoplite general at Athens when the revolution began and remained loyal to Demetrios, his stance will be seen to form a marked contrast with that of his brother Kallias, who fought on the side of the Demos. In order to bring their respective positions into sharper definition, let us consider further the circumstances in which Kallias found himself when the Demos rose in revolt. As the new inscription informs us (lines 19–20), he was like his brother a military officer, the commandant of a Ptolemaic base on the island of Andros. On hearing news of the revolt, Kallias departed at once for Athens, no doubt in accordance with a prearranged plan, taking with him a thousand picked troops and leaving the remainder of his force behind to hold the base in his rear.[195] This means that at a date earlier than the spring of 286 B.C. and before the revolt of Athens, the

---

ment or critical event, Dittenberger, *SIG*^{3}, 409, note 17; Beloch, *Gr. Gesch.* IV^2, ii, p. 85, with date in 252/1 or 256/5; Ferguson, *Tribal Cycles*, pp. 71–72, first year (274/3) after Antigonos' recapture of Peiraieus; *idem*, *AJP* 55, 1934, pp. 332–333, first year (276/5) after Antigonos' accession. 3) πρῶτος means first in rank on the board, Schwahn, *RE*, Suppl. VI, 1935, cols. 1086–1087; Pritchett and Meritt, *Chronology*, pp. 93–94. Fatal to the second interpretation is the fact that an explanation of what event was followed by Phaidros' election "first" must be supposed to have stood where the text is now excised. But Pritchett and Meritt, *loc. cit.*, acutely observed that an uninscribed letter space remains on the stone both before and after the preserved sentence, lines 44–47, which was therefore unconnected syntactically with what went before or after. As it stands the sentence cannot mean "first" after anything. The third interpretation is subject to the objection that, among frequent references in Attic inscriptions to the hoplite general, he is nowhere else qualified as "first" in rank. While it seems probable that he was, in fact, first in rank, there was no need to say so because everybody knew it to be the case. Especially, there was no need to distinguish Phaidros' tenure of the office under Xenophon as "first" when he had previously held the same office with the same priority of rank under Kimon.

[195] If the size of Kallias' force seems ineffectually small, it should be noted that the size of Demetrios' garrison at Peiraieus was two thousand mercenaries after his departure for Asia, Polyainos, V.17.1. In addition to the thousand men under Kallias, Zenon will certainly have had some troops with him. How large a force of mercenaries deserted with Strombichos and how many Athenians Olympiodoros commanded are not recorded.

navy of Ptolemy I had moved in force into the Aegean and had already established a base in the Cyclades, which was strategically located both for an invasion of Attica and for control of the islands.

The evidence of the decree should now be brought into relation with Plutarch's account of the coalition against Demetrios: "For at the same moment Ptolemy, having sailed to Greece with a great fleet, tried to bring it to revolt, while Lysimachos invaded Macedonia from Thrace, and Pyrrhos from the neighboring territory, and both began to lay waste the countryside."[196] As a part of the concerted attack on Demetrios, and at the beginning of the same campaign which ended in his fall and flight, Ptolemy sailed to Greece with a large fleet and tried to incite revolutions in the cities. There need be no doubt that Athens was among his targets, if not his principal objective; but Plutarch evidently understood Ptolemy's descent on Greece to have taken place before the revolt of Athens, which he mentions two chapters later (*Demetr.* 46.1), after describing Demetrios' fall and the partial recovery of his forces in Greece. Having once mentioned Ptolemy's part in the campaign, the biographer makes no further reference to the fleet or its activities; and one is left with the impression that the Egyptian efforts were inconclusive at best. But Plutarch's narrative helps to elucidate the establishment of the Egyptian base on Andros before the revolt of Athens; for Kallias and his mercenaries undoubtedly sailed to Andros with the great fleet, and Zenon's light cruisers will have formed a part of it. The plan was to seize strategic bases safely removed from the Macedonian forts, but near enough to the mainland so that small units could operate, together with anti-Macedonian parties in the various cities, to raise the banner of general rebellion.

This brings us to a second episode in the career of Phaidros, and one which may well reflect from a different point of view some of the events here under consideration. His decree devoted 14 lines to his services as hoplite general in the archonship of Kimon, and thus before the archonship of Xenophon: "Elected by the Demos hoplite general in the year of Kimon's archonship, he continued to strive for the common safety; and when difficult circumstances encompassed the city, he preserved peace in the country, always giving the best possible account of himself, and he was responsible for bringing in the grain and the other crops from the countryside; he advised the Demos to complete...." This is followed by the excision of a full line after which the text resumes: "and he passed on the city to his successors, free and independent, governed by democratic institutions, and with the laws in force" (lines 30–40). Important sections of the next four lines have been excised so as to make the text unintelligible. It is fair to say that these lines have been subjected to as many interpretations as there have been dates proposed for Kimon's archonship.[197] Nevertheless, in view

[196] *Demetr.* 44.1; Appendix **2**. The wording of *Pyrrh.* 10.1 is almost precisely the same.

[197] Kimon is dated 292/1 and the "difficult times" referred to the return of the Athenian exiles and the Boiotian revolt: W. Kolbe, *Die attischen Archonten von 293/2–31/0, Abhandl. Göttingen* N.F. X, iv, Berlin 1908, p. 23; Tarn, *Ant. Gon.*, p. 46, note 20; Dittenberger, *SIG*³, 409, note 15; Johnson, *CP* 9, 1914, p. 253. With a date in 291/0, the "difficult times" are interpreted as the threat of raids by the Aitolians: Ferguson, *HA*, p. 142; Dinsmoor, *List*, p. 51. With a date in 289/8 (before Diokles), Phaidros' activities

of the sequence of events now suggested by the decree for Kallias, there seems to be justification for asking once again what exactly happened at Athens in the archonship of Kimon.

A number of inferences can be drawn from the wording of the text itself. Since Phaidros "preserved the peace for the country", one naturally infers that in this year Athens narrowly escaped war. The danger evidently seemed near at hand, but as a result of Phaidros' efforts there was no fighting in the Attic countryside. Since he was "responsible for bringing in the grain and the other crops" at the critical moment, the conclusion is obvious that the danger lay in an invasion from abroad by forces which would have sought to lay waste the crops, had they not been gathered into the city. Moreover, the threat of invasion came inevitably from forces hostile to the pro-Macedonian government at Athens, and in the period before the liberation, hostile alike to Demetrios and Macedon. On the other hand, the "difficult circumstances surrounding the city" give the impression of internal trouble in addition to the external threat. Indeed, the wording of the passage seems to have been chosen with great circumspection; and it suggests that Phaidros was confronted by the danger of an uprising from within the city. But the fact that he completed his term of office that year with "the laws in force" shows that the revolution did not materialize, and Phaidros' actions successfully averted a change of government.

All this fits perfectly with the course of events which we have deduced from the decree for Kallias and from Plutarch's account of the coalition against Demetrios, if allowance be made for the fact that Phaidros saw the events from the point of view of the Athenian government which was later overturned by the revolt of 286. The threatened invasion of Attica in Kimon's year is to be explained by the arrival of Ptolemy's great fleet and the establishment of the Egyptian mercenary garrison on Andros by Kallias and Zenon. They no doubt acted in concert with the nationalist party at Athens whose members created the "difficult circumstances" at home. But the fruit was judged as yet unripe for the plucking. The Athenian nationalists abided the outcome of the campaign in the north; the government of Phaidros thus successfully restrained the uprising in the city; and the Ptolemaic forces withheld for a time their invasion of Attica. The date should be late in the spring of 287; for Phaidros brought in the grain from the harvest in May and June. The events of Kimon's year thus place his archonship just one year before Xenophon's which saw the successful revolt from Macedon in the spring of 286; and Phaidros' two terms as hoplite general come

---

have been understood as the revolt from Demetrios itself: Ferguson, *Tribal Cycles*, p. 70; Tarn, *JHS* 54, 1934, p. 38. With a date in 282/1, Phaidros averted a threat from Antigonos: Beloch, *Gr. Gesch.* IV², ii, pp. 70f.; Dinsmoor, *Archons*, p. 71. With the same date, Phaidros' difficulties have been associated with the recovery of the Peiraieus in 281/0: Meritt, *Hesperia* 7, 1938, pp. 105–107; Pritchett and Meritt, *Chronology*, p. 93. Kimon is dated, as here, in 288/7 without comment by Dinsmoor, *Hesperia* 23, 1954, p. 314; Meritt, *Ath. Year*, p. 232. Manni, *Historia* 24, 1975, pp. 26–27 places Kimon in 291/0 and Xenophon in 259/8 without comment. The omission of Kimon altogether from the archon list published by Samuel, *op. cit.* (footnote 188 above), p. 213, is presumably an oversight. Cf. Meritt, *Historia* 26, 1977, p. 172.

accordingly to be dated in 288/7 and 287/6. He was in command at the time of the concerted attack on Demetrios and was deposed in his second term at the time of the revolt of Athens. What he did in order to keep Athens loyal to Demetrios was later excised from the stone which bears his honorary decree.

At this point an objection may possibly arise and should be met. Since the two brothers, Phaidros and Kallias, are both said to have brought the crops into the city in a state of emergency, and the latter at the time of the revolt from Demetrios, is it not better to suppose that they cooperated in organizing the same harvest? The temptation may then present itself to revive the suggestion once put forward by Ferguson[198] that the crisis of Kimon's year was actually the revolt from Demetrios. If Phaidros had thus been general in the year of the liberation of Athens, it might explain how he could claim to have "passed on the city to his successors, free and independent, governed by democratic institutions, and with the laws in force."[199]

There are, however, serious objections to dating the activities of Phaidros and Kallias in the same year and the revolt of Athens in the archonship of Kimon. The similarity of the situations described by the two decrees is, in fact, quite illusory. Phaidros "preserved the peace for the country" which implies, as we have seen, that there was no fighting, whereas Kallias was obviously involved in combat. Our text states specifically that the ravages of the Peiraieus garrison had the countryside in a state of war (*τῆς χώρας ἐμ πολέμωι οὔσης*, lines 15–16), and as a result Kallias defended

[198] *Tribal Cycles*, p. 70.

[199] Lines 38–40. This statement has sometimes been taken to mean that he must have served the nationalist cause. So Johnson, *CP* 9, 1914, p. 253; Ferguson, *loc. cit.* (footnote 198 above). The warning of Tarn, *Ant. Gon.*, p. 45, note 16 that any decree should be read with an ear to the politics of its proposers and with regard to the circumstances under which it was passed should be emphasized once again. In the spring of 294 B.C., just after the fall of Lachares, when Demetrios would shortly station his garrisons on the Mouseion and the Mounychia (Plut., *Demetr.* 34.4–5) and would then establish the two-year appointive archonship of Olympiodoros (294/3–293/2, Dinsmoor, *Archons*, pp. 16–28), one of his lieutenants, Herodoros, was praised for being helpful to the Demos, so that it could end the war [*καὶ κομισάμε*]*νος τὸ ἄστυ* (*sc. ὁ δῆμος*) *δημοκρατ*[*ίαν διατελῆι ἔχ*]*ων* (*IG* II^2, 646, lines 22–23). Nobody will suppose that this "democracy" should be equated with that of the nationalist regime (indeed we have seen that Laches and Euchares described it as "oligarchy"), but it was more democratic than the regime of Lachares.

We have found reason to date the publication of the decree for Phaidros in 255/4 (above, p. 11), the year following that of Euboulos (256/5), who is the last named archon in the decree (line 58), and preceding the Great Panathenaia of 254 B.C., at which the honors were to be announced. The statement (lines 38–40) about Phaidros' achievement in office perfectly reflects the climate of feeling in Athens in this year, in so far as it can be reconstructed. In the previous year Antigonos Gonatas had acquiesced in the so-called "liberation of Athens", Ol. 131,1 = 256/5, Eusebios, *Chron. Can.* II, p. 120 (ed. Schoene), p. 201 (ed. Karst). From the end of the Chremonidean War down to that year, the king had kept a garrison on the Mouseion, had governed the city through a single *ἐπιστάτης*, and had replaced the allotment of archons with royal appointment (*F. Gr. Hist.*, 244, Apollodoros F 44). On the urging of many Athenians (Diog. Laert., IV.39), this was changed in 256 B.C. to a mode of government modestly more democratic, but nonetheless *de facto* under Antigonos' domination, cf. Ferguson, *HA*, p. 191; Tarn, *Ant. Gon.*, pp. 327f. This is the spirit of the time which produced the decree for Phaidros, summing up more than forty years of loyal service both to his native Athens and to her Macedonian overlords, as was no doubt in his eyes only practical. In the year after the "liberation" of 256/5, Phaidros' claim that his services helped to make the city free, democratic, and autonomous becomes fully understandable.

the harvest with his mercenary troops. At a later point in the campaign, he was himself wounded in an attack on Demetrios' beleaguering army (line 30). All this is incompatible with Phaidros' claim to have preserved the peace; nor can that statement be easily reconciled with what we know of the revolt, unless it be thought that he kept the peace by means of leading the Demos to expel Demetrios' garrison by force of arms. But this was the special feat of Olympiodoros, and we know that he, not Phaidros, was hoplite general at the time of the revolt.

In the present state of the evidence, an attempt to date the revolt in the archonship of Kimon is equally beset by difficulties; for Xenophon, who necessarily follows Kimon, can no longer be relegated to any conveniently unoccupied later year, but as we have seen, he must be placed in the interval between Nikias I (296/5) and Nikias II (282/1), and thus inevitably between Kimon and Diokles.[200] We shall, therefore, be constrained to suppose that more than a year at the least intervened between the peace with Demetrios at the intercession of Ptolemy's officers (lines 35–36 of the decree for Kallias) and the arrival in Attica of Ptolemaic warships to provision the city, whereupon their commander Zenon, who was present in Athens on Hekatombaion 11 of Diokles' archonship (*IG* II^2, 650), received the city's honors for his struggle in behalf of the "deliverance of the Demos."[201] Likewise inexplicable is the same delay of more than a year in the recall of Demochares, whose return from exile is also dated in Diokles' archonship. Far easier and more compelling is the relation of these two events to the activities of Kallias, and with them a date in 286 B.C., as proposed above. This enables the Ptolemaic military operations in Attica to have taken place wholly before the conclusion of peace with Demetrios; and at the same time Kallias' journey with the Athenian ambassadors to Ptolemy I, immediately after the peace (lines 40–43), can be identified with the embassy proposed by Demochares shortly after his return.

Moreover, the interpretation here placed upon the events of Kimon's year has the great advantage of providing for the first time a satisfactory explanation of the timing of the Athenian revolt as reported by Plutarch (*Demetr.* 46.1–2). Students of these events have been troubled by the fact that, according to Plutarch, Athens did not revolt from Demetrios until he had already had a chance to regroup his forces in Greece after his flight from Macedonia. This apparent difficulty has caused the revolt to be placed in the same campaigning season as the allied attack, and sometimes even

[200] Those who place Xenophon much later, e.g. Beloch, *Gr. Gesch.* IV^2, ii, p. 85 (252/1); Manni, *Historia* 25, 1975, p. 27 (259/8) are forced to argue that only Phaidros' military commands are arranged in chronological order, while his agonothesias under Nikias and Euboulos form a second chronological listing unrelated to the first. But this is surely contrary to the sense of the text.

[201] It should be noted that the decrees of the nationalist period regularly use the phrase ἡ τοῦ δήμου σωτηρία or ἡ τῆς πόλεως σωτηρία to describe services rendered during the revolt of Athens, as in line 32 of the decree for Kallias. Cf. *IG* II^2, 650, line 19; 652, line 4; 654, lines 20–21; 657, lines 32–33; 666, lines 13–14. Phaidros, however, struggled for the common safety: ἀγωνιζόμενος ὑπὲρ τῆς κοινῆς σωτηρίας (*IG* II^2, 682, line 32). There is no mention here of the city or the Demos. To the question who else had a "common interest" in the safety of Athens, the answer is, of course, Demetrios. Phaidros was working as much in the interests of Macedon, which here, in his terms, coincided with those of Athens.

prior to Demetrios' fall from the throne,[202] because Plutarch (*Demetr.* 44.1) speaks of Ptolemy's great fleet as setting out at the same time as Lysimachos and Pyrrhos. But this is to assume that Ptolemy's efforts to raise revolutions in Greece were *immediately* successful, while Plutarch nowhere says that they were. We can now suggest that the Athenian nationalists did, indeed, attempt to revolt at the instigation of Ptolemy's fleet during the archonship of Kimon (spring 287 B.C.); but thanks to the efforts of Phaidros, the attempt did not at first succeed, hence the curious timing indicated by Plutarch's account, and the presence of the Egyptian base on Andros before the revolution.

That the coalition of the kings against Demetrios, and consequently the end of his reign as king of Macedonia, is properly dated in 288/7 finds strong confirmation in independent contemporary evidence. The large fleet which Plutarch attributed to Ptolemy, coupled with his evident freedom to move with impunity and to seize bases as far abroad as the Cyclades, implies that the Egyptians had already gained possession of the great Phoenician navies which, together with their home ports of Tyre and Sidon, had been held since Ipsos by Demetrios.[203] In the case of Tyre, the date at which the city passed into Ptolemy's hands can be established exactly from the history of its coinage, as has been demonstrated by E. T. Newell.[204] The crucial evidence comes from a series of didrachms struck on the Attic standard, regularly employed by Demetrios' mints, but bearing the traditional local types of Tyre. In the field of the reverse, the latest group of these coins shows numerals ranging from 23 to 37. These are taken to indicate annual dates which Newell has shown to be counted from the death of Alexander, that is the so-called Era of Philip Arridaios. The count began in 324/3, the year in which Alexander actually died (June 323), and was reckoned on the basis of the Egyptian year which ran from November 324 to November 323.[205] The dated didrachms of Tyre thus commence in 302/1 (year 23), the year of Ipsos, of Antigonos' death, and of Demetrios' accession to sole rule. Year 37 brings the series to an end in 288/7; and the conclusion is clear that the last dated coin of the group was struck, and Tyre was acquired by Ptolemy, some time between November 288 and November 287.[206] In this connection, it should be noted that the same chronology was also adopted in the Chronicle of Porphyry of Tyre, as preserved in the Armenian version of Eusebios; for the reign of Demetrios Poliorketes as king of Macedonia is there recorded as six

[202] Ferguson, *HA*, pp. 144ff.; Tarn, *Ant. Gon.*, pp. 92, 419; Beloch, *Gr. Gesch.* IV^2, ii, pp. 105ff. But cf. Deprado, *RivFil*, n.s. 31, 1953, p. 35, who reaches the same conclusion adopted here.

[203] Plut., *Demetr.* 32.4.

[204] *Tyrus Rediviva*, New York 1923, pp. 15–23, pl. III: 14–16.

[205] Samuel, *op. cit.* (footnote 188 above), p. 52.

[206] There is no longer any reason to think that Ptolemy's acquisition of Tyre and Sidon involved the defection from Demetrios of Philokles, King of the Sidonians, and the Phoenician fleets. So Tarn, *Ant. Gon.*, pp. 104–105; Beloch, *Gr. Gesch.* IV^2, ii, pp. 327–328. Philokles, who later became Ptolemy's viceroy of the Aegean, is better regarded as a Ptolemaic officer throughout his career. See now, Merker, *Historia* 19, 1970, p. 145; Seibert, *Historia* 19, 1970, pp. 342–343. The date of the Ptolemaic capture of Tyre proposed by Newell still seems more attractive than the date in 296/5 proposed by Merker, *Ancient Society* 5, 1974, pp. 119–126.

years in length, ending in the first year of the 123rd Olympiad. Porphyry thus placed Demetrios' fall in the Olympic year between the summer of 288 and the summer of 287.[207]

Ptolemy's acquisition of the Phoenician cities and their renowned navies very likely made possible his participation in the league of kings against Demetrios. The balance of power in the Aegean was now, at any rate, decisively altered; for the conditions which permitted the establishment of a garrisoned fort in the Cyclades are dramatically different from those which had caused a Ptolemaic fleet of 150 ships to flee from Attic waters in 295/4 upon the appearance of Demetrios' armada for the blockade of Athens (Plut., *Demetr.* 33.4). Now, eight years later, it was feasible to conceive of a concerted three-pronged attack upon all parts of Demetrios' dominions. The attack was timed for the campaigning season of 287 B.C.; and Ptolemy's fleet, newly strengthened in Phoenicia, reached Athens before the harvest in the late spring, when Kimon was still archon at Athens and Phaidros was hoplite general. At the same time, in Macedonia Demetrios was trying to fend off the invasions of Lysimachos and Pyrrhos, but before mid-summer of 287 his army had mutinied, and he was forced to abandon his camp at Beroia and his kingdom as well. That his fall came in the summer, when the trees were in full leaf, is confirmed by a detail of Plutarch's narrative (*Pyrrh.* 11.5); Demetrios' deserting soldiers are said to have crowned themselves with garlands of oak leaves to emulate Pyrrhos' men. Plutarch's chronology of Demetrios' subsequent movements now agrees well with the course of events as here reconstructed. From mid-summer of 287 until the spring of 286, the fugitive king was touring the cities of Greece as a private citizen and gathering new forces to recoup his fortunes, just as Plutarch reports; and we next hear of him in the Peloponnese (line 17) whence he hurried with his army to put down the revolt at Athens.

[207] *F. Gr. Hist.*, 260, F 3, 6. Porphyry placed the first of Demetrios' six years as king of Macedon in Ol. 121, 4=293/2. According to his system of post-dating, whereby the first *full* calendar year of a king's reign is reckoned as Year 1 and the year of his death is counted wholly in his reign (Jacoby, *F. Gr. Hist.*, II D, Kommentar, p. 856), this means that Demetrios became king sometime in the previous year, 294/3. Thus Plutarch, *Demetr.* 44.7, rounded off his reign in the other direction and speaks of seven years. Prior to Year 1 of Demetrios, Porphyry reckoned four years for the sons of Kassandros, Ol. 120, 4=297/6 to Ol. 121, 3=294/3 and gave Ol. 120, 3=298/7 as Kassandros' last year (*F. Gr. Hist.*, 260, F 3, 4). The correctness of this chronology is confirmed by *P. Oxy.* XVII, 2082=*F. Gr. Hist.*, 257 a, F 3 which dates the death of Kassandros in the same year, in the month Artemisios, intercalated, that is April-May, 297 B.C. (Jacoby, *op. cit.*, p. 850).

CHAPTER IV

THE PEACE WITH DEMETRIOS

Before the discovery of the inscription honoring Kallias of Sphettos, the events at Athens following Demetrios' arrival were known only from two brief notices of Plutarch (*Demetr.* 46.1–2; *Pyrrh.* 12.4–5). When the Athenians saw that Demetrios had managed to assemble a much larger army than they expected, they dispatched an urgent appeal for help to Pyrrhos in Macedonia. But Demetrios laid close siege about the city, whereupon the philosopher Krates of the Academy was sent to negotiate the lifting of the siege; and Demetrios, apparently persuaded by the philosopher's eloquence, decided to raise his blockade in order to depart at once for Asia. To this unsatisfactory account, the even briefer mention of the incident in the *Life of Pyrrhos* adds little; for it merely reports Pyrrhos' arrival at Athens, apparently after the siege was lifted, since he entered the city unimpeded. There is here one point of importance, however, the reference to a formal treaty of peace between Pyrrhos and Demetrios, concluded just prior to the latter's departure for Asia.

Euchares treated this same episode in his decree for Kallias (lines 27–40), and his detailed account of the siege and its aftermath, at least as far as it involved Kallias, now for the first time adds flesh and blood to the bare skeleton of events which Plutarch has preserved. Our discussion of the text of the inscription (above, pp. 21–22) sought to bring out the striking differences in the two extant sources which now bear on the siege of Athens and the negotiations for Demetrios' withdrawal. It is difficult to know how to reconcile the evidence of Plutarch with the precise and, at first sight, apparently contradictory statements of the decree. That both present us with the merest scraps of information is beyond doubt, but the task now at hand is to weave these scraps into the fabric of contemporary history, when the pattern of events has now been almost wholly lost.

One approach to the problem may lie in attempting to determine the order in which the various known incidents occurred. The association of the mercenary commanders Kallias and Zenon in the same operations has enabled us to show that the Ptolemaic intervention in Attica came at the latest in June of 286 B.C., and by the middle of July (Hekatombaion 11), when Zenon was thanked for his help, the grain crop was still being brought into the city. Demetrios, then, did not enter Attica with his army until sometime later in the summer; and this is borne out also by the chronological distinction which Euchares was careful to make between the gathering of the harvest and the siege of the city. Now, if Plutarch can be taken at his word, the Athenians did not summon help from Pyrrhos until they actually saw that Demetrios' army was larger than expected. Thus the embassy to Pyrrhos cannot have been dispatched before Demetrios' arrival;[208] but Pyrrhos upon reaching Athens entered freely into the city, offered sacrifice on the Acropolis, and withdrew the same day (*Pyrrh.* 12.4). These actions make it plain that by the time the new Macedonian king had marched south with his forces, Athens was no longer in need of military aid; Demetrios had already been induced to lift his blockade about the city. The same inference is to be drawn from the decree for Kallias; for when Sostratos arrived he was allowed to sail into the Peiraieus (line 35), which of course was still held by Demetrios' garrison. This would surely not have been possible if the city had still been closely invested by Demetrios' siege (*πολιορκίαν περὶ τὸ ἄστυ συνεστήσατο καρτεράν*, *Demetr.* 46.2).

The conclusion seems inescapable that the raising of the siege of Athens, which enabled Pyrrhos and Sostratos to enter respectively into the city and the Peiraieus, was only the first incident in a more complicated chain of events leading ultimately to a formal treaty of peace. The siege itself probably lasted no more than a few weeks, not long enough at any rate to become too severe. Nearly a decade before, the Athenians had succumbed with grievous suffering to those same arts from which the Besieger of Cities drew his name; but now in 286, determined to bring about the "deliverance of the Demos", they tried at first to break the blockade by force of arms. The Ptolemaic mercenaries attacked the besieging forces, and Kallias was himself wounded in battle (line 30). It is no doubt at this point that we should place the embassy of Krates to Demetrios. What he effected was the raising of the blockade itself, so that Athens could open her gates. The incident probably coincided with Pyrrhos' approach and the appearance of the Egyptian navy off Peiraieus, for we shall not suppose that Sostratos traveled unaccompanied. Indeed, the imminent arrival of allied forces coming to the rescue of Athens was probably the decisive factor which made it easy for the philosopher to show the king where his own advantage lay.

Both Plutarch and the inscription present only a fragmentary picture of the subsequent diplomatic negotiations. A key to reconstructing the situation is provided by mention of the peace in both sources. Plutarch states that Pyrrhos made peace with Demetrios after leaving the city of Athens; and this is surely to be identified with the peace between Athens and Demetrios which Sostratos came to negotiate.[209] We have seen that the revolution at Athens transpired in direct consequence of the allied assault upon Demetrios in 287 B.C. It was undoubtedly a part of the strategic plan. Now, in view of the fact that the league of kings had four constituents, Seleukos, Ptolemy, Lysimachos, and Pyrrhos, all of whom had been party to the concerted efforts against Demetrios, and two of whom are known to have participated in the diplomatic negotiations at Athens, it seems likely that all parties now joined in the peace.

[208] Deprado, *RivFil*, n.s. 31, 1953, p. 36 dates Demetrios' arrival and siege of Athens in the spring of 285 B.C., on the basis of the inscriptions mentioning the importation of grain (*IG* II², 651, 653, 654). But this is too late, see below. It is possible that Athens sought the help of the Aitolians at the same time as that of Pyrrhos, as suggested above, footnote 185.

[209] Plut., *Pyrrh.* 12.5; line 36 of the decree for Kallias, see above, p. 22. Cf. Deprado, *loc. cit.*

There is at any rate evidence to suggest that all the kings were represented in the peace conference at Athens during the autumn and winter of 286. Plutarch reports the presence of Pyrrhos in person at the head of his army. Ptolemy's mercenaries led by Kallias were on guard in the city (lines 39–40), his cruisers led by Zenon were anchored in Attic waters (*IG* II², 650), and his minister Sostratos was admitted to the Peiraieus as the king's personal envoy in the negotiations (lines 33–35). No evidence has survived concerning the role of Seleukos. But a very fragmentary decree passed on Elaphebolion 30 of Diokles' archonship (April 285) confers a golden crown and Athenian citizenship upon an emissary of Lysimachos who was also in Athens in this same fateful year. This decree honors a certain Artemidoros, son of Apollodoros, of Perinthos and has survived in fragments of two copies,[210] to one of which reference has already been made. The text has required extensive restorations, partly confirmed by comparison with the second copy; but even though we may not be able to recover the exact wording, several facts emerge clearly. Artemidoros was an aide and confidant of Lysimachos, whose name is preserved in three places on the extant fragments (*IG* II², Add. 662, line 9; 663, lines 3, 18); and in this respect he invites comparison with Sostratos. Furthermore, he had been sent by Lysimachos, apparently more than once, in connection with certain embassies and diplomatic negotiations of interest both to the king and to the Athenians, who publicly commended his ambassador's conduct of the affair (Add. 662, lines 7–8). Finally, after returning to Lysimachos (line 10), he had proved helpful to more than one Athenian embassy dispatched to the king (lines 12–13). All of these services, of course, had necessarily to have been completed before Elaphebolion 30, 285 B.C.

In view of the coincidence in time, the nature of Artemidoros' activities, and the events which transpired in Athens between the summer of 286 and the spring of 285, the temptation is irresistible to relate Artemidoros' mission to the peace with Demetrios. This evidence now greatly strengthens the suggestion that all sides participated in the negotiations: Artemidoros represented Lysimachos, Sostratos represented Ptolemy, Seleukos' envoy remains unknown, and both Pyrrhos and Demetrios were present in person. Indeed, it may well have been as a result of this very occasion that Athens erected in the Agora honorary statues of all four kings of the coalition. In Pausanias' time, the statues of Ptolemy Soter, Lysimachos, and Pyrrhos stood among other monuments before the Odeion; the statue of Seleukos I he saw near the Stoa Poikile.[211] Perhaps some statement in the inscription pertaining to the statue of Lysimachos gave

[210] *IG* II², Add. 662+*Hesperia* 26, 1957, p. 29, no. 2; 663; Appendix **12**, **13**. The honorand of this decree has been recognized by C. Habicht, *Chiron* 2, 1972, pp. 107–109, in an inscription from Ephesos, Hicks, *IBM* III, 464, honoring Artemidoros and his brother, sons of Apollodoros, of Perinthos; and this ethnic should now be restored in *IG* II², 663, line 17; Appendix **13**. On the Agora fragment of *IG* II², 662 only the tau of Artemidoros' name has survived (line 6). Habicht has doubted the reading and proposed that this decree honors rather Artemidoros' brother as in the Ephesian decree. But the tau is clearly visible on the stone and confirms the usual interpretation that two copies of one decree have survived. Cf. the decree for Strombichos, *IG* II², 666, 667.

[211] Statue of Ptolemy Soter, Paus., I.8.6; of Lysimachos, I.9.4; of Pyrrhos, I.11.1; of Seleukos, I.16.1. Cf. Ferguson, *HA*, p. 149, note 3; Deprado, *RivFil*, n.s. 31, 1953, p. 36, note 2; Lévêque, *Pyrrhos*, p. 161.

Pausanias to believe that it had been dedicated more out of self-interest than gratitude: *καὶ Λυσίμαχον οὐκ εὐνοίᾳ τοσοῦτον ὡς ἐς τὰ παρόντα χρήσιμον νομίζοντες ἀνέθηκαν* (I.9.4). No phrase could more succinctly describe the relations between Athens and the kings in 286/5; and it was in furtherance of her own interests at that moment that Athens designated appropriate citizens to plead her cause and represent the position of the restored democracy to all parties. After consultation between the generals and the Council, Kallias was asked to serve as intermediary with Sostratos (lines 37–38), just as Krates had earlier been asked to intercede with Demetrios. These ambassadors, and others of whom we no longer know the names, were undoubtedly chosen because they enjoyed the previous acquaintance and special confidence of the kings and ministers to whom they were dispatched.[212]

If the reconstruction of events here suggested be acceptable, then the date of the honorary decree for Artemidoros will be seen to provide a *terminus ante quem* for the conclusion of the peace. By Elaphebolion 30 of Diokles' year (April 285 B.C.), the embassies of Artemidoros and Sostratos must have been successfully concluded in order for the former to receive a vote of thanks. Demetrios by then had sailed for Asia, whence only in an urn of ashes was he destined to return. Pyrrhos had left for Macedon, with his parting advice to the Athenians that if they had any brains, they would never again permit a king to pass their gates. By that time, too, the peace had surely taken effect, up to which time the Ptolemaic mercenaries commanded by Kallias of Sphettos remained in the city (line 40).

From the sequel it is readily apparent that the terms of the peace were chiefly honored in the breach. For by the time the Athenian assembly voted to honor Artemidoros, it is likely that Demetrios was already seizing Lysimachos' territories in Asia Minor. Certainly in the same campaigning season, Pyrrhos attempted to bring about revolutions in Thessaly and among Demetrios' garrisons in Greece, and Athens attacked his forts in Attica, while in the following year Lysimachos was ready for a showdown with Pyrrhos in Macedonia.[213] In fact, the peace can have been no more than a cessation of hostilities on the basis of the status quo, which nevertheless served to provide legal confirmation for the radical changes in the balance of power which had come about through the efforts of the coalition. Thus, the treaty signed at Athens will have formally recognized Pyrrhos as king of Macedonia and his partition of the country with Lysimachos, a division of the spoils which had occurred *de facto* in the summer of 287.[214] Since Pyrrhos later attacked them, it is plain that Demetrios retained

[212] It is interesting to note that Krates and his teacher Polemon are said not to have favored the democratic party, Diog. Laert., IV.22: *καὶ γὰρ ἤστην οὐ φιλοδημώδεε.* His embassies for the city are confirmed by the "speeches made as ambassador" which were found among his papers at his death, *ibid.*, 23.

[213] For the beginning of Demetrios' campaign in Asia Minor: Plut., *Demetr.* 46.3–4; Pyrrhos' attack on Demetrios' possessions in Greece: *Pyrrh.* 12.5; Lysimachos' attack on Pyrrhos: *ibid.*, 6; Athens' attacks on the garrisons in Attica: below, pp. 82–84.

[214] Plut., *Demetr.* 44.7; *Pyrrh.* 11.6–12.1. The terms of the treaty have been discussed by Beloch, *Gr. Gesch.* IV², i, p. 232 and note 2; Lévêque, *Pyrrhos*, pp. 161–162. The latter on the basis of the evidence then available concluded that Ptolemy did not participate. Tarn, *Ant. Gon.*, p. 98 and note 19 regarded the treaty as bilateral between Pyrrhos and Demetrios.

title to Thessaly and his other Greek territories (*Pyrrh.* 12.5), held in check by the great fortresses at Corinth and Chalkis. Peiraieus, Eleusis, Salamis, and the other forts of Attica were also left to Demetrios,[215] to be governed by his son Antigonos after his departure for Asia. It is also possible that at this time some of the eastern islands, Lemnos and probably Imbros and Skyros, which had in the 4th century belonged to Athens, now passed from Demetrios into the hands of Lysimachos.[216] The history of the ensuing years leaves no room for doubt that those who gained the most were Athens and Ptolemy. For the great old city, the treaty legally confirmed her freedom and autonomy, mere slogans of propaganda in the world of the Hellenistic kings, but the breath of life for the nationalist party, whose seizure of the government the previous spring was now accorded official recognition, and under whose leadership Athens would enjoy more than twenty years of democratic government. And as for Ptolemy, his prize was control of the sea. His hegemony of the Aegean dates from this time, and this together with his acquisition of the Phoenician ports was probably formally acknowledged in the peace with Demetrios, who in return was allowed to move his fleet unmolested to his base at Miletos (Plut., *Demetr.* 46.3). Now, too, begins Ptolemy's suzerainty of the Island League, and in this light his garrison on Andros, commanded by Kallias of Sphettos, can be seen as one of the first steps leading to a generation of imperial dominion in the eastern Mediterranean.[217]

[215] See below, footnote 219.

[216] That Lemnos belonged to Lysimachos before the battle of Kouroupedion emerges from a passage of Phylarchos quoted by Athenaios, VI. 254 f–255 a = *F. Gr. Hist.*, 81, F 29. At the time of their liberation by Seleukos (cf. *IG* II^2, 672, lines 39ff.), the Athenian cleruchs on Lemnos complained of their former treatment: *πικρῶς ἐπιστατουμένους ὑπὸ Λυσιμάχου*. Cf. Deprado, *RivFil*, n.s. 31, 1953, pp. 39–40.

[217] The establishment of Ptolemy's control over the Island League is reflected in the language of the Nesiotic decree, *SIG*^{3}, 390, lines 10–16: *ὁ [β]ασιλεὺς καὶ σωτὴρ Πτολεμαῖος πολλῶν καὶ μεγάλων ἀγαθῶν αἴτιος ἐγένετο τοῖς τε Νησιώταις καὶ τοῖς ἄλλοις Ἕλλησιν, τάς τε πόλεις ἐλευθερώσας καὶ τοὺς νόμους ἀποδοὺς [κ]αὶ τὴμ πάτριομ πολιτείαμ πᾶσιγ καταστήσα[ς κ]αὶ τῶν εἰσφορῶγ κουφίσας*. Since these actions are specifically attributed to Soter before the accession of Philadelphos, they should probably be dated before Dystros 12, 285/4 (end of December 285 B.C.), when the co-regency of Philadelphos began, but they must in any event come before the death of Soter in 283/2, footnote 52 above. Cf. *IG* XII 5, 1004 from Ios, quoted footnote 37 above. Since this decree honors Zenon, the Ptolemaic commander of *IG* II^2, 650 and mentions the same squadron of cruisers which were active in the Athenian revolt, it should date within a year or two of 286/5. It then provides the earliest mention of the Ptolemaic nesiarch Bakchon (line 2), who is already in charge of the League. See Merker, *Historia* 19, 1970, pp. 150–152; Bagnall, *Ptolemaic Possessions*, pp. 136–138.

CHAPTER V

FOREIGN AID FOR THE NATIONALIST REGIME

At Athens, the peace had indeed confirmed the "deliverance of the Demos" from a decade of Macedonian domination, enforced by the spears of mercenaries on the Mouseion; and Athens could now send word to her friends abroad that "the Demos had recovered the city."[218] But except for the possession of freedom, the new nationalist government found itself otherwise in a precarious position. After the first heady days of the revolution, and some months before the treaty with Demetrios had set the stamp of international approval upon the military operations of 286 B.C., it was already brought home to the Athenians that only the city itself (τὸ ἄστυ) was theirs. The port of Peiraieus, the border forts of Eleusis, Phyle, and Panakton, and no doubt Sounion and Rhamnous as well were still manned by Demetrios' garrisons;[219] and in such a situation the city of Athens alone, cut off from the sea and her allies abroad, could all too easily be strangled into submission. The key to the survival of Athens, as Themistokles and Perikles once saw, with a clear vision born of more glorious days, was always the control of the Peiraieus.

In our consideration of the text of Euchares' decree, we had occasion to examine various pieces of evidence which show that the recovery of the Peiraieus was a matter of urgent concern to the new government. It seemed possible to identify signs of considerable efforts to prepare the city for such an assault some three or four years after the liberation, efforts which eventually came to fruition in Olympiodoros' famous exploit in 280 B.C.[220] In these years, Athens clung to life and liberty through the munificence of her foreign friends, whose gifts of money and food enabled the city to prepare herself for the military consequences of an attack on the Peiraieus, and to stay alive in the meantime, while supplies were laid in against an eventual siege. It is important now to emphasize that Olympiodoros' recovery of the Peiraieus in 280 was the happy ending of a story which began in the summer of 286, within a few weeks or months of the revolution. At that time, we find the first evidence for the systematic collection of cash

[218] *IG* II^2, 653, line 22; 654, lines 17–18, the earliest dated reference to the liberation of the city. The decrees honor Spartokos of Bosporos and Audoleon of Paionia, respectively, for contributions of grain and are dated Gamelion 29 and Skirophorion 25, 285/4.

[219] For Peiraieus and the forts: *IG* II^2, 657, lines 35–36 (Appendix **11**). Eleusis is inferred from Demochares' subsequent capture of it, [Plut.], *Mor.* 851 e; Appendix **10**. For the assignment of major fortifications at Rhamnous to the Macedonian period, see J. Pouilloux, *La forteresse de Rhamnonte*, Paris 1954, pp. 64–66, 86. But Rhamnous was in Athenian hands at the time of the Chremonidean War, in the archonship of Peithidemos, *SEG* XXIV, 154, line 7. It must have been acquired from Antigonos later, probably in the settlement of 279 B.C., on which see Tarn, *JHS* 54, 1934, pp. 33ff.

[220] See above, pp. 26–29 and footnote 62.

and grain from abroad, and shortly thereafter come the first attempts to seize the Peiraieus and the border forts from Demetrios' garrisons. An investigation of those incidents will greatly animate our picture of Athens in the first year of the restored democracy and will set the later campaign of Olympiodoros in its proper perspective.

Demochares of Leukonoe has already figured prominently in our discussion of the career of Kallias of Sphettos, but we must return to him once again to consider those services to the city which were later adduced as the strongest recommendation that he was worthy of Athens' highest public honors. Laches' decree describes his part in the nationalist government as follows:

> When he was recalled by the Demos in Diokles' archonship, he first reduced the expenditures for administration and was sparing of the funds existing in the treasury; he went as ambassador to Lysimachos and succeeded in raising thirty talents of silver for the Demos and again one hundred in addition; he moved that an embassy be sent to Ptolemy in Egypt, and those who were dispatched brought back fifty talents of silver for the Demos; he went also as ambassador to Antipatros and raised twenty talents of silver; and he recovered Eleusis for the Demos. He persuaded the Demos to vote for all these measures and he implemented them ([Plut.], *Mor.* 851 e–f, Appendix **10**).

Exactly what office Demochares held in the archonship of Diokles, to which most of these actions can be dated, is not stated and not clear. His financial management which reduced the expenses of the administration sounds like a post analogous to that once held by Lykourgos, and later by his son Habron, who was made ὁ ἐπὶ τῇ διοικήσει after the democratic restoration of 307/6.[221] Possibly Demochares was chairman of the newly created Board of Administration (οἱ ἐπὶ τῇ διοικήσει) which first appears in this year. He concerned himself at once with the collection and husbanding of resources for the defense of Athens, just as he had done during the Four Years' War, and his voice was plainly heard in the assembly advising that Athens apply for foreign aid from the kings who opposed Demetrios. On his motion, he was himself dispatched as ambassador twice to Lysimachos and subsequently to Antipatros.

Something of the negotiations of these embassies in Diokles' year can now be reconstructed. Demochares evidently operated, probably in every instance, through the agency of Athenians who had special influence with the kings. His personal success at the court of Lysimachos has been taken to indicate that he passed part or all of his years of exile in the kingdom of Thrace.[222] Nevertheless, Demochares at first made use of the good offices of Philippides of Kephale, who is said to have been a particular favorite of Lysimachos and had likewise taken refuge with him. The decree for Philippides makes it evident that he was with Lysimachos at the time of the revolution, and states specifically that he then went to work in the city's interests, "begging the king to help with money and grain so that the Demos remains free, and so that it may recover the Peiraieus and the forts as quickly as possible."[223] The decree then goes on to

[221] For Lykourgos' financial management, [Plut.], *Mor.* 841 b, 852 b; for Habron's, *IG* II², 463, line 36.
[222] Ferguson, *HA*, p. 137; Tarn, *Ant. Gon.*, p. 42.
[223] *IG* II², 657, lines 33–36; Appendix **11**; cf. Plut., *Demetr.* 12.5 for his friendship with Lysimachos.

record that the king himself often spoke well of Philippides' efforts to the Athenian ambassadors (lines 36–38). These last will be Demochares and his colleagues, who must have hurried north on their first embassy during the summer of 286; for their mission is exactly parallel to that which sought help from Pyrrhos and departed at Demetrios' first appearance in Attica. Gratified as these ambassadors doubtless were to hear the king's kind words for Philippides, for all his efforts and theirs, they returned home nonetheless with only 30 talents of silver. This would not go far in the defense of Athens: Antigonos Monophthalmos had contributed 140 talents in the Four Years' War against Kassandros (*IG* II^2, 1492, lines 97ff.).

But Lysimachos, as we have seen, also sent Artemidoros of Perinthos to represent his interests in the peace conference with Demetrios. The decree in his honor mentions his return to Lysimachos, presumably after the successful negotiations for the peace, and then praises his cooperation with Athenian embassies dispatched afterwards to the king (*IG* II^2, Add. 662, lines 12–13). It is reasonable to suppose that one of the embassies, in whose behalf Artemidoros used his influence at court, was the second mission led by Demochares, in which case the notable success of his appeal, a contribution of 100 talents, we may plausibly attribute to Artemidoros' good report on the new government at Athens. The date of Demochares' second embassy to Thrace should then be placed at the end of winter or the beginning of spring in 285 B.C., for he must have returned successfully to Athens shortly before the vote of praise for Artemidoros on Elaphebolion 30. There is possibly one other trace of these diplomatic efforts in the extant epigraphical record. That is a tantalizingly fragmentary decree conferring proxeny status on two islanders, Habron and Matrias (*IG* II^2, 651). The mention of grain at the beginning of the citation of their services, now almost totally lost, suggests that the two sea captains may have been honored for bringing foreign grain to Attica. The date of the document, Anthesterion 19 of Diokles' archonship (February 285 B.C.), places their activities at exactly the moment of the embassies discussed above. It will now be recalled that Philippides asked Lysimachos for both grain and money, only the latter being mentioned in the decree for Demochares. Now when we observe that Matrias came from the tiny island of Nesos between Lesbos and the Aiolian coast,[224] and thus in the territory of Lysimachos, it is just conceivable that he and Habron were responsible for transporting to Attica the grain for which Philippides had asked the king the previous summer.

At about this time, if not a bit earlier in the winter, the peace will have been ratified and gone into effect. It was then considered safe for the Ptolemaic mercenaries under Kallias of Sphettos to withdraw from the city, which means that Demetrios had by then sailed for Asia. Once again on the motion of Demochares, the assembly voted to appeal for help, this time to Ptolemy I. The fact that Laches' decree mentions Demochares' motion and the result of the embassy even though Demochares was not one of the ambassadors suggests that it coincided in time with his second embassy to

[224] Cf. *IG* XII 2, 645, line 40, and the map, pl. 2.

Lysimachos, no doubt followed closely by his visit to Antipatros.[225] If, as argued above (p. 25), this is the same embassy which Kallias of Sphettos accompanied to Ptolemy (lines 40–43), it is to be dated just after the conclusion of peace. The description of Kallias' assistance to the Athenian envoys shows that his position was analogous to that of Artemidoros with Lysimachos. As an officer in the king's service he was the influential intermediary, not the ambassador, and thus the decree does not mention the fifty talents which the embassy brought back to Athens as a result of his help.

The nationalist government had weathered its first winter in a position of considerable strength, for Demochares' zealous diplomacy had raised no less than 200 talents of silver and some supplies of grain beside. The language of the decree for Philippides makes clear the argument used by the Athenian ambassadors: the Peiraieus and the forts must be recovered or the city cannot remain free. It was this that persuaded Lysimachos, and for this that he invested his money in Athens;[226] for he contemplated the enormous damage to Demetrios' interests in Greece if the Peiraieus were successfully snatched from him. That the Thracian king was conspiring along these lines just after Demetrios' departure for Asia is confirmed by Plutarch's statement (*Pyrrh.* 12.5) that it was he who persuaded Pyrrhos to attack Thessaly and the garrisons in the Greek cities. The Athenian envoys will also have been made privy to these plans.

There is, indeed, evidence that Athens first attempted to recover the Peiraieus shortly after Demetrios' departure. The episode is recounted among the strategems of Polyainos (V.17.1; Appendix **14**), and it should be placed at this time in the context of the policy and preparations here under discussion. The attempt coincided with Demetrios' march through Lydia (αὐτὸς μὲν ἦν περὶ τὴν Λυδίαν), and the date emerges from Plutarch's description (*Demetr.* 46.3–4) of his first movements in Asia. Upon arrival at Miletos, he consummated his marriage with Ptolemais, then turned at once to attack the cities of Lysimachos (μετὰ τὸν γάμον εὐθύς), among which his capture of Sardis is specifically mentioned. Demetrios was thus in Lydia at the beginning of the long and tumultuous campaigning season of 285 B.C.[227]

[225] The Antipatros to whom Demochares went as ambassador is generally assumed to have been the son of Kassandros, and ex-king of Macedonia. Cf. Ferguson, *HA*, p. 146; Tarn, *Ant. Gon.*, p. 14, note 4, 102; Beloch, *Gr. Gesch.* IV², i, p. 231; Dinsmoor, *Archons*, p. 57. This Antipatros, however, is said to have been assassinated by his father-in-law, Lysimachos, at the time of the concerted attack on Demetrios, Justin, XVI.2.4; cf. Porphyry in *F. Gr. Hist.*, 260, F 3, 5. (Dio. Sic., XXI.7; Plut., *Mor.* 530 c say that he was assassinated by Demetrios in 294 B.C.) Since Antipatros' death cannot have occurred later than the summer of 287 and Demochares' embassy cannot have been earlier than the autumn of 286 (more probably the winter of 286/5 as argued in the text), it is preferable to identify the Antipatros in Laches' decree as the nephew of Kassandros, Antipatros ὁ Ἐτησίας, so named from the Etesian winds because in 279 B.C. he was king of Macedonia for only 45 days, the length of time the summer winds blow. Cf. *F. Gr. Hist.*, 260, F 3, 10; Eusebios, *Chron. Can.* I, pp. 235f. (ed. Schoene); Heinen, *Untersuchungen*, p. 58. That he had taken refuge at Lysimachos' court is suggested by Tarn, *Ant. Gon.*, p. 37.

[226] Cf. *ibid.*, p. 103.

[227] Cf. Ferguson, *HA*, pp. 150f. (with date for the incident in 287/6); Beloch, *Gr. Gesch.* IV², i, p. 239 (date, winter 287/6); Tarn, *Ant. Gon.*, pp. 103–104 and note 28 placed the capture of Eleusis before the attempt on Peiraieus (autumn 286). But if, as is likely, the events in Laches' decree are listed in chronological

To the government at Athens, the moment doubtless seemed remarkably propitious. Demetrios himself had given the signal for the next passage of arms. Within only a month or so of ratifying peace with Athens and the other kings, he had brazenly violated the treaty by attacking Lysimachos' possessions in Asia. Accordingly Pyrrhos, in response to Lysimachos' urging, overran Thessaly and thus effectively drew Antigonos' energies and his arms northward away from Attica. Athens, so it seemed, was left free to move with impunity and the Peiraieus lay just within grasp. It is interesting to observe that the generals employed the same strategy which had so successfully paved the way for the revolt in the city one year earlier. Just as Olympiodoros and the revolutionary generals of Xenophon's year had contrived to reach Strombichos and his mercenaries, so now their successors thought to tamper with the officers of the Peiraieus garrison. The approach was made to a certain Hierokles, who like Strombichos was lieutenant to the commandant. We hear of a secret meeting on the banks of the Ilissos at the dead of night, where Hierokles exchanged oaths with two of the generals to the effect that he would open the gates of the Mounychia and admit Athenian troops by night. But the tactic ended this time in tragic failure; for Hierokles remained loyal to his commander Herakleides. The gates of the fort were indeed thrown open at night according to plan, whereupon the storming party found the mercenary phalanx fully armed and waiting, and 420 Athenian hoplites were cut down to a man.

Something of the bitterness of that desperate moment still reaches out to us across the centuries, as it did also to Pausanias,[228] for chance has preserved the gravestone of one of those who met his death beneath Mounychia's walls.[229] The city gave him a statue and a public grave in the Kerameikos. In the simple elegiac lines of his epitaph ring the familiar phrases with which Greeks for centuries had mourned the dead in war, and their archaic language evokes the heroic battles of Athens' glorious past. But these lines are haunted, too, by the grim reality of the present; for the *δούλιον ἦμαρ* which Chairippos fought to avert was no elegiac tag, but a slavery which Athens had recently known and now had reason to fear might swiftly be re-imposed.

But the city rebounded from the debacle on the Mounychia. The frightful consequences of failure never materialized, perhaps because Pyrrhos had kept Antigonos too harried in the north to think of retaliation. Within a year's time, in fact, Athens was prepared to move again, this time against Eleusis. Now fortune marched with the Athenians. The failure at the Peiraieus had strengthened their resolve, the fortress and

---

order, and the embassies to Lysimachos are correctly identified with those which Artemidoros assisted (*IG* II², Add. 662+*Hesperia* 26, 1957, p. 29, no. 2), then they must be dated before Elaphebolion 30, 285 B.C. The capture of Eleusis comes sometime later.

[228] I.29.10 for mention of their tombs in the Kerameikos.

[229] *IG* II², Add. 5227a; N. Kyparisses and W. Peek, *AthMitt* 57, 1932, p. 146, no. 2:

τλῆτε νέοι, πόδα θέντες ἐναντία δυσμενέεσσιν
θνήισκειν, αἰδόμενοι πατρίδα καὶ γο[ν]έας·
καὶ γάρ σοι, Χαίριππε, καταφθιμένωι μ[έ]γα κῦδος
εἰκόνα δημοσίαι τε εἵσατο σῆμα πόλις,
ἡνίκα Μουνιχίας ὑπὸ τείχεσι δούλιον ἦμαρ
[ῥ]υόμενος πρὸ φίλης πνεῦμα ἔλιπες πατρίδος.

the Eleusinian sanctuary were won back for Athens, and the episode gave rise to celebration. Laches' decree, quoted above, gives credit for the exploit to Demochares; and if we may take Laches at his word, his father both made the motion in the assembly and led the assault. One infers that he was elected to the board of generals for the year of Diotimos (285/4), perhaps on the strength of his diplomatic successes of the previous year.

The date of the recovery of Eleusis can be established within a few months, and it will then emerge as the first major success of the new nationalist government, the sweeter too because it came on the heels of the failure to recover Peiraieus. In the archonship of Isaios (284/3), the comedian Philippides of Kephale was elected to serve as agonothetes, having returned to Athens evidently after the liberation two years before. The familiar decree in his honor was passed early in the following year, and its description of his conduct of this office bears directly upon the recovery of Eleusis. "Elected agonothetes in Isaios' archonship, he complied with the will of the Demos and volunteered the expenses of office from his private means; he conducted the ancestral sacrifices for the gods on behalf of the Demos, and he gave the [. . . . .] to all Athenians at all the festivals; he was also the first to establish an additional festival for Demeter and [Kore] as a memorial of the [liberation] of the Demos" (*IG* II^2, 657, lines 38–45, Appendix **11**). It is obvious that Philippides rose handsomely to the occasion and, in fact, discharged most of the expenses of the agonothesia from his own pocket. There is no easy restoration for the single word which has been lost at the beginning of line 42; but the reference is probably to the wine and sweetmeats which Philochoros says were passed among the spectators throughout the Dionysiac festivals.[230] Philippides is said to have provided such refreshments for the entire populace at all the festivals; and if we may judge from the pointed reference to the fact, his agonothesia must have been memorable for its splendor.

All this is in striking contrast to the frugal policy of austerity and fiscal retrenchment with which Demochares had administered the public treasury just two years before. Indeed, the decree says elsewhere that Philippides spent a lot of his own money (lines 46–47), and without such private donations many of the festivals might not have been celebrated. For our purpose it is of particular interest that Philippides "was the first to establish an additional festival for Demeter and Kore as a memorial of the liberation of the Demos." Although the crucial words are lost, the restoration is generally accepted as certain, and with it we learn that the archonship of Isaios was one of general rejoicing in which the liberation from Macedon was publicly celebrated. Since the memorial festival was in honor of Demeter and Kore, it should now be brought into relation with Demochares' recovery of Eleusis from the Macedonian garrison. That was the event which intervened between the failure at Peiraieus and the celebration of Philippides' agonothesia.

[230] Philochoros in Athenaios, XI.464 f=*F. Gr. Hist.*, 328, F 171: *παρὰ δὲ τὸν ἀγῶνα πάντα οἶνος αὐτοῖς ᾠνοχοεῖτο καὶ τραγήματα παρεφέρετο, καὶ τοῖς χοροῖς εἰσιοῦσιν ἐνέχεον πίνειν καὶ διηγωνισμένοις ὅτ' ἐξεπορεύοντο ἐνέχεον πάλιν*. Cf. Kirchner, commentary on *IG* II^2, 657.

The Eleusinian connection is further suggested by the date of the decree for Philippides. His honors were voted on Boedromion 18 of Euthios' archonship (September 283 B.C.), on the last day for public business before the celebration of the Great Mysteries,[231] and the decree especially cites his management of the Eleusinian festivals in the previous year (284/3). Philippides then celebrated his "additional festival" in the late summer of 284 B.C. Since the celebration was an ἀγών, it should not be interpreted as a part of the Great Mysteries, but rather refers to the Eleusinian games held before the Mysteries in the middle of Metageitnion. Since the festival was ἐπίθετον, that is not a part of the regular festival calendar, it seems a correct inference that the extra games were staged in conjunction with the Eleusinia in order to add unusual splendor to the regular biennial games, which fell in August 284 B.C. during Philippides' agonothesia.[232] We may suggest that the Eleusinian festivals were thus singled out for special aggrandizement because the last previous celebration of the Eleusinia, the biennial games which had been due in August 286, was actually omitted, for the reason that Demetrios' siege had prevented their celebration that summer. We may suggest further that one year later the Great Mysteries themselves had been omitted for the reason that Eleusis had not yet been recovered by the nationalists at the time of the festival in the archonship of Diotimos (285/4). Now, another document of Diotimos' year is a contract for public work on a stoa in the Eleusinian sanctuary, which had been halted and left incomplete and was now to be resumed.[233] The date of the contract is Mounichion 4 (April 284 B.C.) and it provides that some parts of the job must be finished before the end of Diotimos' archonship. Clearly the workmen are to have free access to the sanctuary, and the conclusion is obvious that by this time Eleusis was in Athenian control.

Demochares' successful recovery of Eleusis occurred in all probability between September 285 and May 284, in the archonship of Diotimos. Two other bits of evidence may also bear slightly on the date. On Elaphebolion 5, 284/3, the tribe Aigeis awarded special honors to its prytaneis of Diotimos' year,[234] because they conducted their allotted prytany with unusual success. Indeed, they had already been previously honored by the Boule and the Demos for their good work. We may, at least, ask whether the recovery of Eleusis might not have occurred during the prytany of Aigeis. But the timing of Demochares' attack may well have been prompted by a far more

[231] That the procession to Eleusis for the festival took place on Boedromion 19 is indicated by *IG* II², 1078, line 19; cf. Pfuhl, *de pompis*, p. 39; Deubner, *Attische Feste*, pp. 72–73; J. D. Mikalson, *The Sacred and Civil Calendar of the Athenian Year*, Princeton 1975, pp. 58–59.

[232] The biennial Eleusinian games seem to have been celebrated in the first and third years of each Olympiad, and so were due in 286/5 = Ol. 123,3 and 284/3 = Ol. 124,1 (*IG* II², 1496, lines 126–130; 1028, lines 4–16; 2336, lines 200–203). The quadrennial Great Eleusinia fell in the second year of the Olympiad (*IG* II², 847, lines 9–26; 1304, lines 24–27). See Deubner, *Attische Feste*, p. 91; Mikalson, *op. cit.*, p. 46. Cf. also the useful discussion of Dinsmoor, *Archons*, pp. 209–213 which reaches different conclusions.

[233] *IG* II², 1682 as interpreted by H. Lattermann, *Klio* 6, 1906, pp. 140–168. For Demochares' capture of Eleusis and Philippides' festival, see Ferguson, *HA*, p. 145 and note 4; Tarn, *Ant. Gon.*, p. 103; Deprado, *RivFil*, n.s. 31, 1953, pp. 41–42.

[234] *IG* II², 656 = *Agora* XV, 69; cf. Ferguson, *HA*, p. 146, note 1.

momentous event, which in itself was cause for rejoicing among the nationalists of democratic Athens. Toward the end of the winter of 285/4, after nearly a year of desperate, and at times brilliant, fighting which had lurched from Lydia to the fastness of the Tauros Mountains, and into northern Syria, after a campaign dogged by famine, mutiny, and sickness, Demetrios Poliorketes surrendered to Seleukos.[235] It was the end of an era at Athens; and in view of the chronological coincidence, it is possible that the news sparked the Athenians once more to action. In any event, Eleusis was theirs before Mounichion. The successful liberation of the city from a decade of Demetrios' rule could then be celebrated with special pomp and extra games at the time of the Eleusinia in the late summer. For the moment the revolution could be deemed complete. The city was free; the nationalist government was secure in its position; and thanks to her foreign friends, Athens' autonomy had been legally recognized in the peace treaty with Demetrios. The time for arms and action had given way to the time for celebration and to the awarding of public honors.

[235] The date in the spring of 286 B.C. here adopted for the revolt of Athens, and based largely upon the revised dating of the archon Diokles (286/5, whereas formerly 288/7, see footnote 188 above), necessitates a readjustment in the chronology of Demetrios' final campaign and captivity. Demetrios' crossing to Asia has generally been placed in late 287 or early 286, and his surrender at the end of winter or beginning of spring 286/5: Ferguson, *HA*, p. 151; Tarn, *Ant. Gon.*, p. 100 and note 21; *idem*, *CAH* VII, p. 88; Beloch, *Gr. Gesch.* IV^2, ii, pp. 106–107; Jacoby, *F. Gr. Hist.*, II D, Kommentar, p. 869. Since the peace negotiations at Athens cannot now be placed earlier than the autumn or winter of 286/5, Demetrios' campaign in Asia must now be assigned to the campaigning season of 285. As argued above, the *terminus ante quem* for his departure is Elaphebolion 30, 285. In Plutarch's account (*Demetr.* 46.3–49.5), there is no indication that the events fell in more than one long campaigning season. In *Demetr.* 47.4–48.1 the campaigning season was at an end; Demetrios begged Seleukos for supplies for the winter; and Seleukos agreed to grant him two months in winter quarters. The time is thus November or December 285. Shortly thereafter Demetrios fell sick for 40 days (48.3). The confrontation of Demetrios and Seleukos in north Syria, followed by Demetrios' surrender, falls in January or February 284. Porphyry's date for Demetrios' surrender as given by the Armenian version of Eusebios is Ol. 120,4=297/6, and this being impossible, has been emended to Ol. 12⟨3⟩, 4=285/4, *F. Gr. Hist.*, 260, F 32, 2. Although the date has been questioned by Jacoby, *loc. cit.*, because of the traditional date in 286/5, the emended date is now seen to be correct. But Demetrios' death, dated Ol. 124, 4=281/0, emended to Ol. 124, ⟨1⟩=284/3, in Eusebios, cannot be squared with Plut., *Demetr.* 52.4, where he is said to have died in the third year of captivity (ἔτος τρίτον). Plutarch's statement can, however, be reconciled with the chronology here proposed. Antigonos Gonatas took the royal title and dated his first regnal year in the Macedonian year 283/2, beginning in the autumn. See M. Chambers, *AJP* 75, 1954, pp. 385–394. If Demetrios died in the late summer of 283, his death will have occurred in the Attic or Olympic year 283/2, beginning in mid-summer, and thus in the third such year after his surrender. He surrendered in 285/4 (archon Diotimos), was in captivity during 284/3 (archon Isaios), and died early in 283/2 (archon Euthios).

APPENDIX

LITERARY AND EPIGRAPHICAL TESTIMONIA

1. Decree for Phaidros of Sphettos. *IG* II², 682
ca. 255/4

NΩN–ΣTOIX. 34–45

. . .6. . . ịειαν . . ασε [- -]
[. . . ἐ]πολιόρκησεν τῆς εị[- - - - - - - - - - - - - - - - - - - -]
[.μ]ενος ἃ ἦν ἐν τεῖ τῶν ἐναντίων συμμαχία[ι· Θυμο]
[χά]ρη[ς] δὲ ὁ ὑὸς ὁ τούτου, πατὴρ δὲ Φαίδρου χει[ροτονη]
θεὶς στρατηγὸς ὑπὸ τοῦ δήμου ἐπὶ τὸ ναυτικ[ὸν ἔπλε]
υσεν ἐπὶ τῶν νεῶν ἃς ὁ δῆμος [τῶι τῶν Μακεδόνων στόλωι]
συνέπεμπεν εἰς τὴν Ἀσίαν, ᵛ καὶ συνδιεπολέμησ[εν τ]
ὸν πόλεμον τὸν ἐν Κύπρωι καὶ ἔλαβεν Ἅγνωνα τὸν Τ[ήϊο]
ν καὶ τὰς ναῦς τὰς μετ᾽ αὐτοῦ, καὶ ἐπὶ Πραξιβούλου ἄρχον[τ]
ος Γλαυκέτου καθειληφότος Κύθνον καὶ καταγαγόντ
ος ἐντεῦθεν τὰ πλοῖα τήν τε πόλιν ἔλαβεν καὶ αὐτὸν
Γλαυκέτην καὶ τὰ πλοῖα τὰ μετ᾽ αὐτοῦ καὶ παρεσκεύ
ασεν ἀσφάλειαν τοῖς πλέουσι τὴν θάλατταν· ᵛ Κασ
σάνδρου δὲ πολιορκοῦντος Ὠρεὸν ἀποσταλεὶς στ
ρατηγὸς ἐπὶ τῶν νεῶν τῶν τῆς πόλεως τοὺς πολίτας
τοὺς πλέοντας ἐν ταῖς ναυσὶν παρειτήσατο ὥστε τ
ῶν συμμάχων μόνους Ἀθηναίους ἀλειτουργήτους
εἶναι τῶν ἔργων τῶν πρὸς τὴν πολιορκίαν· ᵛ καὶ αὐ
τὸς δὲ Φαῖδρος τὴν αὐτὴν αἵρεσιν ἔχων τοῖς προγό
{γο}νοις διατετέλεκεν ἑαυτὸν ἄξιον παρασκευάζω
ν τῆς πρὸς τὸν δῆμον εὐνοίας· ᵛ καὶ ἐπὶ Νικίου μὲν ἄρ
χοντος στρατηγὸς ὑπὸ τοῦ δήμου χειροτονηθεὶς ἐπὶ
τὴν παρασκευὴν δὶς πάντων ὦμ προσῆκεν ἐπεμελήθ
η καλῶς καὶ φιλοτίμως· ᵛ καὶ ἐπὶ τὴν χώραν χειροτονη
θεὶς πλεονάκις καὶ ἐπὶ τοὺς ξένους γενόμενος τρὶς
τὴν πᾶσαν ἐποήσατο σπουδὴν ὅπως ἂν οἱ στρατιῶται
ὡς ἄριστα κατασκευασάμενοι παρέχωνται τὰς χρε
ίας τῶι δήμωι· ᵛ πρεσβεύσας δὲ πρὸς τὸν βασιλέα τὸν
πρεσβύτερον Πτολεμαῖον ἐκόμισεν τῶι δήμωι σῖτον
καὶ χρήματα· ᵛ χειροτονηθεὶς δὲ ὑπὸ τοῦ δήμου ἐπὶ τὰ

ὅπλα στρατηγὸς τὸν ἐνιαυτὸν τὸν ἐπὶ Κίμωνος ἄρχοντ
ος διετέλεσεν ἀγωνιζόμενος ὑπὲρ τῆς κοινῆς σωτηρί
ας, καὶ περιστάντων τεῖ πόλει καιρῶν δυσκόλων διεφύ
λαξεν τὴν εἰρήνην τῆι χώραι ἀποφαινόμενος ἀεὶ τὰ κράτ
ιστα, καὶ τὸν σῖτον ἐκ τῆς χώρας καὶ τοὺς ἄλλους καρποὺς
αἴτιος ἐγένετο εἰσκομισθῆναι, συμβουλεύσας τῶι δήμω
ι συντελέσαι [-------------------------]
[. . .], καὶ τὴν πόλιν ἐλευθέραν καὶ δημοκρατουμένην αὐ
τόνομον παρέδωκεν καὶ τοὺς νόμους κυρίους τοῖς μεθ'
ἑαυτὸν [--------------------------]
[--------] διετέλεσε καὶ λέγων καὶ πράττων ἀγαθ
ὸν ὅ τι ἠδύνατο ὑπὲρ τοῦ δήμου [--------------]
[----------------------------------]
[. . .6. . .]v χειροτονηθεὶς ἐπὶ τὰ ὅπλα πρῶτος ὑπὸ τοῦ δήμου
στρατηγὸς τὸν ἐνιαυτὸν τὸν ἐπὶ Ξενοφῶντος ἄρχοντος
διετέλεσε πάντα πράττων ἀκολούθως τοῖς τε νόμοις κα
ὶ τοῖς τῆς βουλῆς καὶ τοῦ δήμου ψηφίσμασιν v [----]
[----------------------------------]
[----------------------------------]
[----------------------------------]
[----------------------------------]
[----------------------------------]
καὶ ἀγωνοθέτης χειροτονηθεὶς ὑπὸ τοῦ δήμου ἐπὶ Νικίο
υ ἄρχοντος ἐπεμελήθη τῶν τε θυσιῶν ὅπως ἂν συντελε[σ]
[θῶσ]ι πᾶσαι κατὰ τὰ πάτρια καὶ οἱ ἀγῶνες ὡς κάλλιστοι
[γένω]νται καὶ ἄξιοι τῆς τοῦ δήμου φιλοτιμίας, καὶ ὕστ[ε]
[ρον] τοῦ ὑοῦ Θυμοχάρου ἀγωνοθέτου χειροτονηθέντος
[τὸ]ν ἐνιαυτὸν τὸν ἐπ' Εὐβούλου ἄρχοντος συνεπεμε
λήθη καὶ τούτων πάντων, φανερὰν ἀποδεικνύμενος
ἐμ πᾶσιν ἣν ἔχει πρὸς τὸν δῆμον εὔνοιαν· v καὶ τὰς ἄλ
λας δὲ πάσας λειτουργίας λελειτούργηκεν φιλοτίμ
ως, καὶ ὅσαι ἐπιδόσεις γεγόνασιν ἐν τῶι δήμωι πα
σῶν μετέσχηκεν· v καὶ ἐπὶ πᾶσιν τούτοις ἐστεφά
νωται ὑπό τε τῆς βουλῆς καὶ τοῦ δήμου· vv ὅπως ἂ
ν οὖν φαίνηται καὶ ὁ δῆμος τιμῶν τοὺς ἀγαθοὺς
ἄνδρας καὶ ἀξίους μνήμης, vv ἀγαθεῖ τύχει δεδό
χθαι τεῖ βουλεῖ, v τοὺς προέδρους οἵτινες ἂν λά
χωσιν προεδρεύειν ἐν τῶι δήμωι, ὅταν αἱ ἡμέραι
αἱ ἐκ τοῦ νόμου ἐξήκωσιν, χρηματίσαι περὶ τού
των, γνώμην δὲ ξυμβάλλεσθαι τῆς βουλῆς εἰς τὸν
δῆμον, ὅτι δοκεῖ τεῖ βουλεῖ, vv ἐπαινέσαι Φαῖδρο
ν Θυμοχάρου Σφήττιον καὶ στεφανῶσαι αὐτὸν

χρυσῶι στεφάνωι κατὰ τὸν νόμον ἀρετῆς ἕνεκ
[α] καὶ εὐνοίας ἧν ἔχων διατελεῖ περὶ τὸν δῆμον τ
ὸν Ἀθηναίων· ᵛ καὶ ἀναγορεῦσαι τὸν στέφανον Δι
ονυσίων τῶν μεγάλων τραγωιδῶν τῶι ἀγῶνι τῶι
καινῶι ᵛ καὶ Παναθηναίων τῶν μεγάλων τῶι γυ
μνικῶι ἀγῶνι· ᵛ τῆς δὲ ποήσεως τοῦ στεφάνου
καὶ τῆς ἀναγορεύσεως ἐπιμεληθῆναι τὸν ἐπὶ
τεῖ διοικήσει· ᵛ στῆσαι δὲ αὐτοῦ τὸν δῆμον καὶ
εἰκόνα χαλκῆν ἐν ἀγορᾶι καὶ εἶναι αὐτῶι σίτ
ησιν ἐμ πρυτανείωι καὶ ἐκγόνων τῶι πρεσβυτ
άτωι ἀεὶ καὶ προεδρίαν ἐμ πᾶσι τοῖς ἀγῶσιν
οἷς ἡ πόλις τίθησιν· χειροτονῆσαι δὲ τὸν δῆ
μον ἤδη τρεῖς ἄνδρας ἐξ Ἀθηναίων οἵτινες
ἐπιμελήσονται τῆς τε ποήσεως τῆς εἰκόνος
καὶ τῆς ἀναθέσεως· ἀναγράψαι δὲ τόδε τὸ ψήφι
σμα τὸν γραμματέα τὸν κατὰ πρυτανείαν ἐν σ
[τ]ήλει λιθίνει καὶ στῆσαι παρὰ τὴν εἰκόνα,
εἰς δὲ τὴν ἀναγραφὴν τῆς στήλης μερίσαι τ
ὸν ἐπὶ τεῖ διοικήσει τὸ γενόμενον ἀνάλωμα.
Λύανδρος Λυσιάδου Ἀναφλύστιος εἶπεν· ἀγα
[θ]εῖ τύχει, δεδόχθαι τῶι δήμωι, ᵛ τὰ μὲν ἄλλα
[πά]ντα πράττειν περὶ τῆς δωρεᾶς ἧς εἴτηκεν
Φαῖδρος κατὰ τὸ πρότερον ψήφισμα ὃ Λύανδρο
ς εἶπεν· τοὺς δὲ θεσμοθέτας εἰσαγαγεῖν αὐτ
ῶι τὴν δοκιμασίαν τῆς δωρεᾶς εἰς τὸ δικαστ
ήριον κατὰ τὸν νόμον. ᵛᵛ ἐπὶ τὴν ἀνάθεσιν τῆ
ς εἰκόνος οἵδε κεχειροτόνηνται· ᵛ Θυμοχάρ
ης Σφήττιος, ᵛ Μένων Ἀχαρνεύς, ᵛ Στράτων
Σφήττιος.

in corona
ἡ βουλὴ
ὁ δῆμος

2. Plutarch, *Demetrios* 44.1–2

αἱρομένης οὖν τοσαύτης δυνάμεως ἐπὶ τὴν Ἀσίαν ὅσην μετ' Ἀλέξανδρον οὐδεὶς ἔσχε
πρότερον, οἱ τρεῖς συνέστησαν ἐπὶ τὸν Δημήτριον, Σέλευκος, Πτολεμαῖος, Λυσί-
μαχος· ἔπειτα κοινῇ πρὸς Πύρρον ἀποστείλαντες ἐκέλευον ἐξάπτεσθαι Μακεδονίας
καὶ μὴ νομίζειν σπονδὰς αἷς Δημήτριος οὐκ ἐκείνῳ τὸ μὴ πολεμεῖσθαι δέδωκεν, ἀλλ'
2 εἴληφεν ἑαυτῷ τὸ πολεμεῖν οἷς βούλεται πρότερον. δεξαμένου δὲ Πύρρου πολὺς
περιέστη πόλεμος ἔτι μέλλοντα Δημήτριον. ἅμα γὰρ τὴν μὲν Ἑλλάδα πλεύσας

στόλῳ μεγάλῳ Πτολεμαῖος ἀφίστη, Μακεδονίαν δὲ Λυσίμαχος ἐκ Θρᾴκης, ἐκ δὲ τῆς ὁμόρου Πύρρος ἐμβαλόντες ἐλεηλάτουν.

3. Plutarch, *Demetrios* 46.1–2

ἐπεὶ δὲ ἅπαξ ὥσπερ εἰς ὁδὸν βασιλικὴν τὴν ἐλπίδα κατέστη καὶ συνίστατο πάλιν
σῶμα καὶ σχῆμα περὶ αὐτὸν ἀρχῆς, Θηβαίοις μὲν ἀπέδωκε τὴν πολιτείαν, Ἀθηναῖοι
δὲ ἀπέστησαν αὐτοῦ. καὶ τόν τε Δίφιλον, ὃς ἦν ἱερεὺς τῶν Σωτήρων ἀναγεγραμ-
μένος, ἐκ τῶν ἐπωνύμων ἀνεῖλον, ἄρχοντας αἱρεῖσθαι πάλιν, ὥσπερ ἦν πάτριον,
ψηφισάμενοι, τόν τε Πύρρον ἐκ Μακεδονίας μετεπέμποντο, μᾶλλον ἢ προσεδόκησαν
2 *ἰσχύοντα τὸν Δημήτριον ὁρῶντες. ὁ δὲ ὀργῇ μὲν ἐπῆλθεν αὐτοῖς καὶ πολιορκίαν*
περὶ τὸ ἄστυ συνεστήσατο καρτεράν, Κράτητος δὲ τοῦ φιλοσόφου πεμφθέντος ὑπὸ
τοῦ δήμου πρὸς αὐτόν, ἀνδρὸς ἐνδόξου καὶ δυνατοῦ, τὰ μὲν οἷς ὑπὲρ τῶν Ἀθηναίων
ἐδεῖτο πεισθείς, τὰ δὲ ἐξ ὧν ἐδίδασκε περὶ τῶν ἐκείνῳ συμφερόντων νοήσας ἔλυσε
τὴν πολιορκίαν, καὶ συναγαγὼν ὅσαι νῆες ἦσαν αὐτῷ, καὶ στρατιώτας μυρίους καὶ
χιλίους σὺν ἱππεῦσιν ἐμβιβάσας, ἐπὶ τὴν Ἀσίαν ἔπλει, Λυσιμάχου Καρίαν καὶ Λυδίαν
ἀποστήσων.

4. Plutarch, *Pyrrhos* 12.4–5

ἐδήλωσε δὲ ὁ Πύρρος· ἐμποδὼν γὰρ αὐξομένῳ τῷ Δημητρίῳ πάλιν ἱστάμενος, καὶ
κωλύων τὴν δύναμιν ὥσπερ ἐξ ἀρρωστίας μεγάλης ἀναλαμβάνουσαν, ἐβοήθει τοῖς
Ἕλλησι καὶ παρῆλθεν εἰς τὰς Ἀθήνας. ἀναβὰς δὲ εἰς τὴν ἀκρόπολιν καὶ θύσας τῇ θεῷ
καὶ καταβὰς αὐθημερὸν ἀγαπᾶν μὲν ἔφησε τοῦ δήμου τὴν πρὸς αὐτὸν εὔνοιαν καὶ
πίστιν, ἂν μέντοι σωφρονῶσι μεδένα τῶν βασιλέων ἔτι παρήσειν αὐτοὺς εἰς τὴν πόλιν
5 *μηδὲ τὰς πύλας ἀνοίξειν· ἐκ τούτου καὶ πρὸς Δημήτριον εἰρήνην ἐποιήσατο, καὶ μετ'*
ὀλίγον χρόνον, εἰς Ἀσίαν ἀπάραντος αὐτοῦ, πάλιν πεισθεὶς ὑπὸ Λυσιμάχου Θετταλίαν
ἀφίστη καὶ ταῖς Ἑλληνικαῖς φρουραῖς προσεπολέμει, βελτίοσι χρώμενος τοῖς Μακε-
δόσι στρατευομένοις ἢ σχολάζουσι, καὶ ὅλως αὐτὸς οὐκ εὖ πρὸς ἡσυχίαν πεφυκώς.

5. Pausanias, I.26.1–3

χρόνῳ δὲ ὕστερον ἄνδρας ἐσῆλθεν οὐ πολλοὺς μνήμη τε προγόνων καὶ ἐς οἵαν
μεταβολὴν τὸ ἀξίωμα ἥκοι τῶν Ἀθηναίων, αὐτίκα τε ὡς εἶχον αἱροῦνται στρατηγὸν
Ὀλυμπιόδωρον. ὁ δὲ σφᾶς ἐπὶ τοὺς Μακεδόνας ἦγε καὶ γέροντας καὶ μειράκια
ὁμοίως, προθυμίᾳ πλέον ἢ ῥώμῃ κατορθοῦσθαι τὰ ἐς πόλεμον ἐλπίζων· ἐπεξελθόντας
δὲ τοὺς Μακεδόνας μάχῃ τε ἐκράτησε καὶ φυγόντων ἐς τὸ Μουσεῖον τὸ χωρίον
2 *εἷλεν. Ἀθῆναι μὲν οὕτως ἀπὸ Μακεδόνων ἠλευθερώθησαν, Ἀθηναίων δὲ πάντων*
ἀγωνισαμένων ἀξίως λόγου Λεώκριτος μάλιστα ὁ Πρωτάρχου λέγεται τόλμῃ
χρήσασθαι πρὸς τὸ ἔργον· πρῶτος μὲν γὰρ ἐπὶ τὸ τεῖχος ἀνέβη, πρῶτος δὲ ἐς τὸ
Μουσεῖον ἐσήλατο, καὶ οἱ πεσόντι ἐν τῇ μάχῃ τιμαὶ παρ' Ἀθηναίων καὶ ἄλλαι
γεγόνασι καὶ τὴν ἀσπίδα ἀνέθεσαν τῷ Διὶ τῷ Ἐλευθερίῳ, τὸ ὄνομα τοῦ Λεωκρίτου

3 καὶ τὸ κατόρθωμα ἐπιγράψαντες. Ὀλυμπιοδώρῳ δὲ τόδε μέν ἐστιν ἔργον μέγιστον χωρὶς τούτων ὧν ἔπραξε Πειραιᾶ καὶ Μουνυχίαν ἀνασωσάμενος· ποιουμένων δὲ Μακεδόνων καταδρομὴν ἐς Ἐλευσῖνα Ἐλευσινίους συντάξας ἐνίκα τοὺς Μακεδόνας. πρότερον δὲ ἔτι τούτων ἐσβαλόντος ἐς τὴν Ἀττικὴν Κασσάνδρου πλεύσας Ὀλυμπιόδωρος ἐς Αἰτωλίαν βοηθεῖν Αἰτωλοὺς ἔπεισε, καὶ τὸ συμμαχικὸν τοῦτο ἐγένετο Ἀθηναίοις αἴτιον μάλιστα διαφυγεῖν τὸν Κασσάνδρου πόλεμον. Ὀλυμπιοδώρῳ δὲ τοῦτο μὲν ἐν Ἀθήναις εἰσὶν ἔν τε ἀκροπόλει καὶ ἐν πρυτανείῳ τιμαί, τοῦτο δὲ ἐν Ἐλευσῖνι γραφή· καὶ Φωκέων οἱ Ἐλάτειαν ἔχοντες χαλκοῦν Ὀλυμπιόδωρον ἐν Δελφοῖς ἀνέθεσαν, ὅτι καὶ τούτοις ἤμυνεν ἀποστᾶσι Κασσάνδρου.

6. Pausanias, I.29.13

ἐτάφησαν δὲ καὶ οἱ περὶ τὸν Ἑλλήσποντον ναυμαχήσαντες καὶ ὅσοι Μακεδόνων ἐναντία ἠγωνίσαντο ἐν Χαιρωνείᾳ καὶ οἱ μετὰ Κλέωνος ἐς Ἀμφίπολιν στρατεύσαντες, οἵ τε ἐν Δηλίῳ τῷ Ταναγραίων τελευτήσαντες καὶ ὅσους ἐς Θεσσαλίαν Λεωσθένης ἤγαγε καὶ οἱ πλεύσαντες ἐς Κύπρον ὁμοῦ Κίμωνι, τῶν τε σὺν Ὀλυμπιοδώρῳ τὴν φρουρὰν ἐκβαλόντων τριῶν καὶ δέκα ἄνδρες οὐ πλείους.

7. Decree for Strombichos. *IG* II², 666
Posideon 11, 26<u>6</u>/5 (Archon Nikias III of Otryne)

NON-ΣΤΟΙΧ. *ca.* 45

[ἐπὶ Νικίου ἄρχοντος] Ὀτρυνέ[ως ἐπὶ τῆς --δος ἕκτ]
ης πρυτανείας, ἧι Ἰσοκράτης Ἰσοκρά[του Ἀλωπεκῆ]θεν ἐ[γ]
ραμμάτευεν· Ποσιδεῶνος ἐν[δεκ]άτει, δω[δεκά]τει τῆς π[ρ]
υτανείας· ἐκκλησία κυρία· τῶν προέδρων ἐπεψήφιζε Μ[νη]
σίστρατος Σωσίππου Κυδαθηναιεὺς καὶ συνπρόεδρο[ι]·
ἔδοξεν τεῖ βουλεῖ καὶ τῶι δήμωι· vv Φύτιος Παμφίλου Θορ[ίκ]
[ι]ος εἶπεν· ἐπειδὴ Στρόμβιχος στρατευόμενος πρότερο[ν]
παρὰ Δημητρίωι καὶ καταλειφθεὶς ἐν τῶι ἄστει μετὰ Σ[πι]
νθάρου, λαβόντος τοῦ δήμου τὰ ὅπλα ὑπὲρ τῆς ἐλευθ[ερ]
[ί]ας καὶ παρακαλοῦ[ν]τος καὶ τοὺς στρατιώτας τίθεσθα[ι π]
ρὸς τὴμ πόλιν ὑπήκουσεν τῶι δήμωι εἰς τὴν ἐλευθερίαν [κ]
[α]ὶ ἔθετο τὰ ὅπλα μετὰ τῆς πόλεως οἰόμενος δεῖν μὴ ἐνίσ[τ]
ασθαι τῶι τῆς πόλεως συμφέροντι, ἀλλὰ συναίτιος γενέσ[θ]
[α]ι τεῖ σωτηρίαι, συνεπολιόρκει δὲ καὶ τὸ Μουσ[εῖ]ον μετὰ [το]
ῦ δήμου, καὶ συντ[ε]λεσθέ[ντ]ων τεῖ πόλει τῶν πρ[α]γμάτω[ν κ]
αὶ τὰς λοιπὰς χρείας ἀπροφασίστως παρασχόμενο[ς διατ]
ετέλεκεν καὶ διαμεμένηκεν ἐν τεῖ τοῦ δήμου εὐ[νοίαι, κα]
ὶ τοῦ πολέμου γενομένου [ἀ]νὴρ ἀγα[θὸ]ς ἦ[ν περὶ τὸν δῆμον κ]
[αὶ] ἀγωνιζόμενος ὑπ[ὲρ αὐτοῦ ἐποίησεν ὅσα παραγγέλλοι ὁ σ]
[τρατηγ]ὸς κα[ὶ ------------------------]

8. Decree for Strombichos, second copy. *IG* II², 667
Posideon 11, 266/5 (Archon Nikias III of Otryne)

NON–ΣΤΟΙΧ. *ca.* 40

[- - - - - - - - - - - - - - - - - - - οἰόμενος δεῖν μὴ ἐνίστ]
[ασθαι τῶι τῆς πόλεως συμφ]έρον[τι, ἀλλὰ συναίτιος]
[γενέσθαι τεῖ σωτηρίαι, συ]νεπολιόρκει δὲ κ[αὶ τὸ]
[Μουσεῖον μετὰ τοῦ δήμου, κ]αὶ συντελεσθέντων
[τεῖ πόλει τῶν πραγμάτων κα]ὶ τὰς λοιπὰς χρείας πα
[ρασχόμενος διατετέλεκεν] καὶ διαμεμένηκεν ἐν τ
[εῖ τοῦ δήμου εὐνοίαι, καὶ τοῦ] πολέμου γενομένου ᵛ
[ἀνὴρ ἀγαθὸς ἦν περὶ τὸν δῆμον] καὶ ἀγωνιζόμενος ὑπ
[ὲρ αὐτοῦ ἐποίησεν ὅσα παραγγ]έλλοι ὁ στρατηγὸς κα
[ὶ εἰς τὸ λοιπὸν ἐπαγγέλλετ]αι χρείας παρέξεσ[θ]
[αι τῶι δήμωι τῶι Ἀθηναίων· ὅπως ἂν ο]ὖν ἐφάμιλλον ε[ἶ]
[πᾶσιν τοῖς βουλομένοις ἀγαθὸν εὑρ]έσθαι παρὰ το[ῦ]
[δήμου εἰδόσιν ὅτι τιμηθήσοντα]ι ὑπὸ τοῦ δήμο[υ],
[ἀγαθεῖ τύχει δεδόχθαι τεῖ βουλεῖ] τοὺς προέδρ
[ους οἳ ἂν λάχωσιν προεδρεύειν ἐν τῶ]ι δήμωι εἰς τὴν
[ἐπιοῦσαν ἐκκλησίαν ὅταν ἐξήκ]ωσιν αἱ ἐκ τοῦ ν
[όμου ἡμέραι χρηματίσαι περὶ τούτων], γνώμην δὲ ξυμ[β]
[άλλεσθαι τῆς βουλῆς εἰς τὸν δῆμο]ν, ὅτι δοκεῖ τεῖ β
[ουλεῖ ἐπαινέσαι Στρόμβιχον καὶ στ]εφανῶσαι χρυ
[σῶι στεφάνωι κατὰ τὸν νόμον ἀρετῆ]ς ἕνεκα καὶ φ[ι]
[λοτιμίας τῆς εἰς τὸν δῆμον· εἶναι δ]ὲ αὐτὸν Ἀθην[α]
[ῖον καὶ τοὺς ἐκγόνους αὐτοῦ καὶ γρά]ψασθαι φυλῆ
[ς καὶ δήμου καὶ φρατρίας ἧς ἂν βούληта]ι κατὰ τὸν ν
[όμον, τοὺς δὲ πρυτάνεις δοῦναι περὶ αὐ]τοῦ τὴν ψῆφ
[ον εἰς τὴν πρώτην ἐκκλησίαν, τοὺς δὲ θεσ]μοθέτ[ας]
[εἰσαγαγεῖν αὐτῶι τὴν δοκιμασίαν τῆς δωρε]ᾶς ὅ[ταν]
[πρῶτον -]

9. Decree for Zenon. *IG* II², 650
Hekatombaion 11, 286/5 (Archon Diokles)

ΣΤΟΙΧ. 33

θ [ε ο ί] .
Ζ ή ν ω ν [- - - - - - - - - - - - - - - - - -]
ἐπὶ Διοκλέους [ἄρχοντος ἐπὶ] τῆς . . .⁷. . .
ίδος πρώτης π[ρυτανείας, ἧι] Ξενοφῶ[ν Νικέ]
ου Ἁλαιεὺς ἐγ[ραμμάτε]υ[εν· Ἑκ]ατομβ[αιῶνο]
ς ἑνδεκάτει, ἑ[νδεκάτει] τῆ[ς πρ]υτανείας· ἐκκ

λησία· τῶν π[ροέδρων] ἐπεψήφιζεν Λυσίας [Λ]
υσιμάχου . . . .⁸. . . . ος καὶ συμπρόεδροι· [ἔ]
δοξεν τ[ῆι βουλῆι κα]ὶ τῶι δήμωι· Ἐπίχαρμ[ο]
ς Καλλι[στρατίδου Κ]ολωνῆθεν εἶπεν· ἐπε
ιδὴ Ζή[νων καθεστηκ]ὼς ὑπὸ τοῦ βασιλέως
Πτολ[εμαίου ἐπὶ τῶν ἀ]φράκτων εὔνους ὢν δ⟨ι⟩
ατε[λεῖ κοινῆι τε τῶι] δήμωι καὶ ἰδίαι ἑκάστω
ι Ἀ[θηναίων ἐπιμελ]ούμενος οἷς ἂν περιτυ
[γχάνηι καὶ λέγων κ]αὶ πράττων ἀγαθὸν ὅ τι
[δύναται ὑπὲρ τῆς] πόλεως· ἐπιμελεῖται δὲ
[τῆς συνκομιδῆς το]ῦ σίτου τῶι δήμωι ὅπως ἂ
[ν ἀσφαλέστατα εἰσ]κομίζηται συναγωνιζό
[μενος τῆι τοῦ δήμ]ου σωτηρίαι· ἀγαθῆι τύ[χ]
[ηι δεδόχθαι τῆι βο]υλῆι τοὺς προέδρο[υς ο]
[ἵτινες ἂν λάχωσι πρ]οεδρεύειν ἐν τῶι δ[ήμωι]
[εἰς τὴν πρώτην ἐκκ]λησίαν χρηματίσ[αι πε]
[ρὶ τούτων, γνώμην δὲ] συμβάλλεσ[θαι τῆς βου]
[λῆς εἰς τὸν δῆμον ὅ]τι δ[ο]κε[ῖ τῆι βουλῆι . .]

For the restoration of lines 17–18, see above pp. 20–21.

10. Decree for Demochares of Leukonoe. [Plutarch], *Moralia* 851 d–f
271/0 (Archon Pytharatos)

D *ἄρχων Πυθάρατος· Λάχης Δημοχάρους Λευκονοεὺς αἰτεῖ δωρεὰν τὴν βουλὴν καὶ τὸν δῆμον τὸν Ἀθηναίων Δημοχάρει Λάχητος Λευκονοεῖ εἰκόνα χαλκῆν ἐν ἀγορᾷ καὶ σίτησιν ἐν πρυτανείῳ αὐτῷ καὶ τῶν ἐκγόνων ἀεὶ τῷ πρεσβυτάτῳ καὶ προεδρίαν ἐν πᾶσι τοῖς ἀγῶσιν, εὐεργέτῃ καὶ συμβούλῳ γεγονότι ἀγαθῷ τῷ δήμῳ τῷ Ἀθηναίων καὶ εὐεργετηκότι τὸν δῆμον τάδε· πρεσβεύοντι καὶ γράφοντι καὶ πολιτευομένῳ . . . οἰκοδομὴν τειχῶν, καὶ παρασκευὴν ὅπλων καὶ βελῶν καὶ μηχανημάτων, καὶ*
E *ὀχυρωσαμένῳ τὴν πόλιν ἐπὶ τοῦ τετραετοῦς πολέμου, καὶ εἰρήνην καὶ ἀνοχὰς καὶ συμμαχίαν ποιησαμένῳ πρὸς Βοιωτούς· ἀνθ' ὧν ἐξέπεσεν ὑπὸ τῶν καταλυσάντων τὸν δῆμον· καὶ ὡς κατῆλθεν ἐπὶ Διοκλέους ἄρχοντος ὑπὸ τοῦ δήμου, συστείλαντι τὴν διοίκησιν πρώτῳ καὶ φεισαμένῳ τῶν ὑπαρχόντων καὶ πρεσβεύσαντι πρὸς Λυσίμαχον καὶ λαβόντι τῷ δήμῳ τριάκοντα τάλαντα ἀργυρίου καὶ πάλιν ἕτερα ἑκατόν· καὶ γράψαντι πρεσβείαν πρὸς Πτολεμαῖον εἰς Αἴγυπτον, καθ' ἣν ἐκπλεύσαντες πεντήκοντα ἐκόμισαν τάλαντα ἀργυρίου τῷ δήμῳ· καὶ πρὸς Ἀντίπατρον πρεσβεύσαντι καὶ*
F *λαβόντι εἴκοσι τάλαντα ἀργυρίου καὶ Ἐλευσῖνα κομισαμένῳ τῷ δήμῳ· καὶ ταῦτα πείσαντι ἑλέσθαι τὸν δῆμον καὶ πράξαντι, καὶ φυγόντι μὲν ὑπὲρ δημοκρατίας, μετεσχηκότι δὲ οὐδεμιᾶς ὀλιγαρχίας οὐδὲ ἀρχὴν οὐδεμίαν ἠρχότι καταλελυκότος τοῦ δήμου· καὶ μόνῳ Ἀθηναίων τῶν κατὰ τὴν αὐτὴν ἡλικίαν πολιτευσαμένων μὴ μεμελετηκότι τὴν πατρίδα κινεῖν ἑτέρῳ πολιτεύματι ἢ δημοκρατίᾳ· καὶ τὰς κρίσεις*

καὶ τοὺς νόμους καὶ τὰ δικαστήρια καὶ τὰς οὐσίας πᾶσιν Ἀθηναίοις ἐν ἀσφαλεῖ ποιήσαντι διὰ τῆς αὐτοῦ πολιτείας καὶ μηδὲν ὑπεναντίον τῇ δημοκρατίᾳ πεπραχότι μήτε λόγῳ μήτε ἔργῳ.

11. Decree for Philippides of Kephale. *IG* II², 657
Boedromion 18, 283/2 (Archon Euthios)

ΣΤΟΙΧ. 40

[ἐ]πὶ Εὐθίου ἄρχοντος ἐπὶ τῆς Ἀ[καμαντίδο]ς τρ[ίτης]
[π]ρυτανείας, εἷ Ναυσιμένης Ναυσικύδου Χολαρ[γεὺ]
[ς] ἐγραμμάτευεν· Βοηδρομιῶνος ὀγδόει ἐπὶ δέκ[α, ἐ]
[ν]άτει καὶ δεκάτει τῆς πρυτανείας· ἐκκλησία κυρ[ί]
α· τῶν προέδ[ρ]ων ἐπεψήφιζεν Ἱερομνήμων Τεισιμάχ
ου ἐκ Κοίλης καὶ συμπρόεδροι· ἔδοξεν τῆι βουλεῖ κ
αὶ τῶι δήμωι· Νικήρατος Φιλέου Κεφαλῆθεν εἶπεν· ἐ
πειδὴ Φιλιππίδης διατετέλεκεν ἐν παντὶ καιρῶ[ι]
ἀποδεικνύμενος τὴν πρὸς τὸν δῆμον εὔνοιαν καὶ ἀ
ποδημήσας πρὸς ṭὸν βασιλέα Λυσίμαχον πρότερόν
τε διαλεχθεὶς τῶι βασιλεῖ ἐκόμισεν τῶι δήμωι δω
ρεὰν πυρῶν μεδίμνους Ἀττικοὺς μυρίους τοὺς δια
δοθέντας πᾶσιν Ἀθηναίοις ἐπ' Εὐκτήμονος ἄρχοντ
ος, διελέχθη δὲ καὶ ὑπὲρ κεραίας καὶ ἱστοῦ ὅπως ἂν
δοθεῖ τῆι θεῶι εἰς τὰ Παναθήναια τῶι πέπλωι ἃ ἐκο
μίσθη ἐπ' Εὐκτήμονος ἄρχοντος· καὶ νικήσαντος Λυ
σιμάχου τοῦ βασιλέως [τὴ]ν μάχην τὴν Ἰψῶι γενομέν
ην πρὸς Ἀντίγον[ον κα]ὶ Δημήτριον τοὺς μὲν τελευτ
ήσαντας ἐν τῶι κ[ινδύνω]ι τῶν πολιτ[ῶ]ν ἔθαψεν τοῖς
ἑαυτοῦ ἀναλώμα[σιν, ὅσοι δ]ὲ αἰχμάλωτοι ἐγένοντο,
ἐμφανίσας τῶι βα[σιλεῖ καὶ] λαβὼν αὐτοῖς ἄφε[σ]ιν, τ
οὺς μὲν βουλομέν[ους στρατ]εύεσθαι διώικησεν ὅπ
ως ἂν καταχωρισθῶσιν [ἐν] ἡγεμονίαις, τοὺς δὲ προα
ιρουμένους ἀπιέναι ἀμφιέσας καὶ ἐφόδια δοὺς πα
ρ' ἑαυτοῦ ἀπέστειλεν οὗ ἕκαστοι ἠβ[ο]ύλοντο πλείο
υς ὄντας ἢ τριακοσίους· παρειτήσατο δὲ καὶ ὅπως ἂ
ν ἀφεθῶσιν καὶ ὅσοι τῶν πολιτῶν κατελήφθησαν ἐν
τῆι Ἀσίαι εἱργμένοι ὑπὸ Δημητρίου καὶ Ἀντ[ι]γόνο
υ, καὶ τοῖς ἀεὶ περιτυνχάνουσιν Ἀθηναίων χρήσιμ
ος ὢν διατελεῖ καθότι ἂν ἕκαστος αὐτὸν παρακαλε
ῖ, καὶ κομισαμένου τοῦ δήμου τὴν ἐλευθερίαν διατ
ετέλεκε λέγων καὶ πράττων τὰ συμφέροντα τεῖ τῆς
πόλεως σωτηρίαι, καὶ παρακαλῶν τὸν βασιλέα βοηθ
εῖν καὶ χρήμασιν καὶ σίτωι, ὅπως ἂν διαμένει ὁ δῆμ

ος ἐλεύθερος ὢν καὶ τὸν Πειραιᾶ κομίσηται καὶ τὰ
φρούρια τὴν ταχίστην, καὶ ὑπὲρ τούτων π[ά]ντων πολ
λάκις μεμαρτύρηκεν αὐτῶι ὁ βασιλεὺς πρὸς τοὺς π
[ρ]εσβεύοντας Ἀθηναίων πρὸς ἑαυτόν· καὶ χειροτον
[ηθεὶ]ς ἀγωνοθέτης ἐπὶ Ἰσαίου ἄρχοντος ὑπήκουσε
[ν τῶι δ]ήμωι ἐθελοντὴς ἐκκ τῶν ἰδίων, τάς τε πατρίο
[υς θυσία]ς ἔθυσεν τοῖς θεοῖς ὑπὲρ τοῦ δήμου καὶ τὴ
[ν . . . .⁸. . . .]ν ἔδωκεν πᾶσιν Ἀθηναίοις πάντας τοὺς
[ἀγῶνας, καὶ ἐπί]θετον ἀγῶνα κατεσκεύασεν τεῖ Δήμ
[ητρι καὶ τεῖ Κόρη]ι [πρ]ῶτος ὑπόμνημα τῆς τοῦ δήμου
[ἐλευθερίας, ἐπεμελή]θη δὲ καὶ τῶν ἄλλων ἀγώνων κα
[ὶ θυσιῶν ὑπὲρ τῆς πόλεω]ς, καὶ εἰς ταῦτα πάντα ἐκ τῶ
[ν ἰδίων ἀναλώσας πολλὰ χρ]ήματα τὰς εὐθύνας δέδω
κεν κατὰ το[ὺ]ς νόμους κα[ὶ οὐθ]ὲν ὑπεναντίον πρὸ[ς δ]
ημοκρατίαν οὐδεπώποτε [ἐποίησ]ε[ν ο]ὔ[τε λόγωι οὔτ']
ἔργωι· ὅπως ἂν οὖν φανερὸν εἶ [πᾶσιν, ὅτι ὁ δῆμος ἐπί]
σταται χάριτας ἀποδιδόναι τ[οῖς εὐεργέταις ἀξί]
ας ὧν ἂν εὐεργετήσωσιν, ἀγαθεῖ [τύχει δεδόχθαι τε]
ῖ βουλεῖ, τοὺς προέδρους οἳ ἂν λά[χωσιν προεδρεύε]
ιν εἰς τὸν δῆμον, ὅταν ἐξέλθωσιν αἱ [ἐκ τοῦ νόμου ἡμ]
έραι τῆς αἰτήσεως χρηματίσαι περὶ τ[ούτων εἰς τὴ]
ν πρώτην ἐκκλησίαν κατὰ τὸν νόμον, γνώ[μην δὲ ξυμβ]
άλλεσθαι τῆς βουλῆς εἰς τὸν δῆμον, ὅτι δοκεῖ τ[εῖ β]
ουλεῖ, ἐπαινέσαι Φιλιππίδην Φιλοκλέους Κεφαλ[ῆ]
θεν ἀρετῆς ἕνεκα καὶ εὐνοίας ἧς ἔχων διατελεῖ π[ε]
ρὶ τὸν δῆμον τὸν Ἀθηναίων καὶ στεφανῶσαι αὐτ[ὸ]ν [χ]
ρυσῶι στεφάνωι κατὰ τὸν νόμον καὶ ἀνειπεῖν τὸν σ
τέφανον Διονυσίων τῶν μεγάλων τραγωιδῶν τῶι ἀγ
ῶνι, στῆσαι δὲ αὐτοῦ καὶ εἰκόνα χαλκῆν ἐν τῶι θεά[τ]
ρωι καὶ εἶναι αὐτῶι σίτησιν ἐν πρυτανείωι καὶ ἐκ
γόνων ἀεὶ τῶι πρεσβυτάτωι καὶ προεδρία[ν] ἐν πᾶσι
[τ]οῖς ἀγῶσι τοῖς ἡ πόλις τίθησιν· τῆς δὲ πο[ι]ήσεως τ
οῦ στεφάνου καὶ τῆς ἀναγορεύσεως ἐπιμεληθῆναι
τοὺς ἐπὶ τῆι διοικήσει· ἀναγράψαι δὲ τόδε τὸ ψήφι
σμα τὸν γραμματέα τὸν κατὰ πρυτανείαν ἐν στήληι
λιθίνει καὶ στῆσαι παρὰ τὸν νεὼ τοῦ Διονύσου, εἰς
δὲ τὴν ἀναγραφὴν τῆς στήλης μερίσαι τοὺς ἐπὶ τῆι
διο[ι]κήσει ΔΔ δραχμὰς [ἐκ] τῶν εἰς τὰ κατὰ ψηφίσματ
α ἀναλισκομένων τῶι δήμωι.

in corona

ὁ δῆ[μος]

12. Decree for Artemidoros of Perinthos. *IG* II², 662 Addenda + *Hesperia* 26, 1957, p. 29, no. 2
Elaphebolion 30, 286/5 (Archon Diokles)

ΣΤΟΙΧ. 43

ἐπὶ Διοκλέους ἄρχον[τος ἐπὶ τῆς Κεκ]ροπίδος ἐνάτης π
ρυτανείας· Ἐλαφηβολ[ιῶνος ἕνει καὶ] νέαι, τριακοστεῖ
τῆς πρυτανε[ίας· ἐ]κκλ[ησία κυρία ᵛ τῶ]ν προέδρων ἐπεψή
[φ]ιζεν vacat [vacat] vacat *ἔδοξεν τῆ*
[ι βο]υλῆι καὶ τῶι δήμωι· [............]τος Ἀφιδναῖος ᵛ
[εἶπεν·] ἐπειδὴ [ᵛ Ἀρ]τ[εμίδωρος ἐμ πίστ]ει καὶ φιλίαι ὢν τ
[οῦ βασιλέως Λυσιμάχου καὶ ἀποστελλ]όμενος ὑπὸ τοῦ β
[ασιλέως πλεονάκις εἰς τὴν Ἑλλάδα κα]τὰ τὰς πρεσβεία
[ς ταύτας χρήσιμος ἦν τῶι τε βασιλεῖ Λ]υσιμάχωι καὶ τῶ
[ι δήμωι τῶι Ἀθηναίων καὶ ἀνελθὼν πρὸ]ς τὸν βασιλέα ἐμ
[παντὶ καιρῶι λέγει καὶ πράττει ὑπ]ὲρ τοῦ δήμου ἀγαθ
[ὸν ὅ τι ἂν δύνηται ᵛ καὶ ταῖς πρεσβεία]ις ταῖς ἀποστελ
[λομέναις πρὸς τὸν βασιλέα συναγωνί]ζεται εἰς ὅ τι ἂ[ν]
[αὐτὸν παρακαλῶσιν ᵛ τύχηι ἀγαθῆι δεδόχθαι] τῆι βου[λ]
[ῆι --------------------------]

13. Decree for Artemidoros of Perinthos, second copy. *IG* II², 663 + Addenda
Elaphebolion 30, 286/5 (Archon Diokles)

ΣΤΟΙΧ. 30

[------------ ἀποστελλό]με[νος εἰς]
[τὴν Ἑλλάδα κατὰ τὰς πρεσβε]ίας [ταύτας]
[χρήσιμος ἦν τῶι τε βασιλ]εῖ Λυσιμ[άχω]
[ι καὶ τῶι δήμωι τῶι Ἀθ]ηναίων καὶ [ἀνελ]
[θὼν πρὸς τὸν βασιλέα] ἐμ παντὶ καιρῶ[ι ᵛ]
[λέγει καὶ πράττε]ι ὑπὲρ τοῦ δήμου [ἀγα]
[θὸν ὅ τι ἂν δύνητ]αι καὶ ταῖς πρεσβε[ία]
[ις ταῖς ἀποστε]λλομέναις πρὸς τὸν [βα]
[σιλέα συναγωνίζε]ται εἰς ὅ τι ἂν αὐτ[ὸν]
[παρακαλῶσιν· τύχ]ει ἀγαθεῖ δεδόχθ[αι]
[τεῖ βουλεῖ τοὺς π]ροέδρους οἵτινε[ς ἂ]
[ν προεδρεύωσιν ἐ]ν τῶι δήμωι εἰς τὴ[ν π]
[ρώτην ἐκκλησίαν] χρηματίσαι περ[ὶ αὐ]
[τοῦ, γνώμην δὲ ξυ]μβάλλεσθα⟨ι⟩ τῆς βουλῆ
[ς εἰς τὸν δῆμον ὅ]τι δοκεῖ τεῖ βουλε[ῖ], ἐ
[παινέσαι Ἀρτ]εμίδωρον Ἀπολλοδώρ[ο]υ
[Περίνθιον ἀρ]ετῆς ἕνεκα καὶ εὐνοί[α]ς
[τῆς πρὸς τὸν β]ασιλέα Λυσίμαχον κα[ὶ π]

[ρὸς τὸν δῆμον] τὸν Ἀθηναίων καὶ στε[φα]
[νῶσαι χρυσῶι] στεφάνωι κατὰ τὸν νόμο
[ν· εἶναι δὲ αὐτὸ]ν Ἀθηναῖον καὶ τοὺς ἐκ
[γόνους αὐτοῦ κ]αὶ γράψασθαι φυλῆς κα
[ὶ δήμου καὶ φρατ]ρίας ἧς ἂν βούληται κ
[ατὰ τὸν νόμον· το]ὺς δὲ πρυτάνεις [τ]οὺς
[πρυτανεύοντα]ς τοῦ Μουνιχιῶνος μην
[ὸς δοῦναι περ]ὶ αὐτοῦ τὴν ψῆφον εἰς τὴ
[ν πρώτην ἐκκλ]ησίαν κα[ὶ τοὺ]ς θεσμοθέ
[τας εἰσαγαγ]εῖν αὐτῶι [τὴν δοκιμασ]ία
[ν ὅταν πληρῶ]σιν τὰ δημόσι[α δικαστή]ρ
[ια, ὅπως ἐφάμι]λλον ἧι πᾶσι χρεί[ας παρ]
[έχεσθαι τῶι δ]ήμωι εἰδότας ὅτι [κομιο]
[ῦνται χάριτα]ς καταξίας τῶν εὐ[εργετ]
[ημάτων· ἀναγρ]άψαι δὲ τόδε τὸ ψή[φισμ]α
[τὸν γραμματέ]α τὸν κατὰ πρυταν[εία]ν ἐ
[ν στήλῃ λιθί]νει καὶ στῆσαι ἐν Ἀγλ[αύ]
[ρου, εἰς δὲ τὴ]ν ἀναγραφὴν τῆς στήλ[ης μ]
[ερίσαι τοὺς] ἐπὶ τεῖ διοικήσει τ[ὸ ἀνά]
[λωμα]. *vacat*

For the restoration of line 17, see Habicht, *Chiron* 2, 1972, pp. 107–109.

14. Polyainos, *Strategemata* V.17.1

Δημήτριος Ἡρακλείδην φύλακα τῶν Ἀθηνῶν συντάξας αὐτὸς μὲν ἦν περὶ τὴν Λυδίαν. οἱ δὲ στρατηγοὶ τῶν Ἀθηναίων ἐν ἀπορρήτῳ βουλευσάμενοι τὸν ξεναγὸν Ἱεροκλέα, Κᾶρα τῷ γένει, ἔπεισαν νυκτὸς ἀνοῖξαι τὰς πύλας καὶ δέξασθαι στρατιώτας Ἀττικούς, οἳ κτενοῦσιν Ἡρακλείδην. ταῦτα μὲν δὴ συνέθεντο παρὰ τὸν Ἰλισσόν, οὗ τὸν καθαρμὸν τελοῦσι τοῖς ἐλάττοσι μυστηρίοις, Ἱππάρχου καὶ Μνησιδήμου στρατηγῶν ὅρκια δόντων καὶ λαβόντων. Ἱεροκλῆς δὲ πιστὸς Ἡρακλείδῃ γενόμενος ἐμήνυσε τὴν πρᾶξιν. ὁ δὲ συνέπραττε νύκτωρ αὐτοὺς εἰσδέξασθαι ἀνοίξαντές τι μέρος [τῶν] πυλῶν. καὶ δὴ νυκτὸς εἰσεδέξαντο τετρακοσίους καὶ εἴκοσι ἄνδρας, ὧν ἡγοῦντο Μνησίδημος, Πολυκλῆς, Καλλισθένης, Θεόπομπος, Σάτυρος, Ὀνητορίδης, Σθενοκράτης, Πυθίων· Ἡρακλείδης δὲ στρατιώτας δισχιλίους ὡπλισμένους ἐπαφῆκεν, οἳ πάντας αὐτοὺς εἰσελθόντας ἐφόνευσαν.

CHRONOLOGICAL TABLE

Year	Archon and Tribal Rotation of Secretary	Events Discussed in Text
307/6	Anaxikrates (II)	Demetrios occupies Peiraieus Restoration of Democratic government at Athens Creation of tribes Antigonis and Demetrias Beginning of Four Years' War
306/5	Koroibos (XI)	Restoration of Secretary Cycle
305/4	Euxenippos (XII)	
304/3	Pherekles (I)	
303/2	Leostratos (III)	
Early summer 303		Democratic uprising against Demetrios Exile of Demochares
Mounichion 302		Demetrios' irregular initiation into Eleusinian Mysteries
302/1	Nikokles (IV)	
Hekatombaion 302		Storm at Great Panathenaia destroys peplos
Spring 301		Philippides of Kephale attacks Stratokles in comedy for "subverting democracy" Exile of Philippides
301/0	Klearchos (V)	
Summer 301		Battle of Ipsos, death of Antigonos Monophthalmos
300/299	Hegemachos (6)	
299/8	Euktemon (VII)	Moderate government in power in Athens; changes evident in financial administration Lysimachos' gifts of grain and mast delivered for Great Panathenaia of 298
298/7	Mnesidemos (VIII)	Lachares' command of mercenaries; stasis of the generals, their arrest and execution; secession of Peiraieus
Spring 297		Death of Kassandros, succeeded by three sons
297/6	Antiphates (9)	
296/5	Nikias I (X)	Phaidros of Sphettos elected general ἐπὶ τὴν παρασκευήν
Elaphebolion 295		Lachares seizes tyranny; dissolution of Boule; cancellation of Dionysia; Phaidros re-elected general
295/4	Nikostratos (XI)	Demetrios' siege of Athens
Elaphebolion 294		Flight of Lachares, surrender of Athens; Demetrios establishes garrisons in Peiraieus and Athens; honors voted for Herodoros
294/3	Olympiodoros (Registrar II)	Demetrios installs oligarchic government at Athens; appointive archons and registrars
Autumn 294		Accession of Demetrios as king of Macedonia

293/2	Olympiodoros (Registrar XI)	Reconciliation of Stratokles and Philippides of Paiania, latter appointed basileus
292/1	Philippos (Registrar –)	Restoration of oligarchic exiles; Deinarchos returns; property confiscated from Kallias of Sphettos (?)
291/0	Charinos (XI)	Resumption of rotating secretary cycle
290/89	Telokles (12)	
Summer 290		Demetrios celebrates Pythia at Athens
289/8	Aristonymos (I)	
288/7	Kimon (2)	Phaidros of Sphettos elected hoplite general
		Coalition of kings against Demetrios; Ptolemy acquires Tyre and Sidon
Spring 287		Lysimachos and Pyrrhos attack Demetrios in Macedonia; Ptolemaic fleet reaches Attica before harvest; attempted revolt of Athens causes "difficult times"; Phaidros keeps peace
		Ptolemaic invasion postponed; Kallias and Zenon establish base on Andros
287/6	Xenophon (3)	Phaidros elected hoplite general "first"
Summer 287		Expulsion of Demetrios from Macedonia; he escapes to Greece; division of Macedonia between Lysimachos and Pyrrhos
Spring 286		Revolt of Athens; restoration of the nationalist democracy; Olympiodoros expels Macedonian garrison from Athens
		Ptolemaic forces in Attica; Kallias and Zenon bring in the harvest
286/5	Diokles (IV)	Demochares returns from exile
Hekatombaion 286		Honors for Zenon voted
Summer 286		Demetrios besieges Athens; embassy to Pyrrhos
Autumn 286		Krates negotiates lifting siege; arrival of Pyrrhos and Sostratos
Winter 286/5		Peace negotiations at Athens; Kallias negotiates with Sostratos
Late winter 285		Peace ratified; Demetrios sails for Asia
		Ptolemy acquires Island League
		Embassies to Lysimachos, Ptolemy I, and Antipatros
Elaphebolion 285		Honors voted for Artemidoros
		Athens' attempt to capture Peiraieus fails
285/4	Diotimos (V)	Demetrios campaigns in Asia; Demochares elected general (?)
Early winter 285/4		Ptolemy II Philadelphos co-regent with Soter
		Demetrios surrenders to Seleukos
		Demochares captures Eleusis
Spring 284		Lysimachos drives Pyrrhos out of Macedonia, begins rule
284/3	Isaios (6)	Philippides of Kephale agonothetes
Metageitnion 284		Philippides celebrates festival for the liberation of Athens at the Eleusinia

283/2	Euthios (VII)	
Late summer 283		Demetrios dies in captivity; accession of Antigonos Gonatas
Boedromion 283		Honors voted for Philippides of Kephale
Early winter 283/2		Death of Ptolemy I Soter
		Kallias of Sphettos resident in Athens
Spring 282		Kallias' embassy to Ptolemy II
282/1	Nikias II (VIII)	Phaidros of Sphettos and Glaukon of Aithalidai agonothetai
Hekatombaion 282		Cancellation of Great Panathenaia
Late winter 281		Battle of Kouroupedion; death of Lysimachos
281/0	Ourias (IX)	Olympiodoros elected general
Late summer 281		Murder of Seleukos; Ptolemy Keraunos king of Macedonia
Spring 280		Olympiodoros captures Peiraieus
280/79	Gorgias (X)	
279/8	Anaxikrates (11)	
Early winter		Ptolemy II celebrates first Ptolemaia at Alexandria; Kallias of Sphettos chief Athenian delegate, sends home gift of ropes for the peplos
278/7	Demokles (12)	
Hekatombaion 278		First celebration of Great Panathenaia after liberation of Athens
277/6	(unknown) (1)	
276/5	Philokrates (II)	
275/4	Olbios (III)	
274/3	Euboulos (4)	
273/2	Glaukippos (V)	
272/1	Lysitheides (VI)	
271/0	Pytharatos (VII)	Honors voted for Demochares
270/69	Sosistratos (VIII)	Kallias of Sphettos stationed in Halikarnassos; helps Athenian embassies
Posideon 270		Honors voted for Kallias

INDEXES

INSCRIPTIONS STUDIED OR CITED

LIST OF PASSAGES CITED

GENERAL INDEX

PLATE I

PLATE II

PLATE III

PLATE IV